The Jewish World
of Sigmund Freud

The Jewish World of Sigmund Freud

Essays on Cultural Roots and the Problem of Religious Identity

Edited by ARNOLD D. RICHARDS

McFarland & Company, Inc., Publishers
Jefferson, North Carolina, and London

"Hidden in Plain Sight: Freud's Jewish Identity Revisited" originally appeared in *Psychoanalytic Dialogues* 17 (2): 197–217. Reprinted by permission of the publisher, Taylor & Francis (http://www.informa world.com).

"Freud's Moses and Viennese Jewish Modernism" appeared in slightly different form as chapter one of Abigail Gillman's book *Viennese Jewish Modernism: Freud, Hofmannsthal, Beer-Hofmann, and Schnitzler* (University Park: Pennsylvania State University Press, 2009).

LIBRARY OF CONGRESS CATALOGUING-IN-PUBLICATION DATA

The Jewish world of Sigmund Freud : essays on cultural roots and the problem of religious identity / edited by Arnold D. Richards.
    p.   cm.
Includes bibliographical references and index.

ISBN 978-0-7864-4424-3
softcover : 50# alkaline paper ∞

1. Freud, Sigmund, 1856–1939. 2. Freud, Sigmund, 1856–1939 — Religion. 3. Jews — Identity. 4. Jews — Europe — Intellectual life. 5. Judaism and psychoanalysis. I. Richards, Arnold D.
BF109.F74J49   2010
200.92 — dc22   2009047872

British Library cataloguing data are available

©2010 Arnold D. Richards. All rights reserved

No part of this book may be reproduced or transmitted in any form or by any means, electronic or mechanical, including photocopying or recording, or by any information storage and retrieval system, without permission in writing from the publisher.

Front cover: Sigmund Freud, 1926 (photograph by Ferdinand Schmutzer)

Manufactured in the United States of America

McFarland & Company, Inc., Publishers
  Box 611, Jefferson, North Carolina 28640
    www.mcfarlandpub.com

To the staffs of the Leo Baeck Institute,
the YIVO Institute and the Freud Museum

Table of Contents

Introduction	1
Hidden in Plain Sight: Freud's Jewish Identity Revisited *Jill Salberg*	5
Assimilation and Affirmation: The Jews of Freud's Vienna *Marsha L. Rozenblit*	22
Being Mr. Somebody: Freud and Classical Education *Richard H. Armstrong*	35
The *Neue Freie Presse* Neurosis: Freud, Karl Kraus, and the Newspaper as Daily Devotional *Leo A. Lensing*	51
Sigmund Freud and Electrotherapy *Sander L. Gilman*	66
Anti-Semitism in the Freud Case Histories *Harold P. Blum*	78
Freud's Theory of Jewishness: For Better and for Worse *Eliza Slavet*	96
Freud and Levinas: Talmud and Psychoanalysis Before the Letter *Ethan Kleinberg*	112
Freud's Moses and Viennese Jewish Modernism *Abigail Gillman*	126
Freud's Michelangelo: The Sculptural Meditations of a Hellenized Jew *Mary Bergstein*	136
Freud, Moses, and Akhenaten *Florence Dunn Friedman*	144
Sigmund Freud in Exile: The End of an Illusion *Frank Mecklenburg*	160

"Leaving This World with Decency": Psychoanalytical Considerations
on Suicide in the Life and Work of Sigmund Freud
  Benigna Gerisch   165

Freud's Jewish World: A Historical Perspective
  Steven Beller   175

About the Contributors   187

Index   191

Introduction

The essays in this book are based on papers presented at a conference held in December 2006 at the Center for Jewish History in New York City. The conference, Freud's Jewish World, was mounted on the occasion of the one hundred fiftieth anniversary of the year of Freud's birth (1856). The sponsors of the conference were the Leo Baeck Institute, the YIVO Institute for Jewish Research and the Sigmund Freud Archives. The Leo Baeck Institute, founded in 1938, is a research and archival center for the study of the German Jewish world. The YIVO Institute for Jewish Research is the world's preeminent resource center for Eastern European Studies; Freud was one of its founding trustees. The Sigmund Freud Archives is dedicated to the collection, conservation, and collation of Freud's papers, correspondence and photographs. Together these three archives provided a significant amount of the primary and secondary source material for many of the contributors to this volume.

Freud's one hundred fiftieth birthday was celebrated all over the world by conferences, exhibitions, and special journal issues and books. These events and publications addressed many aspects of his work, especially his contribution to the culture of his time and to modern scientific, literary and historical thought, but none focused specifically on Freud as a Jew — his Jewish roots, his Jewish identity and his ambivalent attitude toward Judaism. Jerry Victor Diller did a search in 1991 of more than 100,000 thousand books and articles listed in the Index of Psychoanalytic Writings and found that only forty or fifty dealt directly with Freud's Jewish identity or with the relationship between Jews and psychoanalysis.

A more recent search of the Psychoanalytic Electronic Publishing (PEP) CD-Rom of the literature on Freud's Jewishness called up only seventeen entries. Clearly there has not been adequate attention given to the impact that the experience of Freud and his followers growing up as Jews in the Hapsburg Empire had on the creation and development of the discipline of psychoanalysis. I think the matter has to be located in the larger context of the sociology of scientific thought and the sociology of psychoanalytic thought in particular. We are indebted to another Hapsburg Jew, Ludwig Fleck, for the framework of this sociology. Fleck's landmark volume, *The Genesis and Development of Scientific Fact*, in 1936 launched the discipline of the sociology of scientific knowledge by making the case for the centrality of sociological, cultural, political, psychological and personal determinants in the development of ground-breaking scientific ideas. Nevertheless, a coterie of Central European German-speaking analysts tried to eradicate Jewishness from psychoanalysis in the '20s and '30s. When they were forced by the Nazis to emigrate they tried to bleach various facets of an identifiable Jewish ancestry out of the "re-invented selves" or denigrate the religious practices and or the affirmation of the Jewish identity of colleagues or patients. That was the atmosphere of the New York Psychoanalytic Institute where I trained in the '60s. It took some doing to get the instructors to cancel classes on Yom Kippur.

The contributors to this book provide the particulars of the embeddedings of Freud and his followers in the cultural matrix of Jewish Central and Eastern Europe. The chapters begin with the general, sociological, historical, and cultural and move to the particular and the personal — Freud's education, his Jewish identity, and his ideas about the beliefs of Jews and the origins of Judaism.

Jill Salberg sets the stage with "Hidden in Plain Sight: Freud's Jewish Identity Revisited," examining his often neglected relationship with his mother and its impact on the development of psychoanalytic views on women. Marsha L. Rozenblit then describes the Viennese milieu of Jewish life, and Richard H. Armstrong looks at Freud's education in the Viennese gymnasium. Leo A. Lensing examines Karl Kraus and the Viennese press, and Sander L. Gilman's concern is the psychiatric milieu of the era. Harold P. Blum examines Freud's patients and the often hidden place of anti–Semitism for both members of the psychoanalytic dyad.

The volume then turns to the ambivalence of Freud's Jewish identity. Eliza Slavet and Ethan Kleinberg continue the examination of his Jewishness. Freud's Moses and Michelangelo's Moses are reviewed by Abigail Gillman and Mary Bergstein. Florence Dunn Friedman and Frank Mecklenburg offer new perspectives on Freud's final Jewish work, *Moses and Monotheism*. The chapter by Benigna Gerisch, "Leaving This World with Decency: Psychoanalytic Considerations on Suicide in the Life and Work of Sigmund Freud," is a meditation on Freud and the Jews who left their Viennese world — with dignity, but tragically, as well.

The final chapter by Steve Beller could serve both as an introduction and coda. It addresses the larger historical, political and sociologic context in which Freud and his fellow Habsbergian Viennese Jews found themselves during the end of the nineteenth century and the beginning of the twentieth. Vienna has been referred to as the "birthplace of the modern world" because of the unprecedented creativity of its inhabitants, many of them Jews, who broke ground in art, music, literature, science and philosophy. For the Jews, the era, with its rising anti–Semitism, was defined by their failed hopes of acceptance and assimilation. The Jewish Viennese world embodied the tension between tradition and critical modernism, between cultural particularity and universality. In their efforts to locate themselves in these polarities Jews like Freud found intellectuality at the core of their Jewish identity: creative and critical intellectual work was the essence and pole star of Freud's Godless Jews.

On March 13, 1938, at the board meeting of the Vienna Psychoanalytic where it was decided that everyone should flee the country, Freud said: "After the destruction of the Temple in Jerusalem by Titus, Rabbi Jochanan ben Zakkai asked for permission to open a school at Yavneh for the study of the Torah. We are going to do the same. We are after all used to persecution by our history, tradition, and some of us by personal experience."

In November of that year, after arriving in London, Freud responded to a request to help YIVO in its fund-raising effort with the following note to Jacob Melitis:

> We Jews have always known how to respect spiritual values. We preserved our unity through ideas and because of them we have survived to this day. The fact that Rabbi Jochanan ben Zakkai, immediately after the destruction of the Temple, obtained from the conqueror permission to establish the first academy for Jewish knowledge in Yavneh was for me always one of the most significant manifestations in our history.

When Yosef Yerashalmi writes in his "final conversation" with Freud that "I think you believed that just as you are a godless Jew psychoanalysis is a godless Judaism," he had in mind that for Freud the essence of Judaism was indeed intellectuality and morality.

Hidden in Plain Sight
Freud's Jewish Identity Revisited
JILL SALBERG*

Embedded within our memories is the unknown piece of elusive historical truth. Sigmund Freud offered us his memories and dreams as data for his own theories. While numerous authors have mined these texts and produced much needed exploration of Freud *the man*, this is often done within a particular point of view. In revisiting Sigmund Freud's Jewish identity I want to hold in mind multiple perspectives. I will present a broad overview of the historical and cultural lives for Jews in nineteenth century Europe including the effects of anti–Semitism, emancipation and the enlightenment movement. I will also look at Freud's parents' own personal histories, personalities and interpersonal dynamics. Gender will be an important theme, as it is understood within both Jewish minority culture and Christian dominant culture. How these threads became internalized in Freud's inner life will then be understood in terms of the data Freud uses as the basis for his analytic theories. In discussing Freud and his relationships with both parents I will be covering ground long reviewed but rarely held in mind in an intersubjective tension. It is my hope that this contextualizing, integrative approach will further illuminate the complexity of Freud's subjectivity and help advance our understanding of the unconscious influences on his theories.

It is well known that Freud longed to create a science of the mind. The earliest documentation of this project is woven through the Fliess letters, specifically in the "Scientific Project," and attempted again in *The Interpretation of Dreams*, in particular Chapter VII. What these writings, as well as his later Metapsychology papers, have in common is Freud's belief in a rational, scientific approach to understanding intrapsychic phenomena, a model of the mind. In contrast to this are his clinical writings. As early as the *Studies in Hysteria*, Freud writes that many of his case histories read like short stories, sug-

---

*An earlier version of this essay was presented as part of the Jewish Feminist Research Group of the Jewish Theological Seminary. I am indebted to the JFRG director, Ann Lapidus Lerner, Ph.D., for her helpful comments and the interdisciplinary nature of the JFRG group, as well as the thoughtful comments of my two discussants, Daniel Boyarin, Ph.D., and Yael Feldman, Ph.D. For their support in the evolution and review of this essay I am grateful to Lew Aron, Nancy Edwards, Adrienne Harris, Linda Jacobs, Carole Maso and Daniel Shaw.

gesting already his awareness of the literary, associative, narrative quality of how people experience and speak about their lives. These polarities: interpretation and science, theory and technique, infused his work. But they were already derivatives of an earlier longstanding dialogic tension between the Hebraic tradition with its interpretive, meaning derived emphasis on words and text, and the Greek philosophical tradition of *logos*; a belief in the divine logic implicit in creation of the cosmos, giving it form and truth. This should not be surprising, since Freud was raised in a home in the former tradition and educated in the latter, the German gymnasium educational system. I believe that these traditions informed and infused his theoretical writings. Many writers have argued that Freud's interpretative psychoanalytic approach derives from the Rabbinic exegetical hermeneutics of Talmudic textual analysis (Bakan 1958, Freiden 1990, Handelman 1982, Ostow 1982). I am suggesting that Freud's hermeneutics are both Jewish and Greek, exegetical and rationally scientific. I will discuss in particular how I see the evidence of these tensions in his theory of the Oedipus Complex and the Unconscious, two of the most central and pivotal ideas in his work.

For many writers the starting point of inquiry into Freud's Jewish identity has been Freud's relationship with his father. Specifically cited is this frequently recalled memory by Freud in *The Interpretation of Dreams*:

> I may have been ten or twelve years old, when my father began to take me with him on his walks and reveal to me in his talk his views about things in the world we live in. Thus it was, on one such occasion, that he told me a story to show me how much better things were now than they had been in his days. "When I was a young man," he said, "I went for a walk one Saturday in the streets of your birthplace; I was well dressed, and had a new fur cap on my head. A Christian came up to me and with a single blow knocked off my cap into the mud and shouted: 'Jew! Get off the pavement!' 'And what did you do?' I asked. 'I went into the roadway and picked up my cap,'" was his quiet reply. This struck me as unheroic conduct on the part of the big, strong man holding the little boy by the hand. I had contrasted this situation with another which befitted my feelings better: the scene in which Hannibal's father, Hamilcar Barca, made his boy swear before the household altar to take vengeance on the Romans. Ever since that time Hannibal had had a place in my fantasies [1900, p. 197].

Martin Bergmann (1976, 1995, 1998) was one of the first people to seriously address the subject of Freud's Jewish identity. Bergmann believed that this "unheroic conduct" recollection was a critical memory that came out in Freud's self-analysis. This was the moment that Freud lost his idealization of his father and looked elsewhere for a hero to emulate. Freud states that his father told this story sometime between his tenth and twelfth year. This would mean that Freud was already attending Gymnasium, the German-Austrian secular education system and becoming well educated with the expectation that he would continue on to University; something his parents' pre-emancipation generation would not have been able to do.

Europe and the Jews

The great social and political upheavals in Europe during the nineteenth century had specific antecedents in terms of the effects on Jews and anti–Semitism. The earlier, pre-emancipation anti–Semitic laws required: distinctive dress codes for Jews that left them quite visible and consequently vulnerable to attack, the barring of Jews from entering certain occupations, restriction on travel and prohibitions on owning land, among others. Prior to the emancipation laws Jews could either convert as a means to entering the dominant culture, or remain observantly Jewish and therefore easily identifiable. This latter choice sustained their separateness and perceived inferiority. With the Enlightenment movement and the emphasis on rationalist ideas, emancipation became a possibility for Jews. In *Gender and Assimilation in Modern Jewish History* Paula Hyman writes that "Jewish leaders defined the goals of assimilation as the acculturation and social integration of the Jews ... and the shedding of external markers of Jewishness but supported religious, educational and philanthropic institutions that would maintain a sense of Jewish particularlism within the larger society (p. 16)." Many of these goals were outgrowths of the Jewish Enlightenment movement known as the Haskalah. This movement promoted a rationalist agenda focusing on learning and self-improvement as a means of entry and participation in European majority culture. Freud, who in many ways seems to have embodied this assimilationist agenda, was born during these tumultuous events in 1856 to parents who had already lived through a part of this process and experienced the impact of the Haskalah (see Gay 1987).

Following an 1873 stock market crash in Vienna and then Berlin, organized political anti–Semitism became quite prevalent. Specifically Wilhelm Marr, a radical German journalist who actually coined the term anti–Semite, and others wrote about a racialized hatred of Jews who were now seen as causing the ruin of "Germanism." In October 1894 Captain Dreyfus, the only Jewish officer in the upper ranks of the French army, was charged with spying for Germany. He was convicted with no real evidence, stripped of his rank and, while being taken away, he was subjected to crowds yelling "Death to the Jews," (as recorded by Theodore Herzl, reporter for Vienna's *Neue Freie Presse* who later founded the Zionist movement). The 1897 election of a virulent anti–Semite, Karl Lueger, as Vienna's mayor further fueled this tide. Lueger ran on a specifically anti–Semitic, anti-capitalist political platform. Carl Schorske (1961) sees fin-de-siècle Vienna as a rich mix of vibrant cultural changes in music, art, philosophy and of course the birth of psychoanalysis. Alongside of these creative productions Schorske outlines the political backlashes to earlier enlightenment liberal agendas that were occurring. And it is this reaction, which he believes helped fuel the mass political movements of that era: socialism, nationalism, as seen in Pan-Germanism and the later evolution into Nazism, and Zionism.

Given the political and social climate in flux during these decades if we now turn to the "unheroic conduct" memory and look at the surface text it is about the era of waning virulent anti-Semitism in Europe. Bergmann points out that before the emancipation of the Jews in Germany in 1809 they had not been permitted to walk on public sidewalks. By the time of the walk with his father the effects of the emancipation laws, which up until then had depended upon the will or whim of the local government, were finally a reality for many Jews. Clearly life had improved and Jakob Freud wanted his son to be aware of these changes and benefits. But the subtext of the story told is even more telling. I believe that Jakob Freud was also informing his son about his own personal path of assimilation. Freud in his 1930 letter to A. A. Roback, states, "It may interest you to hear that my father did indeed come from a Chassidic background. He was forty-one when I was born and had been estranged from his native environment for almost twenty years" (p 395). Given Jakob's history we can assume that this is a story transpiring on Shabbat, with Jakob dressed in his best clothing and a new fur streiml, the distinctive wide-brimmed fur trimmed hat that Hasidim wear as suggested by Simon (1957). Jakob Freud had raised his two sons from his first marriage, Emmanuel and Phillip, in an orthodox home. By the time Jakob married Freud's mother Amalia it was not in a strictly orthodox service. (There is some controversy about this, given that all marriage certificates were required to be signed by the chief Rabbi Manheimmer, a Reform rabbi. See Rice [1990, p. 56] for a fuller discussion.) It is as if he is saying, "See, we Jews can now walk where we please wearing whatever clothing we like and blend in, not be recognizable as different, as the 'other.'" Although Freud found his father's behavior unheroic, Bergmann (1976) notes that the father's behavior was completely in keeping with how Jews responded to anti-Semitic acts from the Christian world: "A Jew was expected to be able to control his anger, not to be provoked; his feelings of inner dignity were sustained by a belief in his own spiritual superiority which a ruffian and 'goy' can in no way touch" (p. 124). But for Freud his father's conduct becomes coded as unheroic, passive and shameful.

What we can see reflected in this brief overview is a turbulent era in history on political levels across Europe. These ripples then affect the minority Jewish culture, which is mediated by Freud's father to his son Sigmund. This memory becomes emblematic of not only a shift in Jewish assimilation and wished for integration but also what was probably already an ambivalent father-son relationship. I believe that Freud then connected all of these unheroic qualities to Jewish identity as well.

Jewish Identity and Anti-Semitism

Jewish identity within the Diaspora in Europe during the pre-modernity era, specifically male identity, was not necessarily parallel with the dominant

Christian culture. Daniel Boyarin (1997) in his book *Unheroic Conduct: The Rise of Heterosexuality and the Invention of the Jewish Man* argues that within the pre-modernity culture of Ashkenazi Jews the concept of masculinity was quite different from the prevailing culture. He writes, "More than just an anti–Semitic stereotype, the Jewish ideal male as counter type to 'manliness' is an assertive historical product of Jewish culture. Pre-modern Jewish culture frequently represented the ideal Jewish man as feminized, a sort of 'woman.' I am thus not claiming a set of characteristics, traits, behaviors that are essentially female but a set of performances that are read as non-male within a given historical culture" (p. 3–4). The type of man Boyarin is referring to was the "Yeshiva-Bokhur," a young unmarried man devoting himself to the study of Torah and Talmud. This man was seen as softer, gentler, perhaps even passive but was very much a cultural ideal. Jakob Freud certainly fit this description. We are told by a few of Jakob's grandchildren (Anna Freud, Judith Heller and Martin Freud) that he spent much of his time studying the Talmud in the original (Aramaic) at home. This suggests that Jakob had an advanced degree of Talmudic knowledge since Jews rarely studied Talmud without a partner. Clearly Jakob was not out in the world aggressively earning a living.

Additionally the anti–Semitic ideas of Christian Europe included perceiving and labeling Jewish males as females, i.e., femininity in all its negative connotations. Robert Wistrich, in his book *The Longest Hatred: Anti-Semitism* writes, "Among the more outlandish assumptions that underlay the blood libel was the notion that Jewish men menstruated and therefore required Christian blood to replenish themselves, or alternatively that they needed to make up for the blood they lost through circumcision" (p. 31). This view of Jewish men as women is clearly one of a negative female stereotype. Further, Sander Gilman (1993) has written that these beliefs formed a racial identity of the Jew that the Christian dominant culture and medical community documented. In this version the body of the Jew, as evidenced by circumcision, was deemed to be inferior, less masculine, diseased and "other." An ideology of race became part of the culture of science, one that even Jewish doctors and scientists, like Freud, would have been trained within.

While Freud was studying at University anti–Semitism had been on the rise. Freud writes of this time in his essay "An Autobiographical Study," "I found that I was expected to feel myself inferior and an alien because I was a Jew. I refused absolutely to do the first of these things. I have never been able to see why I should feel ashamed of my descent or, as people were beginning to say, of my race" (p. 9). We see in this quote Freud's being asked to take a passive, noncompetitive role in the academic circles of his life. Freud vehemently refuses to feel humiliated by this but we can only wonder if in his unconscious there is already an association with Jewishness and shame. By the time he is trying to establish his practice, writing his early papers with Breuer and unsuccessfully trying to gain professorial promotions at the University, a difficulty he is told has to do with his being Jewish, the anti–Semitic trend was now prevalent in the political landscape. Freud's further comments reveal his typical conscious response of combative defiance, "These first impressions at the University, however, had one consequence which was afterwards to prove important; for at an early age I was made familiar with the fate of being in the Opposition and of being put under the ban of the 'compact majority.' The foundations were thus laid for a certain degree of independence of judgment" (p. 9).

This becomes the persona Freud adopts and purports to be: proud of being a Jew and independent in his thinking. But beneath this image lies the disowned, disavowed representation of the passive, unheroic father and of denigrated status, race and Jewish culture. Freud never informs us about this part of his life. He briefly tells Ernest Jones that his early life was too impoverished to speak about. But it is this world, the one into which his parents were born, nursed, fed upon and attempted to discard, that later infuses the world they try to create for their son. It is a world quite gendered, but gendered differently from the compact majority. Moreover it was ambivalently offered to Freud along with his parents' desire to transform themselves. Freud too attempts to discard this world of his parents and of his own early life but as will be discussed later, *nothing* is lost in the unconscious.

The Role of Jewish Women

In the Jewish European world Boyarin refers to, women were afforded more opportunities to be aggressive and competent in the world outside the home. It was traditional for wealthy families to want their daughters to marry the best Yeshiva students. These wives would often help run entrepreneurial businesses supporting the family while their husbands studied the holy books of Torah and Talmud. Although to our modern ears this may sound progressive, it was not perceived as such. Estelle Roith (1987) reports that the Jewish woman's active role in economic responsibility for the family was completely usual and not outside ghetto culture. She writes, "If anyone is sheltered, it is the scholarly man.... Whereas the scholar ideal was one distinguished by physical passivity, the woman controlled the crucial domestic ritual on which her husband's piety depended. She may have managed the livelihood, as well as the home and the children, and thus have spoken the local language and moved about the countryside more than her husband (p. 80)." Glückl of Hameln,[1] the first Jewish female memoirist writing in the seventeenth century tells, in great detail, of both helping her husband in business and supporting his time at study and prayer. After his death she takes over the business financially supporting herself and their thirteen children. The business was in commodity trading business of pearls, jewelry and money lending, requiring her to travel extensively in Europe. All of this was accepted by the culture, i.e., she was not considered to be behaving in a non-feminine manner. Gender performances were opposite to the prevailing dominant Christian culture at large where convention had a more active father/man and passive mother/woman.

Returning to the "unheroic conduct" memory, we now need to explore the other side of the story, i.e., how it might have been otherwise understood. Freud tells us that he heard the story as a failure, specifically one revealing a lack of courage. The idealization of his father, the strong figure Freud longed for, was fractured. Instead Freud looks to historical, mythic figures to model himself after, telling us about Hannibal. Freud's growing feeling of disappointment in his father also may have derived from Jakob's difficulty in earning a living, relying on the charity of family members and the community.

Boyarin writes that emancipated Jews were influenced by fin-de-siècle Vienna's rise in misogyny and homophobia, an increase in all associations of femaleness much greater than at any prior time. Further, Boyarin sees Zionism and its introduction of a new Jewish male identity as a direct response to this. In discussing the pleasures of male gentile culture, what Jews have referred to as *goyim naches*, Boyarin summarizes, "Goyim naches can now be defined as the contemptuous Jewish term for those characteristics that in European culture have defined a man as manly: physical strength, martial activity and aggressiveness, and contempt for and fear of the female body" (p. 78). I believe that Freud's longing for the hero embodied these conflicting cultural "masculinities." In Freud's rejection of the passive, feminized, unheroic Jewish male we can see his move towards embracing what Max Nordau (1903) decried as a "Jewry of Muscle," i.e., Jews who do not step aside but fight back.

How we read the "unheroic conduct" memory becomes an important aspect of how we *begin* to understand Freud. I am arguing for it to be seen as a moment in history, multiple histories in fact. The incident recounted happens at a time of great change in the social and political lives of Europeans and of Jews. Emancipation and consequently the opportunity for acceptance into the majority culture became irresistible for many Jews. But the complexity of differences found within minority Jewish culture and the majority Christian culture is important to remember. Freud can then be understood as mediating the political, religious and cultural changes along his own personal psychodynamic dimensions. The longing for assimilation and the distancing of anti–Semitic stereotypes that Jews and their own self-identity were struggling with can be traced through this memory across the generations of Freud and his father. But Freud had two Jewish parents. What role did his mother play in all of this?

The Power of the Mother

Louis Breger in "Freud: Darkness in the Midst of Vision" believes that Freud created a new image for himself as the hero. To craft this Freud would only tell the details of his life which he believed painted the picture he wanted to show. This necessitated him to rewrite parts of his own personal history. Freud saw himself as a conqueror and his intellect as his great weapon. (Interesting to note that historically the Rabbis, a group without any political power, believed that their strength, if you will their weapon, was in their intellect.) Part of Freud's reshaping of his personal history I believe included minimizing the importance of his mother. Therefore, the sparse information he does tell us about his mother is notable. I want to look at one memory of his mother he does report, found in *The Interpretation of Dreams*:

> I dreamt as follows: I went into a kitchen in search of some pudding. Three women were standing in it; one of them was the hostess of the inn and was twisting something about in her hand, as though she was making Knodel (dumpling). She answered that I must wait till she was ready. (These were not spoken words.) I felt impatient and went off with a sense of injury.

(Although there is more to this dream I want to jump to Freud's interpretation because his analysis of this dream includes the early memory with his mother.)

> In connection with the three women I thought of the three Fates who spin the destiny of man.... One of the Fates, then, was rubbing the palms of her hands together as though she was making dumplings: a queer occupation for a Fate, and one that cried out for an explanation. This was provided by another and earlier memory of my childhood. When I was six years old and was given my first lesson by my mother, I was expected to believe that we were made of earth and must therefore return to earth. This did not suit me and I expressed doubts of the doctrine. My mother thereupon rubbed the palms of her hands together — just as she did in making dumplings, except that there was no dough between them — and showed me the blackish scales of epidermis produced by the friction as proof that we were made of earth. My astonishment at this ocular demonstration knew no bounds and I acquiesced... [p. 204–205].

Interestingly, in this memory we see the young Freud in awe, in his words "astonished," at his mother's proof of the creation story. He does not initially believe his mother, but the power of her demonstration convinces him. And it is not just any story she is telling him but a story from the Bible on the creation of man (Genesis 2:7). Freud will later recall in his autobiographical essay, "My deep engrossment in the Bible story (almost as soon as I had learnt the art of reading) had, as I recognized much later, an enduring effect upon the direction of my interest" (p. 8). I will return to this memory and what I feel its impact may have been, but first I want to briefly outline what is known about Freud's mother.

Amalia Freud (née Malka Nathanson) was born in eastern Galicia, her family then moving to Vienna. She was raised as an Orthodox Jew and spoke Yiddish, barely learning to speak German. Before her twentieth birthday she married Jakob Freud, a man twenty years her senior. She conceived and gave birth to Sigmund, her firstborn child whom she would always glowingly praise all of his life. Jones tells us, "It was strange to a young visitor to hear her (Amalia) refer to the great Master as 'mein goldener Sigi'" (1953, p. 3). Many writers have noted that Sigmund was clearly Amalia's favored child (See Anna Freud Bernays 1940, Deborah Margolis 1996, Peter Gay). Freud himself stated that, "if a man has been his mother's undisputed darling he retains throughout his life the triumphant feeling, the confidence in success, which not seldom brings actual success along with it" (1917, 17:156).

Early on Amalia worked with Jakob in a family business of wool merchants while Sigmund was taken care of by a Czech nanny. Amalia was fertile, she would have a total of eight children, but she was also often infirmed. When Sigmund was just under a year old, she gave birth to his brother Julius, named for Amalia's beloved younger brother who had died recently. This child died when only eight months old. During Freud's first two years of life his mother could not be fully emotionally available; either she was in mourning or pregnant. Additionally she seems to have had some nonspecific lung ailment, perhaps even tuberculosis, which prompted her to stay for three months annually at a health spa.

Many family members have commented on Amalia's beauty, fiery personality and at times infantile behavior. Judith Heller, Freud's niece who lived with her grandparents for some time states, "My grandmother had a volatile temperament. She was very charming when strangers were about, but I at least, always felt that with familiars she was a tyrant, and a selfish one" (p. 13). Amalia would later tell Freud that after giving birth to him, a peasant woman had predicted she had given the world a great gift (1900). There was no question in Amalia's mind; her "goldener Sigi" was destined for greatness. Clearly Amalia was narcissistically invested in Sigmund as the genius/hero prophesized at birth. At Freud's seventieth birthday Amalia, "announced simply to at least one student of Freud's: "I am the mother" (as quoted in Roazen, p. 46), as if to say she was the one who gave the world such greatness.

His mother was a complicated woman, both fierce and powerful while needy and demanding. Her delight and belief in Sigi's genius propelled Freud toward ambitious achievements but her inconsistent emotional availability created vulnerabilities, specific narcissistic wounds. Many writers have suggested that Amalia continued to rely on Freud in some needful attachment manner throughout her life (See Jones, Gay, Roazen, Margolis and Breger). Freud himself writes, "My Mother will be eighty-three this year and is no longer very strong. I sometimes think I shall feel a little freer when she dies, for the idea that she might have to be told that I have died is a terrifying thought" (as cited by Jones, p. 196). When she does die at age 94 Freud does not attend the funeral, sending his daughter Anna instead.

Freud's tie to his mother was intense, and complicated. Deborah Margolis views this relationship as one shaped by unfulfilled need and longing, love and hate and not enough of his father's attention. She writes, "The protection Freud sorely needed was ... protection by his father against the engulfing tendencies of his mother. But here his father had failed him, abandoning him to his mother and leaving him no recourse but to consign his rage to the unconscious, layering it over with denial and idealization (p. 14)." Just as the unheroic memory of the passive father in the street leaves Freud longing for a hero, his mother, also, increases his need for a strong father who could stand up to her.

I want to further suggest that this powerful, difficult mother mediated Jewishness. This is the mother who explains God's creation of man. In the palm of her hand she unlocks mysteries. She was the strong mother of Eastern European shtetl life. In particular she was someone who Freud both needed and needed to control. We can see, perhaps, his need to control the Jewish woman in his marriage. In marrying Martha Freud, who was originally raised as an observant, Orthodox Jew as was his mother, Freud insisted in her abandoning her Jewish ritual. The first Shabbat after they are married he insisted that she not light the Shabbat candles, a tradition all Jewish wives are required to perform. Her allegiance was to be to Freud, not Jewish tradition, and Martha complied.

Freud and Oedipus

I would like to turn now to the ways in which Freud's theories may have been influenced by his own personal relational world and his feelings about being a Jew. Revisiting the memories with each parent and looking first at Freud's mother, the picture he paints for us is of someone who is spellbinding. She is teaching Freud an early religious lesson but also using a clever trick to make her point. She is masterful, forceful, and maybe even actively mystical in her revealing of God's creation of humankind. And Freud is fully caught up with her compelling proof. He tells us, "My astonishment ... knew no bounds and I acquiesced...." This is a Freud we rarely hear of, one who acknowledges the persuasive power of another and surrenders to it. I believe this early relational configuration with a compelling mother became enmeshed with the other aspects of his relationship with her. The other side to his mother was someone who was burdened with losses (death of her brother and second child), frequent pregnancies and newborns to care for and physically ill due to some unspecified lung ailment. She was often emotionally taxed while the description of her by her grandchildren also suggests a needy, demanding and selfishly vain woman.

It then becomes quite interesting that both religion and femininity are devalued in Freud's theories while rationality and masculinity are elevated and considered the standard. Libido, the life force and sexual energy of Freud's theories, becomes masculinized. Roith suggests that Freud's views on women are directly linked to his early traumatic experiences with his mother. In fact Freud doesn't write his essays on femininity until after she has passed away. Additionally, Freud had difficulty tolerating an image of himself as maternal, even within the transference. H.D. (Hilda Doolittle, the poet) recalls his saying in one of her analytic sessions, "I do *not* like to be the mother in transference — it always surprises and shocks me a little, I feel so very masculine" (p. 52). One might say he found it intolerable to be consciously identified with his mother.

Keeping in mind these important experiences with his mother I want to now hold in tension the father's unheroic conduct story. This is a moment of discovery for Freud of a father found to be passive, lacking in strength and courage, and experienced as a humiliation. Consequently, in his turning to Hannibal and later other conquerors as mythic heroes I believe Freud unconsciously linked Jewishness with passivity, humiliation and, ultimately, femaleness. The Rabbis saw their power in their intellect. For Freud, intellectual strength gets split off from Jewishness, leaving only an imprint of passivity and perhaps shame. He distanced himself from what felt unbearable: his own dependency on a dazzling, narcissistically demanding yet somewhat unavailable mother and a father perceived as too passive to offer protection from the mother directly or via identificatory idealizations. This splitting would be reversing his personal experience in normative Jewish culture. Instead he creates the idea of a hero, as Breger states, "Freud worked hard to create this image; it is an integral part of a personal myth.... His passionate desire was to become a great man, to achieve fame, to be, in his own words, a 'hero'" (p. 1). And for Freud that hero figure was the rational scientist, a masculine conquistador of the mind, not a Talmud scholar.

It is this interplay of culture, both European and Jewish, which becomes mediated by Freud's parents and their own personal dynamics. What we see are mixed identifications and dis-identifications with both parents. Freud rejects his father's perceived passivity but is scholarly like his father. He distances himself from his mother but is similarly narcissistically vulnerable to criticism, demanding attention and loyalty while anxiety-ridden about his health, a probable hypochondriacal identification with her. And within these mixed identifications we can also see the repressive splits. When Freud links in his mind (and consequently in his theory) activity with masculinity he then accordingly connects femininity with passivity. This is the arrangement of his internal object world and not the arrangement in his external family, a family of a more active mother and of a passive father.

This complexity is not evident in some of Gilman's work on Freud and anti–Semitism. Gilman's emphasis on the profoundly pervasive effect of anti–Semitic views of Jews is valuable in revealing the impact on Freud of having both lived and studied within German Christian culture. But Gilman takes the point of view of the Jew as seen by the Christian world, not as experienced by Jews. Gilman does not perceive how the parents became the mediator of the Jewish cultural environment. Nor does he include the possibility of an internal world of complicated identifications. Boyarin, on the other hand, explores the culture of the Jewish world both prior to and after emancipation as lived and seen by Jews. It was this changing Jewish landscape that Freud's parents were products of and transmit to Freud. But Boyarin does not see how this world becomes internalized within Freud through the complex relational configurations with both parents.

A theoretical cornerstone for Freud rested upon his concept of the Oedipus complex. Yael Feldman (1993), in her article "And Rebecca Loved Jacob, But Freud Did Not," notices that Freud, in turning to the Greek myth of Oedipus, finds a master story of filial aggression. In so doing he overlooks his own Jewish myths found in the Bible, specifically the story of Isaac, Rebecca and their twin sons Esau and Jacob; a biblical story not of father-son aggression but of divided loyalties in a family and profound sibling rivalry. Interesting to remember that the first story of a murder in the biblical text is between siblings, of Cain's killing of Abel. This leads me to question why Freud had to abandon the stories, which he said had an enduring effect upon him. He felt compelled to look to a different cultural myth. Was Freud attempting to leave his "Jewishness" behind?

It is within Freud's Oedipal theories where we can find his complex internalized relational configurations. Freud partly discovers and partly creates an Oedipus who both triumphs over his father by killing him and subdues his mother with his own desire. This Oedipus is to some extent Freud's own imaginary creation, not the veritable myth. By starting midway in the Oedipal story Freud ignores the beginning of the Oedipus myth, overlooking the father of Oedipus, Laius. Unlike his own father Jacob, Laius refuses to move out of the way on the road upon meeting the young man whom we know is Oedipus. Laius stands up to Oedipus, the upstart, who kills him. This is not a passive father but a King who holds his ground, literally his spot on the road (not moving aside as Jacob had unheroically done). Further, the Oedipal myth actually starts with attempted infanticide, not patricide. Upon hearing the prophecy from the Oracle, Laius attempts to have Oedipus, his infant son, killed first. Notice that Freud completely omits the powerful aggressive father. (See Garber, 1995, p. 176–77, for further ideas on Freud's "overlooking" the earlier aspects of the myth.)

Schorske points out that Freud ignores that Oedipus is a king and overlooks the powerful political motivation of Oedipus to cure Thebes of the plague. While filled with guilt Oedipus's self-punishment, although personal, is anguish motivated primarily to restore public order. I want to suggest that Freud's truncating of the Oedipus myth was in the service of uncovering his own personal Oedipal drama. I am not suggesting that Oedipal themes aren't powerful or even universal but that what Freud wrote as *theory* was actually his own permutation and personal resolution on the triangular Oedipal conflict within his family. For Freud, and consequently he believed for all men, it became necessary to identify with fathers the character traits of activity and dominance. This resolution required the masculinization of libido and of development in general. Freud then believed that normative heterosexual identity would prevail. Women consequently had to renounce any longings for agency and power while accepting passivity and receptivity as normative female development. Jessica Benjamin (1998) has written that masculinity is created simultaneously with femininity because the girl must contain passivity for the father/male. She writes, "In Freud's usage a girl takes her father as object while fulfilling a passive aim ... her femininity is set up as the passive counterpart of masculine activity" (p. 40). Oedipus becomes the new Freudian ideal, an enlightenment *male* in search of his unconscious motives and meaning — Oedipus *as* Hamlet.

Additionally the Oedipus of Sophocles is not a story of repudiation of desires but of the tragedy of living one's fate. Fate for the Greeks was unchangeable, a truth of life. Freud's Oedipus is about guilt and retaliatory aggression, as seen in castration anxiety, which causes repudiation or sublimation of drives and desires. Bergmann (1989) writes that, "Freud introduced the biblical concept of guilt into the Greek matrix.... The discovery of the Oedipus complex Freud owed to the classical past, but the interpretation of guilt he gave it he had inherited from his Jewish past" (p. 18). Freud has, as well, transplanted the vengeance of the powerful father from the Biblical God, as noted by Feldman, to the family arena — specifically to the father-son relationship. And so we see a son struggling with aggression to triumph over a weaker father, along with a mother who is libidinously desired.

Judith Van Herik (1982) believes that Freud's emphasis on renunciation as a developmental achievement and as a cultural necessity is entwined within his theories of gender. She argues that one needs to read Freud's theories of religion *as* theories of gender. Van Herik states, "Freud manages to explain whatever is civilized, heroic, intellectual, or scientific in terms of renunciation. Renunciation is also assimilated to paternity, masculinity, morality, and in some instances, mental health" (p. 80–81). The Greek Oedipus myth becomes the overarching explanatory story for Freud with a conviction in the superiority of renunciation of wishes; for men repudiation of feminine passive aims, for women the acceptance of passivity.

Freud's Jewish Unconscious

Freud's "Project for a Scientific Psychology" (1895) opens with: "The intention of this project is to furnish us with a psychology which will be a natural science: its aim, that is, is to represent psychical processes as quantitatively determined states of specifiable material particles" (p. 295). Freud then locates everything irrational, i.e., all urges, drives, and passions in the unconscious realm. He proceeds, through his self-analysis, to create a method of understanding the Unconscious through dreams, slips of the tongue, inexplicable thoughts and symptoms relying on entirely nonscientific interpretative means. Jonathan Lear (1998) believes that Freud and psychoanalysis are intellectual descendants of the Greek philosophical tradition, of Plato, Socrates and Aristotle. Lear writes, "Rather than starting, as Socrates does, with an argument that mind must be rational, and then wondering how irrationality can be tacked on, psychoanalysis, when properly understood, begins with the idea that mind must be sometimes irrational" (p. 90).

Perhaps Lear is suggesting that Freud's ideas were a corrective to Socrates but I believe that Freud intertwined the Greek with the Jewish. He layered his theory, locating irrationality and associative connections in the unconscious world of dreams, parapraxes and phantasy while developing rational, logical techniques—a scientific praxis to explore these products of mind. Handelman (1982) states that, "The movement of Rabbinic interpretation is not from one opposing sphere to another, from the sensible to the nonsensible, but rather 'from sense to sense' a movement into the text, not out of it" (p. 21). The data of psychoanalysis clearly falls into this longstanding exegetical tradition. Ostow (1982) and Frieden (1990) have written at length about the similar hermeneutics involved in text study of Talmudic exegesis and Freud's interpretative processes.

Freud needed psychoanalysis to be a science, a product of the enlightenment rationality and German high Kultur. I believe Freud straddled both worlds of Jewish and German cultures. His science attempts to adhere to scientific guidelines of logic. However, his greatest discovery of unconscious phenomena and mental life directly opposes the rationalist scheme of knowing the truth or reality of anything. Everything irrational, mysterious, uncontrollable is located in Freud's Unconscious. Freud then makes clear that the forms of psychoanalysis, the methods by which we discover, uncover and explore these passions are rational and logical—in a way, a Greek hermeneutical form. Ultimately, Freud creates a new field, psychoanalysis, which embraces science (logos) only to subvert it. He undermines his Greek rational logic with Jewish interpretative sensibility. The very process of interpretative examination both reveals and suggests the inability to ever fully know one's own mind, to ever be *only* the object or the subject of investigation. Freud can be seen as arguably one of the great integrators of these diverse worlds.

As Edgar Levenson wrote, "Freud, one might say, wrote Greek and thought Jewish" (p. 21). Why the need to say one thing but think another, one might wonder? Freud maintains equally his pride in being Jewish and being an atheist clearly stated to Oskar Pfister (1918), "Incidentally, why was it that none of the pious ever discovered psycho-analysis? Why did it have to wait for a completely godless Jew?" While continuing on his father's path toward assimilation, Freud was clearly concerned that his creation, psychoanalysis, not be considered a "Jewish" science dooming it to anti–Semitism, hatred or oblivion. But in fact he implanted both his "Jewishness" and his fear of anti–Semitism within his psychoanalysis. Freud failed to fully remember his own concept of the Unconscious—that we are unaware of thoughts, ideas, fantasies and feelings, which at any given point in time we may find unacceptable or unbearable. In some very primary way, he could not know what he knew and these very things can be seen and revealed in his dreams and memories.

I further believe that everything shameful for Freud becomes identified with the passive, the feminine and the Jew and becomes hidden in the unconscious. This split is embedded within the very structure of psychoanalysis, reflected in the conscious and unconscious aspects of mind as well as the split between the psychoanalytic technique for understanding mind and the content of what is being understood.

Conclusion

Rabbi Abraham Joshua Heschel says, "The Torah, we are told, is both concealed and revealed, and so is the nature of all reality. All things are both known and unknown, plain and enigmatic, transparent and impenetrable.... We know and do not know—this is our condition" (p. 23). And this is the exact space inhabited by Freud's Unconscious. He writes in a footnote during his discussion of the Irma Specimen Dream, "I had a feeling that the interpretation of this part of the dream was not carried far enough to make it possible to follow the whole of its concealed meaning.... There is at least one spot in every dream at which it is unplumbable—a navel, as it were, that is its point of contact with the unknown" (p. 111). And later he states, "There is often a passage in even the most thoroughly interpreted dream which has to be left obscure; ... This is the dream's navel, the spot where it reaches down into the unknown" (p. 525). This is the closest I believe Freud came to acknowledging true mystery. All he can do is acknowledge its existence, then have nothing more to do with it. But this rejection of mystery includes femininity, the body and the tie to the mother; for what is the navel but the scar reminding us all of our birth and umbilical tie to a mother?

Again we see him turn away from the unconsciously unknown, which includes femininity and passivity, and from religious experience turning towards the enlightenment agenda believing science explains all. John Cuddihy believes that psychoanalysis was created by and became a byproduct of the clash of Jewish with Gentile cultures. I have tried to show this was, in fact, a collision of multiple worlds—the Jewish with the Gentile, the masculine with the feminine and passivity with activity within Freud's life and mind. I believe there were very specific repressions for Freud resulting from these collisions. Repressions against femininity, Jewishness, passivity and religion, with the complementary idealization of masculinity, activity, science and atheism, which can all be seen threaded through his theories, letters and private remarks. But he never does completely repress and renounce. Instead it becomes embedded within his theory, hidden in plain sight.

Notes

1. An interesting note is that Glückl's memoirs are first translated from their original Yiddish into German by her great-great-granddaughter, Bertha Pappenheim. Pappenheim, best known in psychoanalytic circles as Breuer's Anna O., later went on to found the German Jewish Feminist Movement while remaining an Orthodox Jew.

References

Bakan, David (1958). *Sigmund Freud and the Jewish Mystical Tradition.* New York: Schocken.
Benjamin, Jessica (1998). *Shadow of the Other: Intersubjectivity and Gender in Psychoanalysis.* New York and London: Routledge.
Bergmann, Martin (1976). "Moses and the Evolution of Freud's Jewish Identity." Israel Annals of Psychiatry and Related Disciplines, Vol. 14, No.1, as reprinted in *Judaism and Psychoanalysis* (1982), ed. Mortimer Ostow. London: Karnac.
_____ (1995). "The Jewish and German Roots of Psychoanalysis and the Impact of the Holocaust." *American Imago* 52:3 (243–259).
_____ (1998). "Science and Art in Freud's Life and Work." In *Sigmund Freud and Art: His Personal Collection of Antiquities,* ed. Lynn Gamwell and Richard Wells. New York: Harry N. Abrams in association with State University of New York and Freud Museum, London.
Bickerman, Elias (1962). *From Ezra to the Last of the Maccabees.* New York: Schocken.
Boyarin, Daniel (1997). Unheroic Conduct: The Rise of Heterosexuality and the Invention of the Jewish Man. Berkeley and Los Angeles: University of California Press.
Breger, Louis (2000). *Freud: Darkness in the Midst of Vision.* New York: John Wiley & Sons.
Buber, Martin (1967). *On Judaism.* New York: Schocken.
Cuddihy, John Murray (1974). *The Ordeal of Civility: Freud, Marx Levi-Strauss, and the Jewish Struggle with Modernity.* New York: Basic.
Engelman, Edmund (1976). *Bergasse 19: Sigmund Freud's Home and Offices, Vienna 1938.* New York: Basic.
Feldman, Yael (1993). "And Rebecca Loved Jacob," But Freud Did Not." *Jewish Studies Quarterly* Vol. 1, No. 1 (72–88).
_____ (1998). "Isaac or Oedipus? Jewish Tradition and the Israeli Aqedah." *Biblical Studies/Cultural Studies: Journal for the Study of the Old Testament,* Supplement Series 266, Gender, Culture, Theory 7.
Frieden, Ken (1990). *Freud's Dream of Interpretation.* Albany: State University of New York Press.
Friedman, Susan S. (2002). *Analyzing Freud: Letters of H.D., Bryher, and their Circle.* New York: New Directions.
Freud, Sigmund (1895). "Project for a Scientific Psychology." *Standard Edition,* Vol. I.
_____ (1900). *The Interpretation of Dreams. Standard Edition,* Vol. IV and V.
_____ (1903). Letter to A.A. Roback in *The Letters of Sigmund Freud,* ed. Ernst L. Freud. New York: Basic.
_____ (1917). "A Childhood Memory of Goethe." *Standard Edition,* Vol. XVII.
_____ (1935). "An Autobiographical Study." *Standard Edition,* Vol. XX.

_____ (1954). *The Origins of Psycho-Analysis: Letters to Wilhelm Fliess, Drafts & Notes: 1887–1902.* Ed. Maria Bonaparte, Anna Freud and Ernst Kris. New York: Basic.
Garber, Marjorie (1995). *Vice Versa: Bisexuality and the Eroticism of Everyday Life.* New York: Simon and Schuster.
Gay, Peter (1987). *A Godless Jew: Freud, Atheism and the Making of Psychoanalysis.* New Haven, CT, and London: Yale University Press.
_____ (1988). *Freud: A Life for Our Time.* New York and London: Norton.
Gilman, Sander L. (1993). *Freud, Race, and Gender.* Princeton, NJ: Princeton University Press.
_____ (1993). *The Case of Sigmund Freud: Medicine and Identity at the Fin de Siecle.* Baltimore and London: John Hopkins University Press.
Handelman, Susan (1982). *The Slayers of Moses: The Emergence of Rabbinic Interpretation in Modern Literary Theory.* Albany: State University of New York Press.
Heschel, Abraham Joshua (1955). *God in Search of Man: A Philosophy of Judaism.* New York: Farrar, Straus and Giroux.
Hyman, Paula (1995). *Gender and Assimilation in Modern Jewish History.* Seattle and London: University of Washington Press.
Jones, Ernest (1953–5). *The Life and Work of Sigmund Freud: Vols. I, II.* New York: Basic.
Lear, Jonathan (1998). *Open Minded: Working out the Logic of the Soul.* Cambridge, MA: Harvard University Press.
Levenson, E.A. (2001). "Freud's Dilemma: On Writing Greek and Thinking Jewish." *Contemporary Psychoanalysis* 37 (375–390).
Margolis, Deborah (1996). *Freud and His Mother: The Preoedipal Aspects to Freud's Personality.* New York: Jason Aronson.
Meng, Heinrich, and Ernst Freud (1963). *Psychoanalysis and Faith: The Letters of Sigmund Freud and Oskar Pfister.* New York: Basic.
Nordau, Max (1903). "Muskeljudentum," in *Juedische Turnzeitung* (1903), reprinted and translated in *The Jew in the Modern World: A Documentary History,* Paul Mendes-Flohr and Jehuda Reinharz, New York and Oxford: Oxford University Press, 1980.
Ostow, Mortimer (1982). *Judaism and Psychoanalysis.* London: Karnac.
Rice, Emanuel (1990). *Freud and Moses: The Long Journey Home.* Albany: State University of New York Press.
Rizzuto, Ana-Maria (1998). *Why Did Freud Reject God? A Psychodynamic Interpretation.* New Haven, CT, and London: Yale University Press.
Roazen, Paul (1971). *Freud and His Followers.* New York: Alfred A. Knopf
Roith, Estelle (1987). *The Riddle of Freud: Jewish Influences on His Theory of Female Sexuality.* New York: Tavistock.
Schorske, Carl E. (1961). *Fin de Siècle Vienna: Politics and Culture.* New York: Vintage.
Simon, E. (1957). *Sigmund Freud, the Jew.* Leo Baeck Institute Yearbook, Vol. 2 (270–305).
Van Herik, Judith (1982). *Freud on Femininity and Faith.* Berkeley, Los Angeles and London: University of California Press.
Wistrich, R. (1991). *The Longest Hatred: Anti-Semitism.* New York: Schocken.

Assimilation and Affirmation
The Jews of Freud's Vienna
Marsha L. Rozenblit

In many ways Sigmund Freud was a typical Viennese Jew, although those ways are not necessarily obvious. He was certainly not typical in his fame and his contribution to modern culture. Although a surprisingly large number of Viennese Jews contributed to the creation of modern culture in Vienna, especially in literature and music, in fact, of course, most Viennese Jews were not cultural luminaries pressing the boundaries of bourgeois respectability, probing the dark undersides of the human psyche, exploring the role of the erotic and the sexual in human behavior.[1] He was also not typical in his bourgeois status. Many Viennese Jews had attained success in business and the professions and achieved middle class respectability and more, but most Jews in Vienna, probably two-thirds of the Jews in the city, were poor, too poor to pay the minimum tax to the Jewish religious community.[2] Moreover, he was not typical in his profound aversion to all religious observance. Many Jews in Vienna did secularize, did abandon some or many or even most of the rules and regulations of traditional Judaism, but most of them were not as anti-religious as Freud, one of whose biographers has called him "a Godless Jew."[3]

Freud may not have been typical in his cultural contributions, his bourgeois status, and his religious posture, but in all other ways he was typical: typical in his background, typical in his social and cultural transformation, typical in his view of the role of Jews in society, typical in his political posture, typical, in short, in his Jewish identity.[4] Freud, like most Jews in Vienna, was completely at home in German-Austrian culture, utterly loyal to the Habsburg Monarchy and its emperor, Franz Joseph, and above all, totally convinced that his primary identity was as a Jew, a German-Austrian Jew. It is this interesting mix that makes Freud a representative Viennese Jew. He was Austrian through and through; he was Viennese; he was German by culture, but not by any sense of belonging to the German *Volk*, the German people, defined in terms of descent, in terms of biology, in terms of ethnicity, in terms of race; and he was a Jew, a part of the Jewish people, with whom he shared descent, history, culture, fate, and in his own words, also, "the clear consciousness of an inner identity, the familiarity of the same psychological structures."[5] In other words, he felt more comfortable in the company of other Jews, and indeed, his social and professional contacts were almost exclusively with other Jews.

My focus here is not Freud's Jewish identity, but rather the identity of the Jews in his city. It is best to begin with some numbers. The Jews in Vienna in the late nineteenth and early twentieth century formed one of the largest Jewish communities in Europe. By 1910, about 175,000 Jews lived in the Austrian capital, forming about 9 percent of the total population of just over two million, and in the 1920s and 1930s, 200,000 Jews lived in the city.[6] Most of the Jews in the city were immigrants, not from Eastern Europe, but from other parts of the far-flung Habsburg Monarchy, who had immigrated to the city only in the second half of the nineteenth century. Indeed, before the Revolution of 1848, Jews were not allowed to live in Vienna at all unless they purchased, for exorbitant sums of money, a "Patent of Toleration," giving them permission to live in the city. In 1826, only 135 Jews had such a patent, which means that with their families, employees, servants, and hangers-on only about 2000 Jews lived in Vienna in the early nineteenth century.[7] After the Revolution and subsequent liberal legislation of 1859 removed the restrictions on residence, Jews flocked to Vienna.

The first wave of immigrants, arriving in the 1850s and 1860s, came from the Habsburg provinces of Bohemia and Moravia, today the Czech Republic. Freud's family was part of that wave. They came from Freiberg, Moravia, in 1860, when Freud was four years old. The second wave of Jewish immigrants, coming in the 1860s, '70s, '80s, and '90s, came from what was then the Kingdom of Hungary, mostly from areas of western Slovakia and western Hungary which were very close to Vienna, not from the Hasidic heartlands of eastern Hungary. Many of them came from Pressburg/Pozsony (today Bratislava), the center of non–Hasidic Hungarian Orthodoxy, or from the Burgenland, an area south of Vienna today in Austria, where Orthodoxy dominated. Finally, only at the very end of the nineteenth century and beginning of the twentieth, a large wave of Jewish immigrants from Galicia, that southern Polish territory that Austria annexed when Poland disintegrated in the late eighteenth century, came to Vienna. As a result of this immigration, by the eve of World War I, about 25 percent of the Jews of Vienna were born in Bohemia and Moravia, about 25 percent hailed from Western Hungary, about 20 percent came from Galicia, and about 25 percent had been born in the city, to immigrants from those same regions.[8] During World War I, hundreds of thousands of Jewish refugees fled Galicia, in terror in the face of the invading Russian army. A very large percentage of them, 70,000 at any given time, settled in Vienna. While most of them either returned home or migrated to the United States after the war, the number of Galician Jews in the Jewish population in Vienna in the interwar period was higher than it had been earlier.[9]

The Jews who moved to Vienna from Bohemia, Moravia, Hungary, and Galicia came from very diverse backgrounds. Some were already prosperous, and sought to improve their situation in the big city. Joseph Wechsberg, who grew up in Mährisch Ostrau/Ostrava, Moravia, recalled in his memoirs:

> When someone thought he was becoming prominent, he might move to Vienna where a man's opportunities were less limited and the rewards were higher. Vienna's attractions remained irresistible to the Germans and German-speaking Jews in Ostrau.... My mother's annual visits ... were considered almost a status symbol at home. It was said, perhaps not jokingly, that some people stayed up late at night trying to discover a relative in Vienna whom they might visit, just as a start.[10]

Others were extremely poor, and moved because Vienna offered economic opportunity, escape from poverty, and the ability to earn a living. Some Jews already spoke German, especially the Jews of Bohemia, Moravia, and Hungary, who had Germanized in the first part of the nineteenth century. Indeed, ever since Emperor Joseph II in his Edict of Toleration of 1781/82 had urged Jews to adopt German language and create modern German-Jewish schools, the Jews in the Bohemian lands and in many parts of Hungary eagerly adopted the German language.[11] Other Jewish immigrants, however, in particular the Jews of Galicia, spoke Yiddish (having successfully resisted Joseph's attempts to Germanize them). Some Jews had already modernized, others were eager to modernize, and still others were deeply enmeshed in the world of traditional Jewish culture, especially the Jews of Galicia, where many Jews were Hasidim, and western Slovakia/Hungary, where a large percentage of Jews abided by the pronouncements of the Hatam Sofer, who regarded Jewish religious innovation as apostasy.[12]

Whatever their backgrounds, to all Jewish immigrants the great cosmopolitan city Vienna offered endless possibilities, including freedom from both the mud and the restrictions of life in provincial cities and towns. In his memoirs, the writer Manès Sperber described his arrival in Vienna in July 1916, during World War I, as a 10-year-old boy from Zablatow, Galicia:

> I was absolutely certain that we had now finally reached the place with the gigantic gateway through which I would step into a wide world dedicated to the future. Everything lay before us.[13]

Minna Lachs, also a teen-age refugee to Vienna during World War I from Galicia, remembered in her memoirs how "totally captivated" she was when she arrived in the capital whose "magical beauty" her father had described in such detail. For these Jews, Vienna was more than a beautiful city. Lachs understood that for the Jews of Austria-Hungary Vienna was "not only the Mecca of German-Austrian culture, but also the door to the European intellectual world."[14]

Unfortunately, Vienna was not just the "gigantic gateway" to the future or the door to European culture. Vienna was also the city in which anti–Semitism flourished. Jews were emancipated in Austria-Hungary in 1867, receiving absolute legal and civil equality, and they suffered no official discrimination or persecution anywhere. But, anti–Semitic orators and anti–Semitic political parties flourished in Vienna. They appealed primarily, but not exclusively, to the lower middle class artisans and shopkeepers and clerks who felt threatened by modern economic and political developments and who listened to demagogues who blamed all their problems on "the Jews," who, so they claimed, controlled the economy and the political process. Anti-Semitism was the politics of resentment. It blamed Jews for the ills of modern society and sought to alleviate those ills by restricting the right of the Jews to play prominent roles in economic and public life, by depriving Jews of the very legal rights they had just won. Anti-Semitic parties existed in many places in Central Europe, but only in Vienna did such a party win an electoral victory. In 1895, the Christian Social Party of Karl Lueger won a majority of seats on the Vienna city council, a majority which it maintained (due to a restrictive franchise that prevented the poor from voting) until universal suffrage in 1919. Lueger himself, still beloved in Vienna, was mayor of Vienna from 1897 (the emperor delayed confirming him) until his death in 1910. Since city governments collect garbage, but do not make law, in fact, Lueger and his Christian Socials did nothing formally to hurt the Jews. Still, the anti–Semitic environment of the city reminded Jews that they were not fully accepted into Viennese society and culture.[15]

Despite the chilly anti–Semitic environment, the Jews who immigrated to Vienna took rapid steps to acculturate, to adopt German language and culture if they had not already done so. They also underwent a profound economic transformation, abandoning traditional Jewish occupations in petty trade and peddling to become respectable businessmen, professionals (doctors, lawyers, engineers), and "business employees," that is, managers, salesmen, and clerks in the large-scale commercial enterprises of the city, especially its large banks and insurance companies. In 1870, soon after the large-scale immigration of the Jews to Vienna began, most Jewish men were merchants of one sort or another, many of them only glorified peddlers. Of the Jewish men who got married in that year, 56 percent of them were merchants and 20 percent were artisans. Very few were civil servants (3 percent), industrialists (6 percent), business employees (3 percent), or workers (3 percent), but 11 percent were professionals. In 1910, by contrast, while the percentage of civil servants, industrialists, professionals, and workers remained roughly the same, the percentage of merchants had shrunk to 33 percent of the men who got married while the percentage of "business employees" had risen to 35 percent. The number of artisans also declined to 8 percent. Among the more prosperous dues-paying members of the Jewish religious community a similar economic transformation took place. Fully 62 percent of new members of the community between 1868 and 1879 were merchants and only 7 percent were "business employees," but among new members between 1900 and 1914, only 39 percent were merchants, and 28 percent clerks, salesmen, and managers. Such economic transformation meant not only that Jews spoke German and dressed like the European bourgeoisie, but also that many of them probably no long fully observed the Sabbath, since Saturday was a normal workday in late nineteenth century Europe.[16]

Jews also attended high school and university in record numbers. In a city in which Jews formed only 9 percent of the population, Jews were 25 percent of all students at the university. In 1900, they formed only 18 percent of all students in "Philosophy," which mostly prepared students for civil service or teaching careers, but they formed 23 percent of all students in law, and 40 percent of all students in medicine.[17] The statistics are even more impressive in secondary education. At that time, secondary education was reserved for a very narrow, male elite. In 1900, there were only 5,984 boys in *Gymnasium*, the elite secondary school that focused on Latin and Greek. But, in a city in which Jews were only 9 percent of the population, they formed 30 percent of all students in the *Gymnasium*.[18] This is not because Jews were rich. Indeed, as we have seen most were poor immigrants. The percentage of Jews at *Gymnasium* was so high because Jews understood its worth for upward social mobility and integration. In the areas of the city in which the Jews lived — the first, second, and ninth districts, the *Gymnasien* were overwhelmingly Jewish. In 1900, in the two *Gymnasien* in the first district, which was 19 percent Jewish, Jews formed "only" 35 percent and 44 percent of the student body, but in the *Gymnasium* in the ninth district, where Jews were 18 percent of the population, Jews were 65 percent of all students, and in the *Gymnasien* in the second district, which was 36 percent Jewish, Jews formed 71 percent and 75 percent of the student body.[19] Jews were also a large percentage of students at the *Realschulen*, which focused on math, science, and modern languages and prepared students for the Technical University and careers as engineers or architects.[20] They were even more noticeable in secondary schools for girls, forming 45 percent of the population in such schools, and almost the entire student body in some.[21]

My main point here is that although Jews in Vienna eagerly and thoroughly acculturated, that is adopted Austrian German culture, they nevertheless also remained self-conscious Jews, identifiable as a Jewish group within the larger society, and not just because of anti-Semitism. That Jews formed a separate group in Vienna was literally visible, but not because Jews dressed differently or looked different than other Viennese (which they did not) or because they practiced (or did not practice) a different religion (which they did). Jews were noticeable because they occupied a different niche in the economy than everyone else. Jews may have abandoned traditional Jewish occupations, but they did not "assimilate" economically. They did not become industrial workers, who formed half of the working population in Vienna. Because of de facto discrimination, they also did not work for the imperial, state, or city governments, which employed another large percentage of Viennese. Jews remained concentrated in commerce, they had become professionals, and they worked as employees in the business world, which became a kind of new "Jewish" occupation.[22]

More important, however, than economic clustering for continued Jewish group separateness was the fact that Jews concentrated in certain neighborhoods of the city. Jews were 9 percent of the total population of the city, but they formed about 19 percent of the population of the first district (the inner city), 36 percent of the population of the second district (the Leopoldstadt), known affectionately as "Die Mazzesinsel," the island of Mazzah),[23] and 18 percent of the ninth district (the Alsergrund), where Freud lived his adult life on Berggasse 19, around the corner from Theodor Herzl. Within these districts, which were adjacent to each other, Jews also concentrated in certain areas, so that some parts of the city were — or at least seemed — almost wholly Jewish. While there was some distinctions based on wealth within this Jewish concentration, in general rich and poor Jews lived together in the same neighborhoods, with the richer Jews in nicer apartment houses on the main thoroughfares, and poorer Jews in shabbier buildings on the smaller side streets. Jews lived with each other because they wanted to, not because there was discrimination in housing. Moreover, Jews lived with each other rather than with non-Jews from the same part of Austria-Hungary as they. Vienna contained lots of Czech immigrants, but Jews from Bohemia and Moravia did not live near them in Vienna's tenth district, because the Czechs were mostly Czech-speaking industrial workers and the Jews, no matter how poor, spoke German and mostly worked in the commercial sector of the economy. Moreover, Jews from Bohemia and Moravia identified as Jews, not as Czechs. The fact that Jews clustered in certain neighborhoods had important repercussions. Not only did it serve as a reminder to the Jews and to the non-Jews that the Jews formed a separate group in the city, it also created the setting in which Jews associated primarily with each other.[24]

Certainly the fact that Jewish boys in *Gymnasium* attended school largely in the company of other Jews had an important impact on the way they acculturated and the way they understood their place as Jews in the larger society. Going to school with so many other Jews made acculturation a Jewish group experience, it mitigated the impact of the crucifixes on the walls of the public schools, and it meant that Jewish boys befriended other Jewish boys.[25]

Jews were also distinct because they chose to be so. Jews formed a wide range of organizations in which they could socialize with other Jews. In addition to the "Jewish religious community," to which by law all Jews had to belong and pay taxes (if they could afford it), Jews created charitable, fraternal, gymnastic, musical, and political organizations in which they could articulate old or new Jewish ideologies, receive honor, and foster a sense of Jewish solidarity. One interesting Jewish organization formed in Vienna was the "Austrian-Israelite Union," an organization founded in 1886 both to fight anti-Semitism by taking the anti-Semites to court and also to bolster Jewish self-consciousness and pride.[26] Emphasizing their Austrian patriotism and their "political brotherhood with the peoples and nations among whom ... [we] are born and raised, in whose literature ... [we] are educated by preference and in whose economic and cultural life ... [we] participate," the leaders of this organization stressed their overriding commitment to "Jewish consciousness and its preservation," and stressed that their "holiest duty" was "to uphold our ancient heritage."[27] Joseph Samuel Bloch, the rabbi and newspaper editor who first called for such an organization, never tired of repeating in his weekly Jewish newspaper, the *Österreichische Wochenschrift*, that Jews formed a *Stamm*, literally tribe, but perhaps best represented in English by the term "ethnic group." Jews he argued in an interesting series of articles in 1919, possessed the "ethnological isolation, uniqueness, and exclusivity" of a race as well as a firm sense of belonging to an ethnic community (*Stammesgemeinschaft*)." At the same time, Jews formed "a metaphysical-ethical God-community."[28] Similarly, a spokesman for the Austrian Israelite Union argued that the Jews were not primarily a *Volk*, but rather a religious community whose members shared the same ethnicity (*Stamm*) and blood.[29]

Of course Vienna's Zionists also articulated a very strong sense of Jewish peoplehood and distinctiveness. Vienna was the birthplace, after all, of modern political Zionism. Theodor Herzl was born in Budapest, but he was prominent Viennese journalist who conceived the idea of a Jewish state because of the anti–Semitism he experienced both in Vienna and while a correspondent in France. Herzl inspired a whole generation of followers in Vienna, followers who were mesmerized by his charisma, even if they were already Zionists long before he had galvanized them into action.[30] It was in Vienna where the first Zionist dueling fraternity, Kadimah, was born in 1883. The members of Kadimah rallied around Herzl in 1896 and provided him with loyal shock troops. One such person, Isidor Schalit, recalled the excitement he and his fellow Kadimiahner felt when they read Herzl's call to action. Perhaps not literally, but certainly emotionally, Schalit raced to Herzl's home and cried:

> Herr Doktor, what you have written is our dream, the dream of many young people. What we have sought for so many years but not found is the word that you have now pronounced: the Jewish State. Come with us and lead us and we will create what men are capable of creating.[31]

The Zionist movement in Vienna, like everywhere, was a minority movement for several decades, but it, and its idea that the Jews were a nation, entitled like other nations to nationhood and a home of their own, nevertheless appealed to a growing number of Viennese Jews. The Zionists created a whole raft of organizations and even tried to take over the Jewish religious community, not succeeding until 1932.[32] They and their Jewish diaspora nationalist allies demanded that Austria be re-organized as a federation of autonomous nationalities, each controlling its own cultural, educational, and charitable affairs, and they insisted that the Jews should be counted as one of the nationalities of Austria. Indeed, in their Cracow Platform of 1906, Austrian Zionists embraced a program which focused on political activity in the diaspora.[33] They also ran candidates for parliament on a Zionist ticket, insisting that only Jews should represent the Jews.[34] In their parliamentary efforts they were successful only once, in 1919. When Robert Stricker, the leader of Austrian Zionists in the interwar period who was deported later to Theresienstadt and Auschwitz, took his seat in the Austrian parliament he announced, "I am a Jew."[35]

But even Jews who eschewed the Zionist movement had a strong sense of Jewishness in Vienna. Not only was the structure of their lives largely Jewish, not only did they live in an anti–Semitic environment in which they would naturally prefer the company of fellow Jews, but the very nature of Habsburg Austria itself allowed them the freedom to comfortably assert a Jewish ethnic identity. Pre–World War I Austria was not a nation-state like France or Germany which demanded that its Jews adopt a French or German national identity as they acculturated and modernized in the nineteenth century. Austria was an old fashioned dynastic state, which included many "peoples" who spoke different languages and conceived themselves as nations. There was no "Austrian" national identity, although of course there was Austrian state patriotism and dynastic loyalty. The Habsburg state itself determined that eleven "nationalities" (*Volksstämme*), defined in terms of the languages they spoke, lived in the realm: Germans, Hungarians, Czechs, Poles, Ukrainians, Slovaks, Serbs, Croats, Italians, Romanians, and Slovenes. In 1867, the Habsburg authorities gave the Hungarians quasi-sovereignty and created the Dual Monarchy of Austria-Hungary. The Kingdom of Hungary was essentially an independent country, tied to the rest of the Monarchy in common foreign policy, foreign trade, a common army, and in the person of the monarch. In the rest of the country — in Habsburg Austria — the authorities gave the nationalities the right to develop their national languages and cultures as long as they were also loyal to the state as a whole and to the emperor. The nationalities engaged in a long struggle for more than linguistic rights, and the resultant nationalities conflict proved terribly divisive, paralyzing politics in the Monarchy's last decades. The state, however, never imposed a single national identity or language on anyone, even if German remained a privileged language, and the Germans, who considered themselves the *Staatsvolk*, the people on whom the state rested, resented the demands of the other nationalities.[36] In such a state it was easy for the Jews — officially counted as a religious group, not a nationality — to feel enormous loyalty to the state and to feel comfortable asserting Jewish ethnic identity, far more comfortable than Jews in the nation states of Western Europe.

Indeed, the Jews all over Habsburg Austria developed what I have labeled a "tripartite" identity. They had an Austrian political identity, warmly supporting the Habsburg state, praying that it would not fall apart, and mourning its collapse after World War I. They correctly understood that this state protected them from the anti–Semitism rampant in many of the nationalist movements, acting as an umpire in the nationalities conflict, and insisting on Jewish legal rights. Jews also adored the emperor Franz Joseph, (incorrectly) giving him the credit for their emancipation. Jews in Galicia even affectionately called him "Froyim Yossel." In addition to this Austrian political identity, modernizing Jews also adopted the languages and cultures of the peoples amongst whom they lived. In Vienna Jews adopted a German cultural identity, and shared the German sense of the superiority of German culture. But, they did not necessarily think they were "Germans," members of the German *Volk*. Austrian political loyalty and German cultural affinity left the Jews, in the Habsburg Austrian context, with plenty of room to assert a Jewish ethnic identity in private and in public. Thus Viennese Jews were politically Austrian, culturally German, and ethnically Jewish.[37] This was true not only for the Zionists or the leaders of the Austrian Israelite Union, but for Vienna's rabbis and religious establishment and for ordinary Jews like Sigmund Freud as well. Such a political context made it easier for Jews, including Jews like Freud, to feel politically Austrian, culturally German, and ethnically Jewish all at the same time.

Memoirs of Jews from Vienna emphasize the Austrian and the Jewish, but not so much the German identity of the writers. The writer Stefan Zweig, for example, introduced his memoirs by telling his readers that he was "an Austrian, a Jew, an author, a humanist, and a pacifist."[38] Similarly, the much less famous George Clare emphasized his, his parents', and his grandparents' (all of whom were born in Galicia or Bukovina) Austrian, or German-Austrian identity. His father and his siblings, were "fully integrated Viennese. They were born and grew up as Austrians among Austrians."[39] Sigmund Mayer, a wealthy businessman who wrote his memoirs in 1911, noted that Vienna did not obsess about its German identity, so Jews easily assimilated into the German cultural nation there, but continued to feel part of the Jewish *Volk*.[40] In his unpublished memoirs, the doctor Otto Ehrentheil insisted that "we are children of the tribe which has existed for 4000 years," a tribe formed by "historical circumstances" and by "blood relationships" generating "certain attitudes which are of value."[41] Similarly Vienna's rabbis emphasized that Jews belonged to the Jewish *Volk* or *Stamm*, a people whose culture derived from its unique religion. Jews formed a religio-ethnic group, not just a religious community, and they were German by culture, but not part of the German *Volk*. Adolf Jellinek, Vienna's Reform chief rabbi from the 1865 to 1893, insisted that although the Jews were not a modern political nation, they "belong to one and the same *Stamm* and profess the same articles of faith."[42]

World War I provided the Jews with the perfect opportunity to assert this tripartite identity. Fighting and dying as soldiers in the army or contributing money and time to help those suffering on the home front, Austrian Jews asserted their patriotism and their loyalty to state and emperor. At the same time, however, they saw the war as a Jewish holy war, to defeat the evil Russian Empire and liberate the Jews of Russian-occupied Galicia and of Russia itself. The fact that the bulk of Viennese Jewish work on the home front went to help Galician refugees in the city meant that their patriotic war work also led to increased Jewish solidarity. In the last two years of the war, as war weariness and hunger contributed to escalating antisemitism, and as the nationalist activists began to work toward independence, the Jews of Habsburg Austria fervently wished for the continuity of the supranational state at the same time as they worried that they were "the only Austrians loyal to the state left in the Monarchy," in the words of a liberal Jewish newspaper in Vienna.[43] With some hyperbole, the Viennese Zionist Robert Stricker argued in a speech in November 1917, "We nationally-conscious Jews want a strong Austria. Only it can provide a home to its nations. We believe that an Austria must exist. If there were no Austria, it would be a misfortune for the entire world."[44] When Austria collapsed in late October 1918, one Jewish spokesmen in Vienna mourned:

> We acknowledge openly and honestly the deep pain in our hearts about the gloomy and painful transformation and upheaval. It is with ... deep sadness ... that we bid farewell to the united fatherland, and we stand shocked before the grave of old, familiar, honorable memories and feelings ... that a day of calamity has dashed into ruins. Our only comfort is the thought that we Jews are not guilty for it.[45]

The creation of the Austrian Republic in November 1918 created a real crisis of identity for the Jews of Vienna. They missed the old state, and they were not really quite sure what the new state demanded of them. Indeed, at that point, most people in Austria, considering themselves German, only wanted *Anschluss* with Germany, a step the victorious Allies would not allow. But the Jews did not want to be part of Weimar Germany, because they were Austrian and not German. Indeed, while they naturally possessed German culture, they did not think of themselves as German in a national sense. To them Germanness remained cultural. They continued to think of themselves as Austrian, as German by culture, and primarily as Jews.[46]

The Jews of Freud's Vienna then wanted to be Viennese and to be Jewish, to be Jews of Vienna and Viennese Jews. They succeeded utterly, certainly in the Monarchy, and even in the new, troubled Austrian first republic. They were Austrian Jews who had successfully assimilated into German culture, but continued to affirm their Jewish identities and their sense of belonging to the Jewish people.

Notes

1. The literature on Jewish contributions to Viennese modern culture is vast. For a new and interesting exploration, see Abigail Gillman, *Viennese Jewish Modernism: Genres of Memory* (College Station: Penn State University Press, 2008). Interestingly, many of the Jews or men of Jewish origins who participated in Viennese literary modernism also explored the psychological and erotic underpinnings of human behavior.

2. This is my estimate based on the number of Jews who could afford to pay the minimum tax to the *Israelitische Kultusgemeinde*, the organized Jewish community in the late nineteenth and early twentieth centuries. For lists of taxpayers to the Jewish community see *Verzeichnis der im Wiener Gemeindegebiete wohnhaften Wähler für die Wahlen in den Cultusvorstand und der Vertrauensmänner im Jahre 1900* (Vienna: Israelitische Kultusgemeinde in Wien, 1900), in Central Archives for the History of the Jewish People, AW 50/1.

3. See Peter Gay, *A Godless Jew: Freud, Atheism, and the Making of Psychoanalysis* (New Haven, CT: Yale University Press, 1987).
4. There is an extensive literature on Freud's Jewish identity. See especially, Marthe Robert, *From Oedipus to Moses: Freud's Jewish Identity*, trans. Ralph Manheim (Garden City, NY: Anchor, 1976); Martin Freud, "Who Was Freud," in Josef Fraenkel, ed., *The Jews of Austria: Essays on Their Life, History and Destruction* (London: Valentine, Mitchell, 1967); Peter Gay, *A Godless Jew*, and idem, *Freud: A Life for Our Time* (New York: Norton, 1988); and Yosef Yerushalmi, *Freud's Moses* (New Haven, CT: Yale University Press, 1991).
5. As quoted in Robert, *From Oedipus to Moses*, 35.
6. For 1910 statistics see *Österreichische Statistik*, N.F., vol. 2, no. 1, 33 and *Statistisches Jahrbuch der Stadt Wien* (1910), 25. For the interwar period, see Leo Goldhammer, *Die Juden Wiens: Eine statistische Studie* (Vienna: R. Löwit, 1927), 9.
7. On the history of the Jews of Vienna in the first half of the nineteenth century see Sigmund Mayer, *Die Wiener Juden 1700–1900: Kommerz, Kultur, Politik* (Vienna: R. Löwit, 1917) and Hans Tietze, *Die Juden Wiens: Geschichte-Wirtschaft-Kultur* (Leipzig: E.P. Tal, 1933). For estimates of Jewish population, see Israel Jeiteles, *Die Kultusgemeinde der Israeliten in Wien mit Benützung des statistischen Volkszählungsoperatus vom Jahre 1869* (Vienna: L. Rosner, 1873) and Akos Löw, "Die soziale Zusammensetzung der Wiener Juden nach den Trauungs–und Geburtsmatrikeln, 1784–1848," unpublished Ph.D. Dissertation, University of Vienna, 1952.
8. These figures are the result of my own computer-assisted analysis of a data base I compiled from the birth and marriage records of Viennese Jews in five sample years (1870, 1880, 1890, 1900, and 1910), and from a data base of every fourth taxpayer to the Jewish community whose last name fell between K and Q (the only extant files) between 1855 and 1918. Birth and marriage registers (*Geburtsbücher und Trauungsbücher*) of the Jewish community are located in the offices of the current Jewish community (*Israelitische Kultusgemeinde*) in Vienna. For a full discussion of the results of this analysis for an understanding of Jewish immigration patterns, see Marsha L. Rozenblit, *The Jews of Vienna, 1867–1918: Assimilation and Identity* (Albany: State University of New York Press, 1983), 13–45.
9. On Galician refugees to Vienna see Beatrix Hoffmann-Holter, "*Abreisendmachung*": *Jüdische Kriegsflüchtlinge in Wien 1914 bis 1923* (Vienna: Böhlau, 1995) and David Rechter, "Galicia in Vienna: Jewish Refugees in the First World War," *Austrian History Yearbook* 28 (1997): 113–130.
10. Joseph Wechsberg, *The Vienna I Knew: Memories of a European Childhood* (Garden City, NY: Doubleday, 1979), 137.
11. Hillel J. Kieval, "Caution's Progress: Enlightenment and Tradition in Jewish Prague, 1780–1830," in Hillel J. Kieval, *Languages of Community: The Jewish Experience in the Czech Lands* (Berkeley: University of California Press, 2000), 37–64; Ruth Kestenberg-Gladstein, *Neuere Geschichte der Juden in den böhmischen Ländern, Erster Teil: Das Zeitalter der Aufklärung, 1780–1830* (Tübingen: J.C.B. Mohr, 1969), 41–65.
12. On the Jews of Galicia, see Piotr Wróbel, "The Jews of Galicia under Austro-Polish Rule, 1869–1918," *Austrian History Yearbook* 25 (1994): 97–138, and Israel Bartal and Antony Polonsky, "Introduction: The Jews of Galicia under the Habsburgs," in *Polin: Studies in Polish Jewry* 12 (1999), "Focusing on Galicia: Jews, Poles, and Ukrainians, 1772–1918": 3–24. On the religious posture of Jews in Western Hungary and Slovakia, see Jacob Katz, *A House Divided: Orthodoxy and Schism in Nineteenth-Century Central European Jewry* (Hanover, NH: University Press of New England, 1998).
13. Manès Sperber, *God's Water Carriers*, trans. Joachim Neugroschel (New York: Holmes and Meier, 1987), 99.
14. Minna Lachs, *Warum schaust du zurück. Erinnerungen 1907–1941* (Vienna: Europaverlag, 1986), 45, 44, 122.
15. On Lueger and the Christian Social Party in Vienna see John W. Boyer, *Political Radicalism in Late Imperial Vienna: Origins of the Christian Social Movement, 1848–1897* (Chicago: University of Chicago Press, 1981) and John W. Boyer, *Culture and Political Crisis in Vienna: Christian Socialism in Power, 1897–1918* (Chicago: University of Chicago Press, 1995).
16. Rozenblit, *Jews of Vienna*, 47–70.
17. *Österreichische Statistik*, vol. 70, no. 3 (1904): 2–5.
18. *Österreichische Statistik*, vol. 70, no. 3 (1904): 32–33.
19. *Österreichische Statistik*, vol. 70, no. 3 (1904): 32–33. For Jewish populations of each district, *Statistisches Jahrbuch der Stadt Wien* (1901): 50–51. For a full discussion of Jews in Viennese *Gymnasien* see Rozenblit, *Jews of Vienna*, 99–125.

20. *Österreichische Statistik*, vol. 70, no. 3 (1904): 44–45.
21. *Österreichische Statistik*, N.F., vol. 8, no. 2, pp. 68–71, 102–103.
22. Rozenblit, *Jews of Vienna*, 47–70.
23. For a wonderfully evocative treatment for the interwar period see Ruth Beckermann, ed., *Die Mazzesinsel: Juden in der Wiener Leopoldstadt, 1918–1938* (Vienna: Löcker, 1984).
24. Rozenblit, *Jews of Vienna*, 71–98.
25. Rozenblit, *Jews of Vienna*, 122–125.
26. Rozenblit, *Jews of Vienna*, 146–161. On the OIU, see also Robert Wistrich, *The Jews of Vienna in the Age of Franz Joseph* (Oxford: Oxford University Press, 1989), 270–343.
27. *Österreichische Wochenschrift*, 30 April 1886, 193–195.
28. *Österreichische Wochenschrift*, 27 June 1919, 390–92.
29. *Monatsschrift der Oesterreichisch-Israelitische Union*, vol. 31, nos. 2–4 (February–April 1919), 4.
30. On Zionism in Vienna, see Rozenblit, *Jews of Vienna*, 161–174; Wistrich, *Jews of Vienna*, 347–493; and Adolf Gaisbauer, *Davidstern und Doppeladler. Zionismus und jüdischer Nationalismus in Österreich, 1882–1918* (Vienna: Böhlau, 1988); and for the interwar period, Harriet Pass Freidenreich, *Jewish Politics in Vienna, 1918–1938* (Bloomington: Indiana University Press, 1991), 48–83.
31. Isidor Schalit, "Erinnerungen" of Kadimah, 80, in Central Zionist Archives, A 196/19.
32. Rozenblit, 185–193; Freidenreich, 72–83.
33. The classic statement of this demand was made by the Hermann Kadisch, *Jung Juden und Jung Österreich* (Vienna: Adria, 1912); and Hermann Kadisch, *Die Juden und die österreichische Verfassungsrevision* (Vienna: Wm. Berkelhammer, 1918).
34. Rozenblit, 170–184; Freidenreich, 59–72.
35. As quoted in Josef Fraenkel, "Robert Stricker," in Josef Fraenkel, ed., *Robert Stricker* (London: Claridge, Lewis & Jordan, 1950), 14.
36. The literature on the nature of the Habsburg Monarchy and its nationalities conflict is vast. In English, see C.A. Macartney, *The Habsburg Empire 1790–1918* (New York: Macmillan, 1969); Alan Sked, *The Decline and Fall of the Habsburg Empire, 1815–1918* (London: Longman, 1989); and Pieter M. Judson and Marsha L. Rozenblit, ed., *Constructing Nationalities in East Central Europe* (New York: Berghahn, 2005).
37. For a fuller discussion of this tripartite identity see Marsha L. Rozenblit, *Reconstructing a National Identity: The Jews of Habsburg Austria during World War I* (New York: Oxford University Press, 2001). On Galician Jews calling the emperor Froyim Yossel, see Joachim Schoenfeld, *Jewish Life in Galicia under the Austro-Hungarian Empire and in the Reborn Poland, 1898–1939* (Hoboken, NJ: Ktav, 1985), xx.
38. Stefan Zweig, *The World of Yesterday* (New York: Viking, 1943), v.
39. George Clare, *Last Waltz in Vienna: The Rise and Destruction of a Family, 1842–1942* (New York: Holt, Rinehart and Winston, 1980), 15, 17, 31.
40. Sigmund Mayer, *Ein jüdischer Kaufmann 1831 bis 1911: Lebenserinnerungen* (Leipzig: Drucker und Humblot, 1911), 289, 350, 485.
41. Otto Ehrentheil, "Part of the Honors," unpublished memoir (1977–78), Leo Baeck Institute, New York, 99.
42. *Die Neuzeit*, 10 March 1893, 113. See also Adolf Jellinek, *Die jüdische Stamm: Ethnographische Studien* (Vienna: Herzfeld & Bauer, 1869).
43. *Österreichische Wochenschrift*, 19 July 1918, 441–442. On attitudes of Jews to the war, see Rozenblit, *Reconstructing a National Identity*.
44. *Selbstwehr*, 23 November 1917, 4.
45. *Österreichische Wochenschrift*, 25 October 1918, 673–675.
46. Rozenblit, *Reconstructing a National Identity*, 128–172.

References

Beckermann, Ruth, ed. *Die Mazzesinsel: Juden in der Wiener Leopoldstadt, 1918–1938*. Vienna: Löcker, 1984.
Beller, Steven. *Vienna and the Jews, 1867–1938: A Cultural History*. Cambridge: Cambridge University Press, 1989.

Boyer, John W. *Culture and Political Crisis in Vienna: Christian Socialism in Power, 1897–1918*. Chicago: University of Chicago Press, 1995.
_____ *Political Radicalism in Late Imperial Vienna: Origins of the Christian Social Movement, 1848–1897*. Chicago: University of Chicago Press, 1981.
Clare, George. *Last Waltz in Vienna: The Rise and Destruction of a Family, 1842–1942*. New York: Holt, Rinehart, and Winston, 1980.
Freidenreich, Harriet Pass. *Jewish Politics in Vienna, 1918–1938*. Bloomington: Indiana University Press, 1991.
Gaisbauer, Adolf. *Davidstern und Doppeladler: Zionismus und jüdischer Nationalismus in Österreich, 1882–1918*. Vienna: Böhlau, 1988.
Goldhammer, Leo. *Die Juden Wiens: Eine statistische Studie*. Vienna: R. Löwit, 1927.
Hoffmann-Holter, Beatrix. *"Abreisendmachung": Jüdische Kriegsflüchtlinge in Wien1914 bis 1923*. Vienna: Böhlau, 1995.
Lachs, Minna. *Warum schaust du zurück: Erinnerungen 1907–1941*. Vienna: Europaverlag, 1986.
Mayer, Sigmund. *Ein jüdischer Kaufmann 1831 bis 1911: Lebenserinnerungen*. Leipzig: Drucker und Humblot, 1911.
_____ *Die Wiener Juden 1700–1900: Kommerz, Kultur, Politik*. Vienna: R. Löwit, 1917.
Rechter, David. "Galicia in Vienna: Jewish Refugees in the First World War." *Austrian History Yearbook* 28 (1997): 113–130.
Rozenblit, Marsha L. *The Jews of Vienna, 1867–1918: Assimilation and Identity*. Albany: State University of New York Press, 1983.
_____ *Reconstructing a National Identity: The Jews of Habsburg Austria During World War I*. New York: Oxford University Press, 2001.
Sperber, Manès. *God's Water Carriers*, trans. Joachim Neugroschel. New York: Holmes and Meier, 1987.
Tietze, Hans. *Die Juden Wiens: Geschichte-Wirtschaft-Kultur*. Leipzig: E.P. Tal, 1933.
Wistrich, Robert. *The Jews of Vienna in the Age of Franz Joseph*. Oxford: Oxford University Press, 1989.
Zweig, Stefan. *The World of Yesterday*. New York: Viking, 1943.

Being Mr. Somebody
Freud and Classical Education
RICHARD H. ARMSTRONG

As many scholars have noted, there is something highly typical about Freud in relation to his overall social trajectory, no matter how original and unusual we deem the content of his work.[1] Already the fact that he was born in Moravia and moved to Vienna as a boy of four reflects the general pattern of immigration that would transform Vienna in his lifetime into an urban center bursting at the seams, whose Jewish population would peak at close to 10 percent.[2] Freud grew up in the 1860s and '70s in Leopoldstadt, the former Jewish ghetto and the most Jewish quarter of the city by a very wide margin, and this also marks him as a fairly typical Jewish boy of the age.[3] He later moved to Berggasse 19 in the Alsergrund, Vienna's ninth district, where he would live most of his adult life as a settled professional and family man — and this conforms quite well to a predictable arc of success within the sociological parameters of the time. In the words of Marsha Rozenblit, the Alsergrund with its concentration of Jewish professionals had become "the proper address for a new breed of urban Jew" (1983, p. 85). This move thus signifies Freud's passage from the lower-middle class of shopkeepers and merchants — his father was a wool merchant — to the ranks of the *Bildungsbürgertum*, the educated middle class. Lastly, even his choice of a career in medicine was quite predictable for the times. As Gary Cohen observes, "Among the learned professions, medicine offered Jews much greater career opportunities than did law and government employment or teaching. Thus, the Vienna medical faculty had the highest Jewish enrollments by far among the various university faculties, reaching a peak of around 55 percent of the students in the early 1880s" (1990, p. 182). From all outward appearances, then, Freud was a kind of secular Jewish Everyman.

Certain attitudes of the young Freud — as glimpsed in letters to his friends Emil Fluss and Eduard Silberstein, and to his fiancée Martha Bernays — also appear as predictable for a young man who is attempting to make his way in a world that is changing very fast, and yet not nearly fast enough for a person classed among the *Israeliten* (as the school records put it). In these letters, he is painfully aware of the anti–Semitic currents around him that pose real obstacles; yet he also entertains hopes for advancement through the secular path of *Wissenschaft*, based upon a trait he termed "the industry, the tenacious enthusiasm of the Jew."[4] Like many Jews with a powerful urge to acculturate into some notion of a universal culture, the young Freud was loyal to the basic values of the *Bildungsbürgertum*, looking down on effete aristocrats on the one hand and the rowdy and undisciplined working class on the other.[5] He confesses to feeling more at home with Jewish families who have known something of poverty, like that of his beloved *Gymnasium* teacher Samuel Hammerschlag, than with those of great wealth, like the Schwabs.[6] He was not above making unkind comments concerning uncouth Moravian Jews whose habits greatly annoyed him, nor was he above being thoroughly appalled at bad Jewish behavior displayed at a funeral or a wedding.[7] He was too fiercely proud, however, ever to deny his own Jewishness. His only apparent flirtation with conversion was simply a technicality, a means of being allowed the luxury of a civil wedding in Vienna by declaring himself a Protestant, thus avoiding the ceremonial inconveniences of a Jewish wedding (Jones 1953–57, vol. 1, p. 167; see also Gilman 1998, chapter 3).

For Jewish boys of the time, the gateway to assimilation via the liberal professions was the *Gymnasium*, the elite eight-year humanistic school that fostered the high ideals of *Bildung*—a word we strain to translate in English as "education/self-cultivation." These ideals were rooted in the *Deutsche Klassik*, the great period of German humanism dating from the late eighteenth century and into the early nineteenth. Initially, this German humanism seemed to fit seamlessly together with the rising current of professionalization in Classical Studies, or the formation of *Altertumswissenschaft*, or "the science of antiquity." The Swiss historian Jacob Burckhardt, whom Freud read assiduously in the 1890s, even commented ironically on the supposed *hieros gamos* or "sacred marriage" between the cultures of Greece and Germany since the age of Goethe, an elective affinity supposedly unique in modern times (1998, p. 11). Though the further professionalization of Classical Studies would spin it off into its own overspecialized world, the one place where the "sacred marriage" of Classical and German culture was kept alive was the *Gymnasium*. In their internal publications, *Gymnasium* teachers tirelessly upheld the value of their curriculum against the pressures of a more practical education. In defending the assiduous attention to Latin and Greek, one teacher wrote:

> It is a much higher goal that is sought with these languages[...], that is, a general self-cultivation [*eine allgemeine Bildung*], the cultivation of what is purely human and the ennoblement of the mind and heart.
>
> The student who graduates from *Gymnasium* may well forget both languages and even the content of their literatures, but he can in no way lose the treasure he obtained in their study [Kalberg 1888, p. 14].

Another teacher emphasized the necessity of classical languages with the argument that "without understanding Greek, a thorough understanding of our native literature is impossible: Lessing, Schiller, Goethe are all tied the Hellenic mentality by a thousand fine threads" (Schiller 1875, p. 40).

Altertumswissenschaft itself became a bellwether for the development of critical historiography, archaeology, and textual philology, and its reach in nineteenth-century culture was very pervasive. As for its leavening effect on modern thought, one need only remember its place among the "triumvirate of suspicion," as they are quaintly known: Nietzsche, the professional classical scholar; Marx, who dissertated on Epicurus' philosophy of nature, and Freud, the amateur archaeologist and excavator of myths and religions. I have written at length (Armstrong 2005) about the various intersections of the archive of antiquity with Freud's own projects, but I am more interested here in underlining the peculiarly *Jewish* aspect of the *Gymnasium* education in Vienna.

That might well sound like an odd way to begin, since this form of schooling was, as I already said, the gateway to mainstream *assimilation*. One could easily assume that spouting your Latin and Greek — as well as your Goethe and Schiller — would be the best means of declaring your suitability for polite society, i.e., of declaring your thorough de–Judification. But I contend that classical education is not simply to be arrayed with all things gentile over and against all things Jewish; Latin and Greek can indeed constitute a third something between Jewish tradition and the dominant culture. I take it as emblematic of this triangulation that when Joseph Breuer explained to the militant Jewish student group Kadimah his position as an assimilated Jew, he defined himself as *gente judaeus, natione germanus:* "by clan or *gens*, a Jew; by nation, a German" (Hirschmüller 1989, p. 219). In other words, he defined himself as a German Jew, but used Latin to say it — not German, not Hebrew, not Yiddish.

The demographic analysis of Viennese education produced by Steven Beller, Marsha Rozenblit and others shows that, whatever the initial intentions were on the part of the dominant culture in allowing Jews access to *Gymnasium* education, the results were certainly hard to control.[8] The striking over-representation of Jewish students in the *Gymnasien* of Vienna cannot simply be taken as *prima facie* evidence of a rush to assimilate completely, or even as an overzealous fulfillment of the norm. The very concentration of Jewish students, particularly in Freud's school in Leopoldstadt, could easily be seen as creating a different kind of homogenization: not the dissolution of Jewish identity into a Christian Austrian mainstream, but rather the jelling of a secular Jewish identity caught at the crossroads. The *Gymnasium* can thus be read as a space where young Jewish men could negotiate an identity on the one hand *separate* from the Jewish traditions of their families (a separation made easier by the fact of immigration to Vienna in itself, which released many Jews from the kind of supervision that existed in older communities in the provinces), and on the other hand, *distinct* from the dominant Catholic culture of Austria and the Habsburg regime. As Ya'acov Shavit has argued more generally, the confrontation with Greco-Roman antiquity is fundamental not just for this particular Jewish social class, but also for secular Jewish identity as a whole (1999). So this Viennese snippet of Jewish history has much wider reverberations.

The history of Freud's *Gymnasium* itself reflects the dynamic population explosion of nineteenth-century Vienna, and some mention of this must be made here. The school was opened in 1864 as a *Realgymnasium*, part of a city-wide effort to address the lack of schools for the growing population. At the time, Vienna had a total population of 552,052 residents and yet contained only four overcrowded *Gymnasien* dating from a time when Vienna was only a third as large. In this respect, Vienna was far behind the rest of the Austro-Hungarian Empire and Germany, and ought to have been operating 11 or 12 *Gymnasien* to service its population (Pokorny 1865, pp. 2–6). A *Realgymnasium* was a combination of curricula, one for those students headed for the more practical *Realschulen*, and another for those headed for the more elite, humanistic *Obergymnasium*, though there was enough overlap for combined instruction to function in the first two years (Pokorny 1865, p. 21). The school expanded by one class per year, and in October of 1868, it had its first *quinta* or fifth grade and thus became in addition an *Obergymnasium*. When in July of 1872 the first group of *Obergymnasium* students sat for their *Matura* examination (the Austrian equivalent of the German *Abitur*, which allowed them to apply for university admission), the *Leopoldstädter Communal-Real-und Obergymnasium* was at last complete as an institution, though it still did not have its own proper school building. Thus when Freud sat for his *Matura* on July 9, 1873, he was only in the second such class to do so in the school's history.

The school's chronicle during Freud's time reflects the overall cultural and political transformation of Vienna (see Pokorny 1874, pp. 31–32). It closed on May 1, 1865, for the opening of the *Ringstrasse*. The school year ended early in 1866 on account of the Austro-Prussian war. It was on holiday on May 21, 1867, for the ceremonial opening of the *Reichsrat*, the dysfunctional Cisleithanian parliament that would later be housed in Theophilus Hansen's glorious neoclassical building on the Ringstrasse. The school closed early in July of 1873, Freud's final year, on account of the *Weltausstellung*, the world's fair held practically in the school's back yard in the Prater, in which the *Gymnasium* participated with an exhibition. While the students were overwhelmingly German speaking, there were students whose mother tongue was Czech, Polish, Hungarian, or Romanian, reflecting the multi-ethnic composition of the Empire (Pokorny 1874, p. 44). It is impossible to guess how this diverse student body felt when it was marched out to the twenty-fifth anniversary celebration of the Emperor Franz Josef's accession to the throne in that same year.

Of course, the dynamic population growth in Leopoldstadt was disproportionately an increase in its *Jewish* population, and this clearly reflected in the student body. When Freud's school opened in October of 1864, there were 42 Catholic vs. 32 Jewish students. Within ten years, the ratio was 110 Catholics to 335 Jewish students (the larger number of students overall was again due to the expansion of the school to upper classes). While the majority of students were born in Vienna and lived in Leopoldstadt, the next-largest group was born in Moravia, like Freud, the third-largest group was born in Hungary, and the fourth-largest in Galicia — all regions that contributed heavily to the Jewish immigration in Vienna (Pokorny 1874, pp. 44–45). Marsha Rozenblit's comments on the *Gymnasium* generally are very apposite to Freud's situation growing up.

> In short, at the *Gymnasium*, middle-class Jews absorbed the European cultural legacy in the company of other Jews. They were initiated into secular learning as a group. Despite complete acculturation, Jewish *Gymnasium* students experienced no compulsion to meet and befriend gentiles. Acquiring secular knowledge was a Jewish group activity, and the group nature of this experience modified and attenuated assimilation. An educated Jew was not an anomaly in a (hostile) gentile environment, but rather enjoyed the company of other similarly educated and acculturated Jews [1983, p. 125].

And it must be remembered they were given instruction in Jewish history and the Jewish religion by a teacher certified by their own community, using books written by none other than Joseph Breuer's father, Leopold (1855, 1869). In Freud's case, we must recall the powerful influence of Samuel Hammerschlag, his teacher in these classes and the tireless librarian of the Jewish Community Library in Vienna, who would remain a friend and even financial supporter long after Freud graduated.

When Hammerschlag died in 1904, Freud wrote an obituary for the *Neie Freie Presse* that shows us Freud's image of an acculturated Jew, a kind of *Bildungsideal* from his youth. "A spark from the same fire which animated the spirit of the great Jewish seers and prophets burned in him and was not extinguished until old age weakened his powers," Freud wrote in celebration of Hammerschlag's Jewish character (1904, p. 255). But he hastened to add, "the passionate side of his nature was *happily tempered* by the ideal of humanism of *our German classical period* which governed him, and his method of education was based on the foundation of *the philological and classical studies* to which he had devoted his own youth" (1904, p. 255; my emphasis). Note how this Jewish character was "happily tempered," that Hammerschlag was *governed* by a rational, humanistic ideal, and his *method* had the appropriate grounding in *Altertumswissenschaft*. It is clear that Jewish fire by itself seems to suffer from a legitimation crisis, and that additional form and focus are needed to shape it. And yet that "spark" promises an element of historical continuity and positive *difference* that fits uniquely together with German classical culture to form something new.

One senses, then, that Hammerschlag himself represents a third something between Jewish tradition and European high culture, a Jewish intensity wedded to a classical ideal and *wissenschaftlich* standard or method. Freud's gesture towards "*our* German classical period" can certainly be explained by the fact that he wrote for the general readership of the *Neue Freie Presse*, which, while heavily liberal and secular, was not exclusively Jewish. But that does not mean the phrase's "our-ness" is insincere; he appeals here to the notional, unifying *Kultur* of the liberal reading public.

Finally, we should note the manner in which Freud characterizes Hammerschlag's pedagogical objectives, which were not those one would expect of a more traditional teacher of religion. Rather, we see instead a surprisingly secular bent, one that steers clear of concrete political or religious teachings and creates instead a kind of aestheticization of Jewish tradition. "Religious instruction served him as a way of educating *towards love of the humanities*, and from the material of Jewish history he was able to find means of tapping the sources of enthusiasm hidden in the hearts of young people and making it flow out far *beyond the limitations of nationalism or dogma*" (1904, 255; my emphasis). Naturally we should suspect Freud is telling us what *he* got from Hammerschlag's teaching and not what the latter's explicit objectives truly were. Even so, the obituary shows how Freud, in retrospect, characterizes the negotiation of identity in the *Gymnasium* for young Jewish men at the hands of this "paternally solicitous friend" (1904, p. 255).

In summary, I wish to characterize the *Gymnasium* not as a site of Jewish mainstreaming, but rather as a site of Jewish solidarity and even mischief; or at least as a site of Jewish self-differentiation that has multiple outcomes. The old Yiddish proverb has it that *Alle Yevonim hobn die selbe Ponim*: All Greeks have the same face. I wish to prove rather the opposite. The "Greeks" bred in the *Gymnasium* had many different faces and different aspects. A first point to be made, and made for *all* groups entering the *Gymnasium*, is that the classical curriculum had *always* contributed a destabilizing element in European education, and was not a seamless edifice that inculcated conformity. The rhetoric of foundationalism all too often strips classical education of its subversive potential — a factor of reception Hans Robert Jauss once termed "the cunning of tradition," a modification of Hegel's cunning of history.

Study of ancient pagan culture provided a critical distance from the values of Christian culture and could be variously adopted by those at odds with the strands of Christianity that impeded free thought, political emancipation, sexual freedom, self-expression in the arts, or any number of underdog causes. As such, classical education provided a number of positions of *opposition* to the mainstream as much as it might be said to homogenize the ruling elites of Europe into bureaucratic drones. We should study the phenomenon of *Gymnasium* education in the light of *particular* appropriations, and my concern here is to point out particular Jewish appropriations, not in order to define or locate an *essentially* Jewish-Viennese culture — that could prove very problematic from the outset — but rather, to trace particular Jewish trajectories through the maelstrom of transformation that was nineteenth- and twentieth-century

Vienna. While some of these trajectories might be seen as leading to the "cultural suicide" of total assimilation, many others did not. And in Freud's case, we see the classical past was always a landscape of mischief, one that afforded him critical distance not just from mainstream Catholic culture, but also from his own Jewish past.

Herr Aliquis, *or the Archaeology of Pedantry*

In outline this is a huge prosopographical project, of course, and I cannot honestly deliver adequate results in this short chapter. But let me at least begin to urge this thesis with a reading of a Freudian *locus classicus*. The passage is one of Freud's most famous — actually, notorious — analytic vignettes, the so-called *Herr Aliquis* episode from *The Psychopathology of Everyday Life*. The passage merits a careful reading on many levels. Though ostensibly the episode is the chief example of the forgetting of foreign words, the whole passage is a gem of mini-analysis that casts the author in the role of master detective. Freud presents himself as a sleuth who, with the slightest of clues, quickly discovers that what is troubling his young companion is a highly delicate situation: the possible pregnancy of his Italian lover. The exact identity of this *Herr Aliquis* is a matter of heated debate; it seems likely that this is another instance of Freud's use of a fictional figure in order to disguise personal information of some kind. Whether this young Jewish companion was actually his brother Alexander or, as Peter Swales would have it, Freud himself who is covertly confessing his affair with his sister-in-law Minna (1982, 1998), is not a matter I wish to settle here.[9] Rather, I am more interested in Freud's literary portrait of two Jewish intellectuals on their holiday trip, which, even if it *is* a fiction — and I think this is likely — is still highly resonant for our theme. Like Freud's ideal portrait of Hammerschlag, *Herr Aliquis* is a relevant character in the drama of Jewish assimilation and frustration.

Freud's characterization of this young man would certainly not have been far off the mark for describing himself:

> We had fallen into conversation [...] about the social status of the race to which we both belonged; and ambitious feelings prompted him to give vent to a regret that his generation was doomed (as he expressed it) to atrophy, and could not develop its talents or satisfy its needs. He ended a speech of impassioned fervor with the well-known line of Virgil's in which the unhappy Dido commits to posterity her vengeance on Aeneas: "Exoriare..." Or rather, he *wanted* to end it in this way, for he could not get hold of the quotation and tried to conceal an obvious gap in what he remembered by changing the order of the words: "*Exoriar(e) ex nostris ossibus ultor*" [1901, p. 9].

Note that this young man, first of all, was "of academic background" (*von akademischer Bildung*) and laments his inability to enter into a suitable career in order to develop his talents. He is, it would seem, one of the marooned mandarins so well educated by the *Gymnasium* system yet, through the increasing anti-Semitism of the 1890s, made ineligible by official and unofficial means for proper advancement. The line from the *Aeneid* is especially telling in this regard: it is the curse of the impassioned Carthaginian Queen who has failed in her attempt to get hold of the Roman hero Aeneas and make him stay in Carthage. She thought they were effectively married, but a higher destiny has called him to Rome. Dido is a figure of shattered identity; like Aeneas she is a refugee, but unlike him, she has done remarkably well for herself until his arrival. Loving Aeneas has cost Dido her reputation among her own people, and has caused her to abjure her posthumous fidelity to her first husband, whom she will shortly join in the Underworld. Thus this curse comes from the lips of a Semitic Queen who hates Troy/Rome for not keeping troth with its newfound and quickly abandoned friend, and from that hatred comes a vague intimation of eternal warfare between Carthage and Rome that the reader knows to be the real historical reflection of this fictional incident: namely, the Punic Wars.

The verse in question is syntactically rather intricate and means literally, "May you arise, somebody, from our bones as the/an avenger" (*Aeneid* 4.625). In fact, the very difficulty of the line was enough to lead Sebastiano Timpanaro to conclude this parapraxis can be simply explained by the verse's intrinsic complexity and the consequent effects of "banalization" (1985, chapter 3). But I will stress instead the verse's remarkably appropriate tenor, which makes us rather wonder about its possible unconscious motivations. After all, the young man's identification with Dido is greatly accentuated by his apparent misquotation, in that *Exoriar*— if that is what is meant by the printing *Exoriar(e)* [sic]— means, "may *I* arise from our bones as the avenger," as if to make the wish one where the *speaker* himself will be the avenger he invokes.[10]

We should first read the cultural situation of the young man in light of the verse. Though he has learned the language of Rome and has made a good effort to become acculturated to the basic values of Roman Catholic Austria; and though he has perhaps even turned his back on his Jewish past and thrown himself into the arms of this conquering culture, all the same, this young man finds himself left like a jilted lover to languish with all the promises unfulfilled. In his free associations, it is interesting to note how initially his mind is absorbed with Christian saints and their relics, like Simon of Trent, Augustine, Origen, Benedict, San Gennaro, and Paul. This leads him to remember, however, the recent accusations of ritual blood sacrifice, perhaps a reference to the Leopold Hilsner case in Bohemia; but this too may be conditioned by the practice of child sacrifice among the Carthaginians. The accusation of blood sacrifice is itself a reminder of how difficult it is to escape the racial caricatures of the dominant culture, just as our entire view of Carthage is controlled by Roman propaganda like the *Aeneid* to this day. Carthage and Jerusalem are two sister cities in that they share the distinction of having been annihilated by Rome.

With the departure of Aeneas, Dido ceases to be a significant agent in history. She kills herself in despair, dying "before her time," Virgil stresses (*ante diem* — *Aeneid* 4.697); she is no longer in step with history. Here the gender issue is worth stressing. To be dis-invited from the march of history is to be denied an active role in what Freud saw as "civilization," which is fundamentally the work of men (1930, p. 103). Hence, the danger of being the dominant culture's jilted lover is that one is reduced to passivity in the historical process—that is, one is placed on a par with women and the other Others in history's deadly sweep. Indeed, the Virgilian echo here is important in linking femininity with the Other of history, since many who resist the grand patriarchal spectacle of Rome's rise to greatness in the *Aeneid* are female, like Dido, Amata, and Camilla among mortals, and Juno and the fury Allecto among the divinities. In their opposition to Rome's future, they seem to reflect that "retarding and restraining influence" Freud alleges of women in general by the time of *Civilization and Its Discontents* (1930, p. 103).

At this point, then, we might venture a preliminary reading of this vignette: it is the elegy of the marooned mandarin who has learned enough of the dominant culture to curse it, whose fear of being left a passive victim instead of a manly actor by historical forces disturbs him greatly. This gives the citation a remarkable resonance in the context of the Jewish situation, in which it reverberates more deeply than in the other political uses of this Latin verse in the nineteenth century.[11] The linkage of Jewishness and femininity in Freud's work and beyond is vital here, though we can only allude to it (see Gilman 1993a and 1993b, and Boyarin 1997). Heroic "manliness" was the *goyish* obsession of the *Gymnasium*, which at its earliest levels raised its students on the lives of *viri illustres*, "illustrious men," whose dynamic individualism made them worthy of admiration and imitation (cf. Freud's Latin textbook, Schmidt and Gehlen 1865). This approach was defensively adopted by the Jewish religion teachers as well (L. Brever 1869). But for all his *Bildung* and ambition, this young man must sit passively on the sidelines in envy and despair.

The irony, of course, is that though initially he invokes Dido and plays the victim, the real predicament is his *own* illustrious virility. By possibly impregnating an Italian lover, as the text claims, the young man has in fact been playing the role of Aeneas all along, who leaves Dido to fulfill his people's destiny by marrying the Italian princess Lavinia. Lavinia will bear him a son, Silvius, progenitor of the kings of Alba Longa and part of a crucial lineage that leads up to Romulus; and Aeneas' marriage itself formally marks the ethnogenesis of Latins and Trojans into one people, the not-yet-Roman *Latini*. Aeneas is not just the primal father of the Roman Empire, but also a strikingly good case of successful assimilation. Thus by Freud's own description, his young interlocutor is caught between the anguish of Jewish suffering and the embarrassment of his own sexual conquest and assimilation.[12] He is clearly caught up in the ambivalence he has towards his desires. He desires a future avenger, an illustrious hero to save his people, but that wish suddenly makes him fear the real prospect of having a bastard descendant. We might also read here some ambivalence in his passionate yearning for social inclusion through acculturation, which forces him confront the hideous caricatures of the Jews that the dominant culture trades in. This in turn leads him to curse the very culture he wishes to join. As we have seen, a curse upon Aeneas is a curse upon the successfully assimilated. Thus *Herr Aliquis* sadly seems hemmed in by his own actions and desires in addition to historical circumstances.

So much for *Herr Aliquis* and his quandaries. Where is Freud in the vignette? Freud's chief commitment in this text is to his own method, though he is clearly highlighting his own solidarity with the Jews, despite the vague reference to them as simply "the race [*Volksstamm*] to which we both belonged" (1901, p. 9). He casts himself as the know-it-all interlocutor who comes to his poor friend's aid. This is one of those moments of classical pedantry that was all too familiar in the competitive school environment, even years after the fact:

> At last he said irritably: "please don't look so scornful: you seem as if you were gloating over my embarrassment. Why not help me? There's something missing in the line; how does the whole thing really go?"
>
> "I'll help you with pleasure," [original: *Gerne*] I replied, and gave the quotation in its correct form: *Exoriar(e) ALIQUIS nostris ex ossibus ultor* [1901, p. 9].

What we see enacted initially is simply the repetition of the schoolboy's testing anxiety; Freud was well enough aware of this phenomenon that he had given the examination nightmare a special status among recurring dreams. He remembered well how the *Matura* examination, which effectively controlled one's entire future, loomed in his mind as a boy like the *dies irae, dies illa* or Doomsday, couched in good Catholic Latin no less (1900, pp. 209–210)![13] It was a test of any young man's abilities, but especially so, we might assume, for a young Jew whom many might like to see fail and climb no higher. With an effortless superiority, Freud the character in this drama, the former *Gymnasium* student who was almost always the first in his class, delivers the verse that he read in the *Septima* (or roughly, the Junior class) at age 15. It is just the first show of calm mastery in this vignette, which will soon extend from the *Gymnasium* curriculum to the path-breaking insights of psychoanalysis, as he boldly unearths his companion's unconscious conflicts and shows the incisive power of his new science of the mind.

But the vignette is far more subversive than it appears on the surface. Like the motto of the *Interpretation of Dreams*, there is reason to suppose that Freud had been acquainted with this verse not just directly from his reading of the *Aeneid* in the *Gymnasium*, but from its pointed redeployment by the German-Jewish socialist writer Ferdinand Lassalle (1825–1864) (Swales 1998). It is a known fact the *Acheronta movebo* verse that is the motto for the *Interpretation of Dreams* was suggested by Freud's reading of Lassalle, so this is not unreasonable.[14] This additional perspective on the verse gives the passage an added twist of social unrest, one that shows how even for the Jewish *Bildungsbürgertum*, the proper response to social inequality might be a revolutionary one — or rather, the *fantasy* of a revolutionary one. Needless to say, Freud knew very well that this was a response made by Jews in Vienna. His old *Gymnasium* friend, after all, was Heinrich Braun, a restless soul who had gotten the young Freud interested in politics and had nearly convinced him to take up a career in the law in order to pursue social change.[15] Braun later became a very influential socialist leader. And for whatever uncanny reason, Freud thought he had taken up quarters on the Berggasse in the flat that once belonged to Viktor Adler, the prominent Social Democrat, himself a graduate of the *Schottengymnasium* and like Freud, a former German nationalist. Thus far, then, we can see how the verses *Exoriare aliquis nostris ex ossibus ultor* and *Flectere si nequeo superos Acheronta movebo* were given new currency by Lassalle, the Jewish socialist, and were in turn picked up in the spirit of opposition by a Jewish scientist (or scientists, as the case may be here). Of even greater relevance in the case of the *Psychopathology* is the fact that Freud knew very well Lassalle had died in a duel over a love affair, and was an example of a man who "wasted his life for a woman" (1900, p. 230). So we might see here another resonance of how manly resolve, social change, and the threat of the feminine are linked.

For Freud, the notion of being a Jew is inherently caught up with being in the opposition against the "compact majority," and this oppositional status, he claimed, was great training for being a scientific *conquistador*.[16] In light of this, the care he takes to describe or orchestrate this vignette has always struck me. Very subtly it alludes to his own boyhood "Hannibal complex," since the avenger invoked by Dido in this verse is Hannibal, though she herself does not know it. Many things, in other words, seem to be attached to the indefiniteness of this indefinite pronoun *aliquis*. Why indeed should the young man hesitate over the word "somebody," a word that ought to be safe in its vagueness? It is because the indefiniteness of this pronoun is itself a *fiction*; it very definitely refers to someone. The "somebody" is Hannibal in the Virgilian text, as yet unborn and so unnamed; and *aliquis* alludes to the possibility of an unborn child in the *Psychopathology*'s analysis, a real descendant who will live to avenge the embittered young Jew (1901, p. 14). But to this day, of course, *Herr Aliquis*, Mr. Somebody, refers to the young man himself, who seems to be a figure in whom mysterious things are entombed. Whether he existed or not, it is Freud who gives him pride of place in the text, who has given us the dialogue that expresses the contradictions of a Jewish *Gymnasium* graduate, and who has thus subtly raised the specter of Hannibal.

Hannibal, as Freud made very clear in the *Interpretation of Dreams* only the year before the publication of the *Psychopathology*, was indeed a figure of cultural triangulation. He was the greatest enemy of Rome, whose implacable hatred symbolized for the young Freud the opposition between "the tenacity of Jewry and the organization of the Catholic Church" (1900, p. 151). As he confesses to the reader in the *Interpretation of Dreams*, Hannibal was a figure of great contrast to his own Jewish father, who, by relating his social humiliation at the hands of Christians, failed to supply the young Sigismund with the heroic narrative he needed. This is the very kind of personal appropriation I set out to look for, and it centers again on the need for a self-narrative of illustrious virility. As Freud knew, it was quite common for students to identify with Hannibal simply as an underdog, just as it was common for people in need of vengeance to cite Virgil's *exoriare* verse. But his own appropriation of Hannibal was as a kind of alternative Semite, a killer Semite we might say, one cut of more heroic cloth than his Galician father. As he later said about the psychology of the *Gymnasiast*, one goes to school to get oneself a father substitute (*Vaterersatz*) in order to get over the dissatisfaction with one's own father (1914, p. 244).

And Freud seems to intervene like a benign father substitute to aid this *junger Mann* through the revolutionary technique of psychoanalysis. At first one might suspect that his analytic persona is deliberately trying to defuse the political statement made at the outset with the description of the young man's passion and discontent. We might even say the political surface narrative is dismissed when the "real plot" of sexuality is uncovered, as if to say the young man's *real* concerns are very much with his own behavior, not that of the anti–Semites. But I would rather argue that we must not forget when the young man fails to curse his gentile adversaries, it is *Freud* who curses them for him by citing Dido *wie es richtig lautet*, "in the correct form," and it is *Freud* who inserts the *aliquis* and thus raises Hannibal.

Moreover, it is Freud who leads the young man through a series of free associations on Christian themes that ends with the bathetic assimilation of the miracle of San Gennaro's flowing blood with the lover's problematic menstrual flow. This is the brilliant inference the character Freud makes in true Holmesian fashion, to the young man's surprise. He goes so far as to praise the young man's unconscious by saying, "In fact, you've made use of the miracle of St. Januarius to manufacture a brilliant allusion to women's periods" (1901, p. 11) (his term for "allusion" is originally *eine prächtige Anspielung*, which keeps the notion of *Spiel* or "play" more to the fore). Since the young man claims to have visited Naples with his Italian lover and San Gennaro is that city's patron saint, the connection is clear. And if you have gone to *Gymnasium*, you will also know that Naples is where Virgil was buried, and where he lived on in Neapolitan folklore as a kind of wonder worker. In the end, all roads lead to Naples in this analytic tale.

Freud is clearly delighting in this demonstration of his new science, which rather mercilessly makes *eine prächtige Anspielung* that links the holiest of miracles—the regular liquifaction of San Gennaro's blood was long attested and touted as a fact — with the naughtiest of sexual intimacies. Even if we take Freud's word for it that another Jew's unconscious has performed this clever transformation while he, the scientist, merely observes it, the fact is Freud *the writer* has made this very public and given it pride of place in his menagerie of misstatement. *Herr Aliquis*, whoever he is, clearly represents a good opportunity for Freud to revisit (already in chapter 2!) the plight of his own people, to curse enemies who are equally his own, to get his own blood flowing by renewing a passionate political side of himself that seems to rest like a relic under the calm edifice of his scientific enterprise. He had resurrected this side of himself before in the *Traumdeutung*, when he first made his Hannibal complex public knowledge. But in this instance, he has more deftly struck out behind somebody, *aliquis*, and scored some points for his science while dragging a host of Christian saints down to the mire of biological reality. With the patient and tenacious enthusiasm of the Jewish scientist, Freud works his own miracles here, using his *Bildung* and keen observation to turn the anti–Semitic vulgarity of blood-libel into the dubious miracle of San Gennaro's blood, itself a standing indictment of Christian credulity; and he transforms this in turn to the obtruding and unpleasant (*unangenehm*) reality of menstrual blood, all of which serves to show his mastery of the mental processes that make up our common humanity. With impeccable manners and a rational method, he has brought us to the brink of unspeakable scandal.

* * *

Now a free association of my own occurs that may serve to conclude this discussion. When Joseph Breuer responded to the dueling fraternity Kadimah for its savage criticism of assimilated Jews, he deftly pointed out that they were in fact quite well assimilated themselves, since they had made Jewish honor a matter for *ritterliche Satisfaction*, "chivalrous satisfaction"; they had formed a dueling fraternity in the *echt* gentile manner (Hirschmüller 1978, p. 216). In fact, Martin Freud later joined Kadimah, which clearly delighted his father, much to Martin's surprise (M. Freud 1958/1983, pp. 164–165). Sigmund Freud later even became an honorary member of Kadimah. The point is that the Freud we know came from a secular Jewish culture born in the competitive crucible of the *Gymnasium* and the University; he learned to use his *Bildung* with great skill when dueling with his adversaries.[17] No amount of bourgeois propriety and classical pedantry can obscure the simmering struggle behind the scenes. For Freud, the drama of education for the Jewish *Gymnasium* graduate was not a case of mere gentile play-acting or wanna-be mimicry; it was a game of *competitive mastery*. As Breuer, the self-confident assimilator, said: "If we wish to deprive anti–Semitism of its foundations by ensuring that the Jew is *manifestly* superior in each class so that he can command respect, that can hardly be described as betraying the cause" (Hirschmüller 1978, p. 217).

Notes

1. See for example, Wistrich 1989, chapter 16; Beller 1990.
2. For general histories and demographic analyses of Viennese Jewry, see Rozenblit 1983, Wistrich 1989, Beller 1989 and Rossbacher 2003. For Moravian Jews in particular, see Wistrich 1989, pp. 45–47.
3. Rozenblit (1983, pp. 76–77) states that in 1880 (when we have the first reliable statistics), Leopoldstadt housed 48.3 percent of the Jews in Vienna.
4. Letter to Martha, October 23, 1883. Freud relates to her the story of Benedikt Stilling (1810–1879), founder of the theory of the vasomotor nervous system, whose diligent researches were carried out privately alongside his practice as a doctor. "All this shows the industry, the tenacious enthusiasm of the Jew [*der Fleiß, die zähe Begeisterung des Juden*], not even coupled with the talent normally expected from Jews. This we can also do" (E. Freud 1960/1992, p. 71).
5. Freud's letter to Eduard Silberstein of August 22, 1874 provides a humorous look at the Crown Prince Rudolph on the advent of his sixteenth birthday (Boehlich 1990, pp. 52–53).
6. Letter to Martha, January 10, 1884; E. Freud (1960/1992), pp. 86–87.
7. A rather harsh description of some Moravian Jews is found in a letter to Emil Fluss (September 18, 1872). For a 16-page satirical description of a Jewish wedding, see letter to Martha, May 16, 1884. For his embarrassment at the funeral of Nathan Weiss over the behavior of "a savage, merciless Jew," see the letter to Martha, September 16, 1883 (E. Freud 1960/1992, pp. 58–66).
8. Excellent demographic analysis can be found in Rozenblit 1983, chapter 5; Beller 1989, chapter 4 and 1990; Cohen 1990.
9. On *Herr Aliquis*, see Hirschmüller 2002 and Skues 2001; on the Freud-Minna controversy, see now especially Maciejewski 2006, Hirschmüller 2007, and Lothane 2007.
10. Technical point: the final vowel of *Exoriare* would normally be elided before *aliquis* in Latin verse, but it would *never* be printed *Exoriar(e)* in a Latin text. I conclude Freud thus punctuates the verb to reflect the actual pronunciation *exoriar*, which would be normal in citing from memory.
11. For example, this verse was reputedly shouted by Diego de Leon y Navarrete at his execution in Madrid in 1841 under the Espartero regime; the poet Ferdinand Freiligrath made it the refrain of a poem "Aus Spanien," which depicted the defiant bravery of the general (1844/1994).
12. It seems strange that Freud missed another explanation for the misquotation. The correct citation itself is suggestive: *exoriare aliquis nostriS EX ossibus ultor*, which might be translated: "may you arise, whoever you are, from our sex bones as an avenger." By changing the position of *nostris* to *ex nostris ossibus*, the man avoids saying "sex."
13. The *dies irae* is a Latin hymn used as the sequence in Requiem masses, ascribed to Thomas of Celano. For a pun on *Matura* and martyrdom (*Märtyrer*), see Letter to Emil Fluss, June 16, 1873 (Ernst Freud 1960/1992, p. 5).
14. See Freud's letter to Werner Achelis, January 30, 1927 (E. Freud 1960/1992, p. 375).
15. See the letter to Braun's widow, Julie Braun-Vogelstein of October 30, 1927 (E. Freud 1960/1992, pp. 378–380). In this letter, Freud mentions his belief that Victor Adler had previously occupied his quarters at Berggasse 19, which is not true in point of fact. See also Knoepfmacher 1979.
16. Letter to the Members of the B'nai B'rith Lodge, May 6, 1926 (E. Freud 1960/1992, p. 366–367).
17. For further views on the *Gymnasium*'s influence on the Psychoanalytic Movement, see Winter 1999.

References

Armstrong, R. (2005). *A Compulsion for Antiquity: Freud and the Ancient World*. Ithaca, NY: Cornell University Press.
Beller, S. (1989). *The Jews of Vienna 1867–1938: A Cultural History*. Cambridge: Cambridge University Press.

_____ (1990). "Why Was the Viennese Liberal *Bildungsbürgertum* Above All Jewish?" In Don and Karady (1990), chapter 6.
Boehlich, W., ed. (1990). *The Letters of Sigmund Freud to Eduard Silberstein 1871–1881.* Trans. A.J. Pomerans. Cambridge: Harvard University Press.
Boyarin, D. (1997). *Unheroic Conduct: The Rise of Heterosexuality and the Invention of the Jewish Man.* Berkeley: University of California Press.
Breuer, L. (1855). *Leitfaden beim Religionsunterrichte der israelitischen Jugend.* Vienna: Klopf and Eurich.
_____ (1869). *Biblische Geschichte und Geschichte der Juden und des Judenthumes bis zum Abschlusse des Talmuds, nebst einem kurzen Ueberblicke der weitern Geschichte der Juden bis auf unsere Tage.* Part 1. Third revised and expanded edition. Vienna: Wilhelm Braumüller.
Burckhadt, J. (1998). *The Greeks and Greek Civilization.* Ed. Oswyn Murray. Trans. Sheila Stern. New York: St. Martin's.
Cohen, G. (1990). "Jews Among Vienna's Educated Middle Class Elements at the Turn of the Century." In Don and Karady 1990, chapter 7.
Don, Y., and Karady, V., ed. (1990). *A Social and Economic History of Central European Jewry.* New Brunswick, NJ: Transactions.
Freiligrath, F. (1844/1994). *Ein Glaubensbekenntniss: Zeitgedichte.* Reprint, Mainz: Philipp von Zabern.
Freud, E., ed. (1960/1992). *Letters of Sigmund Freud.* Trans. Tania and James Stern. New York: Dover.
Freud, M. (1958/1983). *Sigmund Freud: Man and Father.* New York: Jason Aronson.
Freud, S. (1900). *The Interpretation of Dreams.* Trans. Joyce Crick. Oxford: Oxford University Press.
_____ (1901). *The Psychopathology of Everyday Life.* Standard Edition 6: 1–310.
_____ (1904). Obituary of Professor S. Hammerschlag. *Standard Edition* 9: 255–256.
_____ (1914). Some Reflections on Schoolboy Psychology. *Standard Edition* 13: 241–244.
_____ (1930). Civilization and Its Discontents. *Standard Edition* 21: pp. 64–145.
Gilman, S. (1993a) *The Case of Sigmund Freud: Medicine and Identity at the Fin de Siècle.* Baltimore: Johns Hopkins University Press.
_____ (1993b). *Freud, Race, and Gender.* Princeton, NJ: Princeton University Press.
_____ (1998). *Love + Marriage = Death.* Stanford, CA: Stanford University Press.
Hirschmüller, A. (1989). *The Life and Work of Josef Breuer: Physiology and Psychoanalysis.* New York: New York University Press.
_____ (2002). "Kritische Glosse: Wer war 'Herr Aliquis'?" *Psyche* 56: 396–402.
_____ (2007). "Freud and Minna Bernays: Evidence for a Sexual Relationship between Sigmund Freud and Minna Bernays?" *American Imago* 64: 125–128.
Jones, Ernest (1953–57). *The Life and Work of Sigmund Freud.* New York: Basic. 3 vols.
Kalberg, J. (1888). "Wert der lateinischen und griechischen Sprache als Lehrgegenstände am Gymnasium." *Programm des K. K. Staats-Obergymnasiums zu Mitterburg* 15: 5–14. Mitterburg: Verlag des K. K. Gymnasiums.
Knoepfmacher, H. (1979). "Sigmund Freud in High School." *American Imago* 36: 287–300.
Lothane, Zvi (2007). "The Sigmund Freud/Minna Bernays Romance: Fact or Fiction?" *American Imago* 64: 129–133.
Maciejewski, F. (2006). "Freud, His Wife, and His 'Wife.'" *American Imago* 63: 497–506.
Pokorny, A. (1865). "Entstehung und Einrichtung der Wiener Communal-Realgymnasien." *Erster Jahresbericht des Leopoldstädter Communal-RealGymnasiums.* Vienna: Selbstverlag des Leopoldstädter Realgymnasiums.
_____ (1874). "Das erste Decennium des Leopoldstädter Communal — Real — und Obergymnasiums (1864–1874): Ein historisch-statistischer Rückblick." *Zehnter Jahresbericht des Leopoldstädter Communal — Real — und Obergymnasiums in Wien.* Vienna: Verlag des Leopoldstädter Real — und Obergymnasiums.
Rossbacher, K. (2003). *Literatur und Bürgertum: Fünf Wiener jüdische Familien von der liberalen Ära zum Fin de Siècle.* Vienna: Böhlau.
Rozenblit, M. (1983). *The Jews of Vienna 1867–1914: Assimilation and Identity.* Albany, NY: State University of New York Press.
Schiller, H. (1875). "Das Griechische im Gymnasium." *Pädogogische Zeitfragen: Beilage zum Programm des Grossh. Gymnasiums zu Konstanz für 1874/75.* Constance: Stadler.

Schimdt, C., and O. Gehlen (1865). *Memorabilia Alexandri Magni et aliorum virorum illustrium selectasque fabulas Phaedri.* Vienna: Sommer.

Shavit, Y. (1999). *Athens in Jerusalem: Classical Antiquity and Hellenism in the Making of the Modern Secular Jew.* Trans. Chaya Naor and Niki Werner. London: Littman Library of Jewish Civilization.

Skues, R.A. (2001). "On the Dating of Freud's *aliquis* Slip." *International Journal of Psychoanalysis* 82: 1185–1204.

Swales, P. (1982). "Freud, Minna Bernays, and the Conquest of Rome." *New American Review* 1982:1–23.

───── (1998). *In Statu Nascendi: Freud, Minna Bernays, and the Creation of Herr Aliquis.* Unpublished manuscript.

Timpanaro, S. (1985). *The Freudian Slip.* Trans. Kate Soper. London: Verso.

Winter, S. (1999). *Freud and the Institution of Psychoanalytic Knowledge.* Stanford, CA: Stanford University Press.

Wistrich, R. (1989). *The Jews of Vienna in the Age of Franz Joseph.* New York: Oxford University Press.

The *Neue Freie Presse* Neurosis
Freud, Karl Kraus, and the Newspaper as Daily Devotional
LEO A. LENSING

> The *Neue Freie Presse*, the oracle of my fathers and the home of those anointed seven times over.—Stefan Zweig, *The World of Yesterday*

The satirical writer Karl Kraus is easily the most controversial and possibly the most important among those of Freud's contemporaries excluded from or marginalized within his "Jewish World." It is only a slight exaggeration to say that he figures in most biographies as the otherwise unimportant author of the famously infamous aphorism "Psychoanalysis is that mental illness for which it considers itself the therapy" (Kraus 1986a, p. 351). By contrast, Kraus scholars have displayed a keen interest in the writer's relationship to Freud and his reception of psychoanalysis and would undoubtedly point to other, more subtly critical or comically disarming aphorisms. Three examples of the many worth quoting reflect the complexity of Kraus's attitude towards Freud, the theory, and the movement. There is, for example, an equally aggressive definition that not merely pronounces judgment, but actually mimics psychoanalytic argumentation: "A certain psychoanalysis is the occupation of lecherous rationalists who trace everything except their occupation back to sexual causes" (Kraus 1986a, p. 222). In a calm mood, even Freud himself might have been amused by the sexually ambiguous imagery in this metaphorical characterization of his brainchild: "Psychoanalysis: a rabbit swallowed by a boa constrictor just wanted to investigate what it looked like in there" (Kraus 1986a, p. 350). Calm would have been the last emotion he felt, however, if he came across the suggestion in a later aphorism that the youth of Vienna had been better off sexually active under the protection of "Sigi Ernst," one of the "condom kings" of the city, than they now were in therapy with "Sigi Freud" (Kraus 1986a, p. 348). This kind of onomastic pun directed at his own name (Ernst = seriousness, Freud = gaiety) was something Freud abhorred, even though, in *The Interpretation of Dreams*, he admitted indulging in it himself as an act of retribution against others (Freud 1999, p. 159).

During the early positive phase of Kraus's reception of Freud's work, he had in fact cited the controversial physician as an authority, not only by name but also with his professorial title. In an article defending the physiologist and university lecturer Theodor Beer, who had been accused of homosexual activities and pederasty, Kraus explicitly appealed to Freud's medical expertise: "Let us have the insight and courage to declare, together with Professor Sigmund Freud, that the homosexual belongs neither in prison nor in the insane asylum" (Kraus 1905, p. 21). In a letter of January 12, 1906, to Kraus, Freud in fact begins by noting that he must owe the frequent mention of his name in recent issues of the writer's satirical journal *The Torch* to "the partial congruence of our ideas and endeavors" (Anz/Pfohlmann 2006, p. 214). Even as Kraus begins with subtle wit to question the insights of Freud's theory, he still refers to him respectfully, if now more discreetly, as "F.," for example, in an aphorism about *The Interpretation of Dreams*: "If I were to dream that F.'s Interpretation of Dreams tails off in digressions, how would one even go about interpreting that!" (Kraus 1907, p. 4). Indeed, as Kraus begins to intensify his attacks against the excesses of psychoanalytic forays into literary history and biography, he pillories "neurologists" ("Nervenärzte") or the "new psychologists" in general, even using the old-fashioned term "Seelenärzte" (literally "soul doctors"). Except for an admonition to the "professor" who has let his "students" get out of control, he suppresses Freud and Freud's name entirely. This changes only gradually and not until after Freud has failed to condemn a psychoanalytic screed directed at the satirist himself. In 1913, Kraus will coin the comic term "Freudknaben" (Kraus 1986a, p. 532) — a pun that can mean both "Freud's boys" and "boy prostitutes" — to describe young people deformed by psychoanalysis into sublimating their physical desires.

Kraus's most aggressive aphoristic critiques of psychoanalysis appeared between 1910 and 1915 in *The Torch*, in the long, disastrous wake of the quasipublication of another famously infamous document. In January 1910, the young physician Fritz Wittels read a paper to Freud and his circle on what he called "The *Fackel*-Neurosis," an unprecedented attack on a living writer masquerading as a scientific investigation. Between 1906 and 1909 Wittels had been a frequent contributor to Kraus's journal as well as a regular attendee and presenter at the Wednesday sessions of the Vienna Psychoanalytic Association. Karl Kraus, thanks to an informant, learned of the presentation almost immediately. He would recall it in 1923 with fresh indignation as the work of a "symptom hunter" who once traced back "my abhorrence of the Neue Freie Presse to my 'father complex' — in public!" (Kraus 2005, p. 649). It is this one event that has monopolized the imagination of Freud's most prominent biographers. Ernest Jones, who knew better, set the tone by focusing on its disastrous consequences for any further cooperation between Freud and Kraus (Jones 1955, p. 118).[1] Despite access to a then unpublished, spectacular new source, Peter Gay followed suit (Gay 1988, pp. 214f).[2] Even Annette Meyerhöfer, the author of a massive new German biography published in 2006, rehearses the same tired material, citing Ronald Clark as her primary source (Meyerhöfer 2006, p. 346).

If these biographers and many others cared little about Freud's interaction with Kraus, why should we? The answer is simple. During the crucial years in which the Wednesday Psychological Society was metamorphosing into the Vienna Psychoanalytic Association and Freud was writing most of what are now considered his canonical works, Karl Kraus played a stimulating, ultimately explosive role in his intellectual and emotional life. In the early phase of their relationship, the two men corresponded and probably met each other personally as well. The aftershocks of their encounter lasted well into the 1920s.

The partial congruence between Freud's and Kraus's ideas about sexuality — including their refusal to pathologize homosexuality and their shared disdain for the hypocrisy of the prevailing moral code towards sexuality in general — has understandably attracted the attention of scholars of the satirist anxious to situate his work within the larger context of *fin-de-siècle* Vienna (Carr 1982, Timms 1986, Waldvogel 1990).[3] Rather than broadening the focus of such positive parallels, this essay will explore instead the contrasting reactions of these two psychological thinkers to one of the most conspicuous aspects of the pathology of modern life: the daily newspaper.

Kraus's sustained, devastating critique of the *Neue Freie Presse*, a newspaper often compared with the *Times* of London in his day and certainly comparable to the *New York Times* of today, is well known and indeed constitutes the foundation of his satirical œuvre. This critique, which also constituted a response to the rising power of the mass media in general, is summed up succinctly in the first two lines of a song from the play *Literature* (1921): "In the beginning was the Press / and then the world appeared" (Kraus 1989, p. 57). From Kraus's perspective, the press had displaced the sacred *logos* and interrupted the connections between the word and the world. In the age of mass media, he believed, we no longer experience reality, but rather the inevitably distorted report of reality.

How did Freud respond to the *Neue Freie Presse*? His biographers often mention that he read the paper regularly or that it was his "daily fare," as though it were edible (Gay 1988, p. 17; Schur 1972, p. 100). In the early nineteenth century, Hegel had already proclaimed that the daily habit of reading the newspaper was something at once less innocuous and more inspiring than eating breakfast. He famously called it "a kind of realistic morning prayer" (Hegel 1971, p. 547: "Das Zeitungslesen des Morgens ist eine Art von realistischem Morgensegen."), an observation that would soon become a cultural commonplace and familiar quotation. For Freud and his liberal middle-class contemporaries, perusing the morning newspaper had indeed become a kind of secular prayer, performed automatically, almost unconsciously one might say.

This development is vividly illustrated in a satirical fairy tale that Kurt

Tucholsky, writing under one of his pseudonyms (Ignaz Wrobel), published in 1913 in *Die Schaubühne* (The Stage), a cultural weekly that was an important Berlin counterpart of *The Torch*. In "The Man Who No Longer Read Newspapers," Tucholsky tells the story of a man whose life is dominated by the newspapers he reads. The most important of these is *The Daily Morning Prayer*, a title that carries an obvious allusion to Hegel's famous dictum. One morning the man awakes from a nightmare in which he had been crouching against the ceiling of his room perched on a huge pile of issues of *The Daily Morning Prayer*. Although he subsequently liberates himself from his dependence on the daily press, he soon dies and then fails to realize he is actually dead until he goes to a newsstand and reads about his death in the newspaper (Tucholsky 1913, pp. 1030–33).

Tucholsky himself was, like Freud and Kraus, a more or less assimilated, non-observant Jew. The notion that the ostensibly secular *Daily Morning Prayer* might be Jewish in some important sense does not inform this particular text, but for readers of the *Neue Freie Presse* such a connection was unavoidable. At the very beginning of Karl Kraus's own literary career, after he had flirted with and rejected the possibility of becoming a regular contributor to the great journal, he underlined its pseudo-religious function in the world of Viennese journalism. In May 1899, in one of the earliest issues of *The Torch*, Kraus published the following characterization:

> The paper has played divine providence in the Inner City for more than thirty years; its life consists not of issues, but of revelations. And in keeping with Old Testament custom, there is no earthly possibility of entering into direct contact with the editors of the *Neue Freie Presse*, who, it is said in humble admiration, deal even with bank directors only through middle men. Young writers are expected to wait for a "sign," and contracts are drawn up entirely through dreams and visions [Kraus 1899, p. 8].

That this pointed critique of the indiscriminate mixture of religion, journalism and mercantilism in the famous newspaper filtered down into popular culture can be see in *Armin Berg's Treasury of Anecdotes*, a collection of jokes and stories told by the famous Jewish comedian in Viennese cabarets and hotel ballrooms before and during the First World War. Between 1907 and 1913, Berg had also acted in the German-Jewish dialect farces and comedies of the Budapester Orpheumgesellschaft, a vaudeville acting troupe extravagantly praised by Kraus in *The Torch*. In an anecdote illustrated by a simple, but telling cartoon, Berg plays on two meanings of the verb *halten*, "to observe" and "to subscribe":

> Goldstein comes on Saturday to his friend Sami and says: "Please, what kind of Jew are you? Today, on Saturday, you've got your shop open?"—"My dear friend," Sami says, "I got a wife, I got six kids, I got to make money, I can't observe Schabbes any more."—"Now, now," says Goldstein, "but you will observe the high holidays?"—"Those I won't observe either," says Sami, "I told you, I got to make money."—"But, for God's sake, surely you'll observe Rosh Hashanah?'—"I definitely won't observe that."—"Well then, tell me, don't you subscribe to anything Jewish any more?"—"Yes," says Sami, "the *Neue Freie Presse*" [Berg n.d., p. 19].

The text of the anecdote makes the point on its own that the only thing observant about the peddler Sami is his subscription to the *Neue Freie Presse*, but the illustration adds an ironic twist to the situation. In spite of the apparent shabbiness of his attire, Goldstein wears a top hat and, seen from the back as he is, could pass for an assimilated Jew whose daily reading might indeed include the *Neue Freie Presse*. Sami, however, bearded, wearing a yarmulke and sitting next to suspenders and other small articles he offers for sale, clearly fits the stereotype of the *Ostjude* or Eastern European Jew, for whom the famous newspaper would normally have been anathema.

This association of the *Neue Freie Presse* with an inauthentic, compromised Judaism is articulated more directly in Joseph Roth's *Juden auf Wanderschaft* (1927), translated recently as *The Wandering Jews*. Here the top hats, beardless faces, and the famous newspaper, alluded to but not named, are linked with the assimilationist subterfuges of what Roth calls the "Western Jew":

> They no longer pray in synagogues or tabernacles, but rather in boring temples, in which the service is as mechanical as in any half-way decent Protestant church. They become temple Jews, that is, well-brought up, smoothly shaven gentlemen in frockcoats and top hats, who pack their prayer books in the leading article of their favorite Jewish newspaper because they believe people are less likely to recognize them with this leading article than with the prayer book [Roth 1927, p. 24f].

That regular consumption of journalistic information produces confusion and disorientation rather than enlightenment is already the satirical point behind Tucholsky's simple admonitory tale of 1913. In the great anti-war drama *The Last Days of Mankind*, first published in 1918–1919, Karl Kraus takes the problem of the press's destructive power to what he saw as its fatal extreme. Among the recurring characters in the prologue, all five acts, and the epilogue are the "Subscriber," "the Old Subscriber" and "The Oldest Subscriber" as well as Old Biach, who is also a subscriber to the *Neue Freie Presse* and whose Yiddish-inflected speech identifies him as Jewish. In the first act, Old Biach approvingly cites a reverent description of the paper as "the prayer book of cultured people everywhere" (Kraus 1986b, p. 107: "das Gebetbuch aller Gebildeten"), a phrase in keeping with the quasi-religious veneration with which he routinely speaks of Moriz Benedikt, its fabled editor-in-chief. In the fifth act, Biach, whose lines consist almost entirely of titles and phrases quoted from the opinion pages of the *Neue Freie Presse*, will literally choke to death on the increasingly contradictory messages in Benedikt's editorials about the war, as journalistic attempts to smooth over the illogic of government propaganda begin to fail.

What little is known so far about Freud's own, nonfatal perusal of the *Neue Freie Presse* is to be found chiefly in his correspondence.[4] The paper figures there as an indispensable part of everyday life: a venue for publicizing Freud's work, a measure of social and professional success, a source of reliable news. In a letter of February 15, 1901, to Wilhelm Fliess, for example, he mentions cancelling a lecture that had been advertised in the *Neue Freie Presse* because its sexual content was deemed too controversial by the Philosophical Society that had scheduled it (Freud 1985, p. 437). In November 1911, Freud congratulated his niece Lilly on the notice that the "Neue Fr[eie] Presse" has taken of her success on the stage (Freud 2004, p. 63). On September 17, 1907, on the evening of his arrival in Rome for an extended sightseeing stay, Freud wrote a letter to his family, describing the routine he expected to initiate the next day: "Beginning tomorrow I'll read the Neue [Freie] Presse in the cafés regularly and at least find out several days later what is going on in Vienna" (Freud 2005, p. 214). These examples constitute typical evidence, which crops up in several other letters as well, of an unswerving and generally uncritical devotion to the leading newspaper of the Austro-Hungarian Empire, the only journalistic organ of international reputation published in the Habsburg capitol and the favored daily reading of the liberal Jewish middle class. Nothing, however, could illustrate more tellingly the difference between Freud and Karl Kraus than the Roman travel vignette from 1907. For the editor of *The Torch*, the notion that you could find out what was happening in Vienna or anywhere else by reading a newspaper in a coffeehouse, particularly the *Neue Freie Presse*, belonged to the grand illusions of modern life.

Kraus had learned this lesson the hard way. Like many aspiring writers in late nineteenth-century Vienna, he had seen being published in the *Neue Freie Presse* as the first step on the ladder to a brilliant career. In one of the earliest issues of *The Torch*, however, Kraus felt compelled to contradict the rumor that he had founded the new journal out of revenge for not being asked to join the staff as a regular contributor or, as he himself phrases it, "to feed at the 'trough' of liberalism" (Kraus 1899, p. 3). In this witty autobiographical statement of purpose with the provocative title "I and the 'Neue Freie Presse,'" Kraus ironically begs indulgence for his earlier attraction to the revered paper. If "graying university professors, social politicians and publicists versed in economics are lured from the heights of modern knowledge into [the editorial offices in] the Fichtegasse," he contends, then "the mistakes of an impressionable youth with a naïve faith in liberalism" should not be judged too harshly (Kraus 1899, p. 6). He goes on to explain that he was, in fact, offered an attractive position, as the successor of the famed Daniel Spitzer, the author of the immensely popular column *Walks through Vienna*. He declined, however, when the famous editor Moriz Benedikt warned him that he, like Spitzer, would have to submit his articles for editorial approval. Kraus concludes with a statement that confirms the prestige of the *Neue Freie Presse* while reaffirming his own commitment to passionate opposition: "There are two beautiful things in the world: to belong to the *Neue Freie Presse* or to despise it. I did not hesitate for a moment how I had to choose" (Kraus 1899, p. 11).

Freud, who around 1900 also felt himself to be in the opposition, at least to the medical establishment, was in no position to despise or dispense with the *Neue Freie Presse*. As a medical author seeking a wider readership for his new psychological theories and as a practicing physician, he depended on its advertising clout and class-conscious publicity machine. Moreover, the *Neue Freie Presse* became briefly, between 1900 and 1905, a prominent venue for his own publications. Of the mere dozen articles and reviews he published during this period — roughly between *The Interpretation of Dreams* and *Jokes and their Relation to the Unconscious* — five appeared in its pages. These were chiefly brief reviews of books on neurasthenia, sleep and other familiar topics. One of them, an obituary for his religion teacher and erstwhile patron Samuel Hammerschlag, afforded Freud the opportunity to pay tribute to his fatherly friend who shared "in the spirit of the great Jewish prophets and truth tellers" (Tichy / Zwettler-Otte 1999, p. 112).

For Freud then, the *Neue Freie Presse* seems to have been not an object of critical analysis, but instead a fact of life; and, indeed, in one instance, in *The Psychopathology of Everyday Life*, a reliable or at least a neutral source of material for his psychoanalytic investigations.[5] By the time Freud began to publish in the *Neue Freie Presse*, Kraus's practice of attacking the paper's lapses in logic, faulty grammar, typographical errors, sloppy reporting, and contradictory opinions was well developed. Nevertheless, there is no reason to think that he would have held either Freud's act of intellectual filial piety towards Hammerschlag or the handful of exercises in reviewing for a wider audience against him. He is unlikely, however, to have overlooked a detailed, admiring review of *The Psychopathology of Everyday Life* that appeared in the *Neue Freie Presse* during this same period, on April 10, 1904. The reviewer's enthusiastic explication of the subtitle — "Forgetting, Slips of the Tongue, Bungled Actions, Superstitions and Errors" — as referring to "the entirety of the typographical errors of the human brain" (Tichy / Zwettler-Otte 1999, p. 113) made use of a metaphor central to Kraus's own satirical practice. While this paraphrase of the book's examination of parapraxes, verbal and written slips and mistakes of all kind, might have struck a sympathetic chord, he would have undoubtedly remained skeptical about the intellectual competence of the reviewer. The awkward style of Julian Sternberg, the editor of the daily "Chronicle" column in the *Neue Freie Presse*, had already made him one of Kraus's favorite journalistic targets. Just a few weeks after the appearance of his review of Freud's book, Kraus took him to task in *The Torch* for an incompetent review of Gerhart Hauptmann's great naturalistic drama *The Weavers*. Kraus emphasizes the bad judgment of the paper's editors in sending to the performance a "local reporter whose has just enough wit to write about crowded conditions on the streetcars and whose seriousness is entirely equal to the problem of gas pipes" (Kraus 1904, p. 16).

Whatever Kraus may have thought of this first positive reception of Freud's work in the *Neue Freie Presse*, he seems not to have responded to it in *The Torch*. That he ignored *The Psychopathology of Everyday Life* itself seems unlikely. The first book edition appeared in 1904 when Freud first wrote to Kraus, congratulating him on his courage in excoriating sexual hypocrisy in the public sphere. The second, third, and fourth editions appeared in 1907, 1910, and 1912, respectively, years during which his relationship to Freud reached both its apogee and nadir. An intertextual comparison of the text with Kraus's commentaries in *The Torch* during these years may still turn up examples of cryptic commentary.

More pertinent to this investigation are the surprisingly frequent references to the press in *The Psychopathology of Everyday Life* and indeed Freud's autobiographical vignettes of himself as a consumer of the news. He appears, particularly in his commentary on "Misreadings and Slips of the Pen," as a normal, distracted newspaper reader. At the very beginning of this chapter, he describes himself in a coffeehouse, inadvertently misunderstanding a headline in an illustrated journal (Freud 1960, p. 106). In the next example, Freud pursues the meaning of his misreading "in a newspaper one day" of the phrase "on foot [zu Fuß]" across Europe as "in a tub [im Faß]" across Europe (Freud 1960, p. 107). Remembering that he has been reading a book on art in the age of Alexander the Great, he begins with a digression that links the tub with Diogenes and Alexander's famous remark that if he were not Alexander he would rather be Diogenes. Freud then recalls another newspaper article that reported on curious means of transportation that people chose for traveling to the International Exhibition in Paris in 1900, including a certain Hermann Zeitung's decision to pack himself into a trunk for the trip. At first, the man's last name, Zeitung, which means "newspaper" in German, leads to the recollection of a patient with a "pathological anxiety about reading newspapers." Freud explains this as a reaction to his "pathological *ambition* to see himself in print and to read of his fame in the newspapers" (Freud 1960, p. 108). Rather than pursuing the fear and anxiety aroused by the newspaper or even the symbolic importance of Hermann Zeitung's name, Freud focuses on the connection between the double meaning of *Beförderung*—"means of transportation" and "promotion"—and the link provided by "ambition." He brings these key words together to reveal feelings of envy towards his younger brother Alexander, an expert on tariffs and transportation, who at the time was on the verge of receiving a professorship before Freud himself but then found his promotion blocked. Having made the connection between Alexander the Great, his brother Alexander, and his own ambition, he explains his original misreading of the newspaper in terms of a repressed sibling rivalry: "I had behaved as if I was reading of my brother's appointment in the newspaper and was saying to myself: 'How curious that a person can appear in the newspaper (i.e. can be appointed professor) on account of such stupidities (which is what his profession amounts to)!'" (Freud 1960, p. 108). However compelling this analysis may be, it fails to account for the striking motif of the newspaper that seems overdetermined in ways that cry out for interpretation.

In an example added to the chapter on "Slips of the Tongue" in the second edition in 1907, Freud describes a speech witnessed by Max Graf,[6] a music critic and journalist well known to Karl Kraus:

> At the General Meeting of the "Concordia," the Society of Journalists, a young member who was invariably hard-up made a violently aggressive speech, and in his excitement spoke of the "*Vorschussmitglieder* [lending members]" (instead of "*Vorstandsmitglieder* [officers]" or "*Ausschussmitglieder* [committee members]." The latter have the authority to sanction loans, and the young speaker had in fact put in an application for a loan [Freud 1960, p. 88].

For Freud, this anecdote merely augments "linguistic material" that he has gathered for his study; it provokes neither commentary nor interpretation. For Kraus, the "Concordia" was the embodiment of journalistic corruption, a view documented by the more than two-hundred critical references to its misdeeds in *The Torch* between 1899 and 1907. He would have understood the inadvertent pun "Vorschussmitglieder" not as a financially strapped young member's slip of the tongue, but rather as a revealing expression of the leadership's venality.

Freud seems never to have returned to the neurosis involving "fear of the newspaper" (Freud 1960, p. 108), as the condition of the patient mentioned in the anecdote about "on foot" and "in a tub" should more properly be translated. Neither the influence of the press in general nor of the *Neue Freie Presse* in particular appear in any substantial way in his published work. At the meetings of the Vienna Psychoanalytic Association, however, the topic comes up more than once. It makes sense, therefore, in this instance to follow Freud's biographers after all and return to Fritz Wittels's paper on "The *Fackel*-Neurosis" (Nunberg/Federn 1967, pp. 382–393).[7]

Wittels announces at the outset that he will analyze Kraus and *The Torch* in terms of the artist pathography and demonstrate how "extraordinary intellectual gifts" can be so diverted by "neurotic countercurrents" that they produce neurosis instead of art. This was a bold move given that Kraus had already published an aphorism that reads like a preemptive strike on such investigations: "Neurologists who supply us with the pathology of a genius should have their skulls bashed in with his complete works" (Kraus 1986a, p. 82). It is particularly ironic that the third of the three problems that Wittels proposes to investigate is why Kraus has fallen so low as to become an aphorist when the aphorism is the "least passionate" literary form. The first and the second problem consist — in Wittels's view — of Kraus's having suddenly transformed himself from a feature writer, an essentially affirmative journalist, into an "anti-corruptionist" or muckraker for personal reasons and then of losing interest in attacking journalists and directing his attention to sexuality. In his conclusion, he will argue that Kraus's "hatred for journalists" can be traced to his "*neurotic* attitude" towards a specific newspaper. He concludes by reminding his colleagues that the starting point for any neurosis is the "Oedipus motif."

While there would be much more to say about this fascinating exercise in unwitting self-exposure, it is Wittels's description of finding the psychoanalytic key to the "*Fackel*-Neurosis" that is most revealing in this context. He begins by reporting that one day he had a "vision" in which he saw his own father reading the *Neue Freie Presse,* and then offers an account of the famous journal's significance: "This newspaper is a colossal power in Austria, especially within the Jewish community. It belongs to the household of the bourgeois family; it is at the same time the newspaper of the father." Wittels adds that he told an acquaintance about this "vision," who provided further commentary: "the *Presse* is the organ of the father that corrupts the entire world. The *Torch* is only a small organ, but it is capable of destroying the big organ." Otto Rank, who kept the minutes, then inserts his own observation that Wittels preferred not to go any further into these symbolic implications because they would not meet with any understanding at all outside their circle. Wittels concludes with the remark that it would be almost too perfect if the founding of the journal had been a reaction to the death of the father, but that is not correct because the *Torch* began publication a year earlier. Suffice it to say, that in what follows Wittels cancels out his own argument before he can develop it.

What is crucial here is not whether *The Torch* was a neurotic reaction to the *Neue Freie Presse,* but rather that reading the *Neue Freie Presse* seems to have been perceived by these psychoanalytic thinkers as a potential neurotic symptom in its own right. This becomes clear during the discussion. Tausk, certainly one of the most brilliant members of the psychoanalytic circle at this time, remarks that Kraus justifiably attacks the deleterious effect of the *Neue Freie Presse* on thought and feeling and adds that he cannot agree that the relationship to the newspaper is a mirror image of the "father neurosis." Stekel, rather than focusing on Wittels's paper, upbraids Tausk, insisting that "it is not right to make such absolutely negative judgments about the newspaper and journalists." Hugo Heller, the book dealer and cultural impresario, is disappointed not to have heard more about the transference from the father to the *Neue Freie Presse.* It might have been possible to "reach new insights into the relationship between the older and the younger generation in general and in particular." Clearly, this central idea of Wittels's paper, which can be understood independently of Kraus, generated excitement and debate.

But what did Freud say? Wittels's comment, for example, about Kraus's "column dedicated to 'nailing' the misprints, errors and mistakes in the *Neue Freie Presse,*" seems formulated to provoke a comparison with the similar material treated in *The Psychopathology of Everyday Life.* Freud, in essence, said nothing, or at least nothing about the vulnerability and the power of the phallic newspaper of the father. He specifically approves of some of the points Wittels has made—"the father complex," the "influence of the milieu," and "Judaism"—and then goes on to talk about his own dashed hopes for Kraus's support and about what he perceives as the satirist's histrionic behavior and lack of character. It is in every way an evasive, ambiguous, lackluster performance.

Freud's apparent lack of interest in the symbolic significance of the *Neue Freie Presse* and the press in general stands in stark contrast to further debate that the topic generated in meetings that took place a few months later, in the spring of 1910. In the most focused of three sessions devoted to the problem of suicide among school children, held on April 20, the high school classics professor David Oppenheim presented a paper on a new book on the subject by Abraham Baer that singled out conditions in the middle schools as a prime factor (Nunberg/Federn 1977, pp. 444–52).[8] Oppenheim rejects this argument, but concurs with Baer on the importance of imitation, or the copycat factor, and of the power of suggestion. Somewhat suddenly, Oppenheim then launches into a tirade against the "modern press," which he describes as "one of the strongest means of suggestion created by the development of human culture." He goes on to assert that only the Catholic Church in its best times had a similar power of suggestion at its disposal and earned the justified scorn of atheists who sought independence from its influence. He concludes that Voltaire's famous blasphemous imperative "Ecrasez l'infâme" might now be justifiably applied to the "new despot [Zwingherrin] in the realm of the spirit, the press." Oppenheim's following words, which begin with the exclamation "Meine Herren!" (Gentlemen!), suggest that he expected his listeners to be surprised or to object. He goes on to assure them that, although they may be astonished by his "sudden expression of deep resentment," they will soon acknowledge its justification in this instance. The only respondent to allude to this outburst is Isidor Sadger, who says: "Even if the charge of the press that high school professors are directly responsible for student suicides is not justified, there is still a grain of truth in the accusation" (Nunberg/Federn 1977, p. 455).

In his own long comment on the paper (Nunberg/Federn 1977, pp. 455–57), Freud passes over Oppenheim's diatribe against the press without comment and focuses instead on what he sees as the failure of teachers to concern themselves sufficiently with their students' sexuality. When he exercises similar restraint in the session held just a little over a month later towards Stekel's claim that the newspaper plays a substantial role in the symbolism of masturbators and, citing Wittels, that it is "a substitute for the father" (Nunberg/Federn 1977, p. 509), his silence begins to look calculated. In his paper on "Choice of Profession and Neurosis" given on November 2, 1910, Stekel will again, after claiming that the newspaper can symbolize "something vaguely resembling a prostitute," refer to Wittels's idea that "the newspaper represents ... the father" (Nunberg/Federn 1974, p. 36). Despite the glaring contradictions of Stekel's wild theorizing, Freud again avoids making a comment. He proposes, after several respondents have already spoken, postponing the discussion until the next session, which he then fails to attend.

Freud's refusal to be drawn into the debate over the *Neue Freie Presse* and journalism in general seems to present a clear case of resistance, not only to the topic but also to Karl Kraus himself. Stekel's comments, superficial and self-serving though may be, both cite Wittels's paper on "The *Torch*-Neurosis" and, therefore, summon up the letter if not necessarily the spirit of the satirist. Given Freud's low regard for Stekel's intellectual gifts, it may have been easy for him to ignore these remarks, which in any case do not question the press as an institution. David Oppenheim's passionate condemnation of the baleful influence of journalistic sensationalism presented a more complicated challenge. For readers of *The Torch*, which most of the members of Freud's circle clearly were, it must have seemed as though Oppenheim were speaking with Kraus's voice. One of Oppenheim's closest friends during the years before he met Freud was the young writer Otto Soyka, who had published a very positive review of *Three Essays on Sexuality* in *The Torch* in 1905 and belonged to Kraus's circle at least until 1908.[9] As it happens, speaking with Kraus's voice or even mentioning his name in the Vienna Psychoanalytic Association had been prohibited by Freud in the meantime so he was in one sense simply following his own rules.

Less than three months after Wittels's presentation of "The *Fackel*-Neurosis," Karl Kraus published a series of aggressive aphorisms about psychoanalysis including the one decrying the profession as the "occupation of lecherous rationalists." At the very next meeting of Freud's circle, on April 13, 1910, item number IX on the agenda was "Discussion of the Kraus Affair," meaning the attack in *The Torch* and other repercussions from Wittels's activities. Adler reported the decision to maintain strict silence about the affair in public. Freud's brief comment demanded that the matter be suppressed entirely: "Prof. Freud added the further admonition that all remarks about this matter should also be avoided in private. As far as the Vienna Psychoanalytic Association is concerned, there is no Kraus Affair" (Nunberg/Federn 1977, p. 439). With this injunction, Freud was duplicating the strategy of the *Neue Freie Presse*, which early on had banned Kraus's name and the title of his journal from its pages. Kraus himself called it "totschweigen," to maintain absolute silence about something or, literally, to "to silence something to death."

Although the reason for this drastic action cannot be deduced from the *Minutes* themselves, Freud seems to have feared that any further discussion of Kraus and *The Torch* that reached his ears would provoke further satirical attacks on psychoanalysis.[10] As Freud reported in a letter of February 13, 1910, to Ferenczi, Kraus seems to have threatened such action very soon after Wittels's presentation. There he remarks sarcastically that "the negative popularity provided by the Torch is almost as unpleasant as the positive" and indicates that he has already issued the order of "absolute suppression of any reaction" (Freud/Ferenczi 1993, p. 213). Ironically, just as the conflict with Kraus was reaching its highpoint, Freud received a request from the *Neue Freie Presse* to write an article about psychoanalysis, an unparalleled opportunity to disseminate his ideas more widely than ever before. According to Ernest Jones, "he refused, feeling that he was already conspicuous enough in Vienna" (Jones 1955, p. 78). In a letter to Jung of May 26, 1910, on which Jones bases this report, Freud reports that he turned down the offer because he had to "be especially careful in Vienna" (Freud/Jung 1974, p. 322). This suggests that Freud realized that writing about psychoanalysis in the *Neue Freie Presse* would amount to waving a red flag in front of Kraus's punitively poised wit. What else could possibly have held him back from seizing the opportunity to introduce his new "science" to the readership of what was arguably the most respected newspaper in Europe? Although Freud strategically withheld his own presentation of psychoanalysis from the *Neue Freie Presse* in 1910, eight of the twenty-seven references to Freud and his theory that had appeared in the paper since 1895 were published in that year (Tichy/Zwettler-Otte 1999, p. 109). After the First World War, coverage skyrocketed so that between 1920 and 1938 there were more than five-hundred-and-seventy mentions. The *Neue Freie Presse*, which remained Kraus's bête noire, became a major vehicle for publicizing the Psychoanalytic Movement (Tichy/Zwettler-Otte 1999, p. 110).

In 1912, during the final phase of his concerted aphoristic campaign against psychoanalysis, Kraus wrote in *The Torch* that he did not even have to read the front page of the newspaper anymore. He had it in his power to reconstruct "the face of the modern world" out of what he calls, playing on the word for the classified section at the back of the paper, the "backside" composed of advertisements and personals. There, he says, "they speak in their sleep" (Kraus 1912, p. 31). The hidden anal voices of the newspaper speaking from the realm of dreams: this searing comic image of the Unconscious reads like a pointed travesty of psychoanalytic theory addressed to its great articulator. This is yet another reason for Freud's future biographers to think again about what exactly he consumed in his daily portion of the *Neue Freie Presse*.

Notes

1. When Jones writes that Freud did not take Kraus's attacks in *The Torch* "seriously enough to be worth replying to," he misrepresents the letters to Ferenczi that he cites as evidence.
2. Because Gay does not survey the full spectrum of evidence in *The Torch*, he mistakenly believes that Kraus was "never disrespectful of Freud himself." Although he cites the memoir of Fritz Wittels, who attempts to come to terms with Freud and Kraus as his "two spiritual fathers," he fails—in keeping with his general diffidence towards the Viennese context of Freud's work—to realize how important the episode with Kraus was.
3. The best overview of the interaction between Freud and Kraus is still Worbs 1983, pp. 149–77. See also Anz/Pfohlmann 2006, pp. 207–92, which includes most of the relevant texts and documents.
4. Since there is still no central database for Freud's correspondence, it is possible that a thorough survey of the letters will reveal more specifics about Freud's attitude to the *Neue Freie Presse* and to the press in general. Michael Schröter (Berlin) has been kind enough to share references he found to the *Neue Freie Presse* in his own database of Freud's published and unpublished letters.

5. In the Standard Edition, the reference to the newspaper has been removed to the bibliography. See, for example, the third edition of 1910, where it is still cited in the text: "In einem kleinen für weitere Kreise bestimmten Aufsatz (Neue freie Presse vom 23. Aug. 1900: 'Wie man sich versprechen kann')" (Freud 1910, p. 41).

6. In a meeting of the Vienna Psychoanalytic Association in 1910 Graf revealed that he had known Kraus since high school, i.e., since the early 1890s (Nunberg/Federn 1967, p. 390).

7. All quotations in the following discussion of "The *Fackel*-Neurosis" are taken from this source unless otherwise indicated.

8. Unless otherwise indicated, the following quotations are taken from Oppenheim's paper, which was entered into the *Minutes* in his own manuscript.

9. In his biographical study of his grandfather, Peter Singer gives a brief account of this friendship and mentions that Soyka's first article for *The Torch* was on Oscar Wilde (Singer 2003, pp. 23–24). He seems to be unaware of the Freud review. On David Oppenheim, see also Mühlleitner 1992, pp. 239f.

10. The situation was further complicated by Wittels's imminent publication of a *roman à clef* that slandered Kraus and others in his circle. Kraus asked Freud to put pressure on Wittels to suppress publication of the novel. Wittels resisted Freud's efforts and soon found himself forced to resign from the Vienna Psychoanalytic Association. See Lensing 1989, Timms 1990, and Lensing 1996. Timms's edition of Wittels's memoirs under the sensational title *Freud and the Child Woman* (Timms 1995), which conflated two versions of the text and included some re-writing of selected passages, produced more confusion than clarity.

References

Anz, T., and O. Pfohlmann, O. (2006), eds. *Psychoanalyse in der literarischen Moderne. Vol. 1. Einleitung und Wiener Moderne. Hermann Bahr, Hugo von Hofmannsthal, Arthur Schnitzler, Karl Kraus.* Marburg: LiteraturWissenschaft.de

Berg, A. (n.d.). *Armin Berg's Anekdoten-Schatz.* Vienna: Kommissionsverlag J. Linschütz.

Carr, G. (1982). "Karl Kraus and Sigmund Freud." In *Irish Studies in Modern Austrian Literature.* Ed. G.J. Carr and E. Sagarra. Dublin: Trinity College Dublin.

Freud, S. (1910). *Zur Psychopathologie des Alltagslebens.* 3rd expanded ed. Berlin: Karger.

——— (1960). *The Psychopathology of Everyday Life.* Standard Edition Vol. 6. London: Hogarth.

——— (1974). *The Freud/Jung Letters. The Correspondence between Sigmund Freud and C.G. Jung.* Princeton, NJ: Princeton University Press.

——— (1985). *The Complete Letters of Sigmund Freud to Wilhelm Fliess 1887–1904.* Ed. and trans. J. M. Masson. Cambridge, MA, and London: Harvard University Press.

——— (1999). *The Interpretation of Dreams.* Ed. R. Robertson. Trans. J. Crick. Oxford, New York: Oxford University Press.

——— (2004). "Briefe an Maria (Mitzi) Freud und ihre Familie." Ed. C. Tögel and M. Schröter. *Luzifer-Amor.* Vol. 17. No. 33: 51–72.

——— (2005). *Unser Herz zeigt nach dem Süden. Reisebriefe 1895–1923.* Ed. C. Tögel with M. Molnar. Frankfurt a. M.: S. Fischer.

Gay, P. (1988). *Freud. A Biography for Our Time.* New York, London: W.W. Norton

Hegel, G.W.F. (1971). *Jenäer Schriften 1801–1807.* In *Werke.* Vol. 2. Ed. E. Moldenhauer and K. M. Michel. Suhrkamp: Frankfurt a. M.

Jones, E. (1955). *The Life and Work of Sigmund Freud. Vol. 2 Years of Maturity 1901–1919.* New York: Basic.

Kraus, K. (1899). Ich und die "Neue Freue Presse." *Die Fackel.* No. 5. Mid-May 1899. 3–11.

——— (1904). Theater, Kunst und Literatur. *Die Fackel.* No. 162. May 19, 1904. 16–21.

——— (1905). Die Kinderfreunde. *Die Fackel.* No. 187. November 8, 1905. 1–28.

——— (1907). Illusionen. *Die Fackel.* No. 237. December 2, 1907. 1–16.

——— (1912). Ich pfeife auf den Text. *Die Fackel.* Nos. 354–356. August 29, 1912. 31–33.

——— (1986a). *Aphorismen.* (= Schriften. Vol. 8). Ed. C. Wagenknecht. Frankfurt a. M.: Suhrkamp.

——— (1986b). *Die letzten Tage der Menschheit* (=Schriften. Vol. 10). Ed. C. Wagenknecht. Frankfurt a. M.: Suhrkamp.

_____ (1989). *Dramen* (= Schriften. Vol. 11). Ed. C. Wagenknecht. Frankfurt a. M.: Suhrkamp.
_____ (2005). *Briefe an Sidonie Nádherný von Borutin 1913–1936*. 2 vols. Ed. F. Pfäfflin. Göttingen: Wallstein Verlag.
Lensing, L.A. (1989). "'Geistige Väter'" und "'Das Kindweib'": Sigmund Freud, Karl Kraus & Irma Karczewska in der Autobiographie von Fritz Wittels." *Forum* (Vienna). Vol. 36: 62–71.
_____ (1996). "'Freud and the Child Woman' or 'The Kraus Affair'? A Textual 'Reconstruction' of Fritz Wittels's Psychoanalytic Autobiography." *German Quarterly* 69: 322–332.
Meyerhöfer, A. (2006). *Eine Wissenschaft des Träumens. Sigmund Freud und seine Zeit*. Munich: Knaus.
Mühlleitner, E. with J. Reichmayr (1992). *Biographisches Lexikon der Psychoanalyse. Die Mitglieder der Psychologischen Mittwoch-Gesellschaft und der Wiener Psychoanalytischen Vereinigung 1902–1938*. Tübingen: edition diskord.
Nunberg H., and E. Federn, eds. (1967). *Minutes of the Vienna Psychoanalytic Society. Vol. II. 1908–1910*. Trans. H. Nunberg. New York, International Universities Press.
_____ (1974). *Minutes of the Vienna Psychoanalytic Society. Vol. III. 1910–1911*. Trans. M. Nunberg with H. Collins. New York: International Universities Press.
_____ (1977). *Protokolle der Wiener Psychoanalytischen Vereinigung. Vol. II. 1908–1910*. Frankfurt a. M.: S. Fischer.
Roth, J. (1927). *Juden auf Wanderschaft*. Berlin: Verlag Die Schmiede.
Schur, M. (1972). *Freud: Living and Dying*. New York: International Universities Press.
Singer, P. (2004) *Pushing Time Away. My Grandfather and the Tragedy of Jewish Vienna*. New York: HarperCollins.
Tichy, M., and S. Zwettler-Otte. (1999). *Freud in der Presse. Rezeption Sigmund Freuds und der Psychoanalyse in Österreich 1895–1938*. Vienna: Sonderzahl.
Timms, E. (1986). *Karl Kraus. Apocalyptic Satirist. Culture and Catastrophe in Habsburg Vienna*. New Haven, CT, and London: Yale University Press.
_____ (1990). "The 'Child Woman': Kraus, Freud, Wittels, and Irma Karczewska." *Austrian Studies* I: 87–107.
_____, ed. (1995). *Freud and the Child Woman. The Memoirs of Fritz Wittels*. New Haven, CT, and London: Yale University Press.
Tucholsky, K. (1913). "Von dem Manne, der keine Zeitungen mehr las." *Die Schaubühne*. Vol. 9. No. 43. 22 October 1913: 1030–1033.
Waldvogel, A. (1990). "Karl Kraus und die Psychoanalyse: Eine historisch-dokumentarische Untersuchung." *Psyche*. Vol. 44. No. 5. Mai 1990: 412–444.
Worbs, M. (1983). *Nervenkunst: Literatur und Psychoanalyse im Wien der Jahrhundertwende*. Vienna: Europäische Verlagsanstalt.
Zweig, S. (1944). *Die Welt von Gestern. Erinnerungen eines Europäers*. Vienna: Bermann-Fischer.

Sigmund Freud and Electrotherapy

SANDER L. GILMAN

The twenty-first century (re-)appearance of electrotherapy for the treatment of mental illness recalls how very important such therapies were for the treatment of analogous problems for over a hundred and fifty years (Morus 1992, 1998, 1999; Bryan 1966; Henke 1970). They flourished in Western medicine, as we shall see, from the end of the nineteenth century to the post–World War I period. Between the end of World War I and the mid–1960's mention of electrical stimulation for treatment of mental illness all but disappears as the focus moved from a somatic understanding of mental illness to one that mixed somatic and psychological etiologies and then became "brain disease." Even the analogous treatment, Electro-convulsive Therapy, developed out of insulin and camphor therapy for schizophrenia (itself developed out of malaria therapy for General Paralysis of the Insane) by Ugo Cerletti and Lucio Bini in 1937 at a point when electrotherapy had fallen out of fashion, has made a public "come back" for the treatment of profound depression.

A hundred years ago the "age of electricity" saw the application of this "new" medium to medical therapy, as a late nineteenth-century advocate noted (Hedley 1900, iii). As with virtually every technological innovation since the discovery of fire and the invention of the wheel, electricity was immediately applied to the treatment of pathologies, including those of the voice. It was the case with the Greeks' invention of smelting metal — which became Aristotle's model for the heart and lungs but also for therapeutic interventions; it will in the twentieth century be similar with the discovery of vitamins and the assumption that virtually all illnesses could be "cured" with these newly discovered substances. Yet in each stage different meanings were attached to the function of "electricity" and certainly to the question of what it meant to provide succor to that most amorphous of human products, the voice. This tale provides a double insight into how electrotherapy for depression was constituted in the light of technological innovation as well as the implications of the historical record for the present (nascent) fascination Vagal Nerve Stimulation by pacemaker as well as Cranial Electrotherapy Stimulation.

Now it is clear that by the end of the nineteenth century electrotherapy in its many forms was the treatment of choice for a wide range of illness including mental illnesses such as hysteria. Electrotherapy was espoused for the treatment of "nervous" or "mental disorders" from the eighteenth century by Richard Lovett and became a commonplace in the nineteenth century in the work of neurologists such as S. Wier Mitchell, of "Rest Cure" infamy (Lovett 1756, 109; Mitchell 1898, 96–106). But there were always dissenting opinions. William Beven (1842: 176), at the beginning of the electrophysiological era, called such therapies "another instance of those chimerical fancies of the day, which are perpetually disgracing our profession, and bringing it into contempt with the public; that, like mesmerism, it will meet with a similar fate — to be merely had in memory, and as a tale that were told." The fact is that it does not vanish but becomes institutionalized with all of its far-reaching therapeutic claims.

Perhaps the most important figure to recognize the limitations as well as the rationale for success of the electrotherapy for the treatment of mental illness was the Viennese neurologist Sigmund Freud. For the young Freud, newly returned from study in Paris in 1886 with the neurologist Jean Martin Charcot, hysteria is the "contrary" of neurasthenia; it too is a modern disease, but one which has its roots in a trauma of the central nervous system which results in "invisible" lesions. Its treatment needed to address the somatic nature of the disease. Thus, in addition to hypnosis (understood as a somatic therapy), Charcot indeed used electrotherapy, including static electrical sparks, in the treatment of his hysterics.

One of the central symptoms that defined this new way of seeing hysteria as a result of neurological trauma is the "well-known … *globus hystericus*, a feeling referable to spasms of the pharynx, as though a lump were rising up from the epigastrum to the throat" (Freud SE 1, 42). Yet Freud is quite aware, given his tutelage in Paris, that hysteria is no way a disease of women, as "hysteria in males gives the appearance of a very severe illness" (SE 1, 52). Yet he warns that hysteria is overdiagnosed and that somatic illness can be the cause of symptoms that mimic hysteria: "a stomach with a catarrhal affection can give rise to hysterical vomiting, *globus hystericus* and anesthesia or hyperaesthesia of the skin of the epigastrum." For all of these symptoms electrotherapy was the treatment of choice. Thus after Freud's colleague Joseph Breuer "successfully concluded" the cathartic cure of the first patient to experience this, "Anna O." (Bertha Pappenheim) was admitted to Bellevue Sanatorium in July of 1882 was treated further with electrotherapy (Hirschmüller 1989, appendix).

Freud abandoned electrotherapy (as well as hydrotherapy, massage, the "rest cure," and hypnosis) to treat his "neurotics" to explore the "cathartic method" (the talking cure) after 1895, seeing electrotherapy as having no value whatsoever. He had used electrotherapy extensively, even having purchased an expensive machine through a loan from his wealthy friend Ernst Fleischl von Marxow, whose morphine addiction he later unsuccessfully treats with cocaine (not electrotherapy) (Anzieu 1986, 39). His treatment of his patients in 1887, whom he saw suffering from lesions of the nerves, incorporated electrotherapy, as in the case of a "post-diptheritic paralysis of the legs." Another case in 1888 of "cerebral neurasthenia" treated with "galvanization" showed "steady improvement." By 1892, being "satisfied with symptomatic methods" as "the patient does not demand anything other than this" did not seem sufficient to Freud (Masson 1985, 16, 18, 21).

As Freud recalled a decade later in his "The History of the Psychoanalytic Movement" (1914): "I had embarked upon physical therapy, and felt absolutely helpless after the disappointing results from my study of Erb's *Elektrotherapie* [1882], which put forward a number of indications and recommendations. If I did not at the time arrive on my own account at the conclusion which Möbius established later, that the successes of electrical treatment in nervous patients are the results of suggestion, there is no doubt that only the total absence of these promised successes was to blame" (*SE* 14, 9). It turned out to hold no more "reality than some 'Egyptian' dreambook, such as sold in cheap bookshops" (Killen 2006, 52). Freud was among a growing number of therapists in the 1890s who became to judge electrotherapy as unsuccessful since it was deemed to be only effective through suggestion, not as was claimed through a direct action on the nervous system. Yet their powerful associations with the newest technologies of the dynamo and mass electrification made it remain seductive. Among these was, as Freud noted the famed neurologist Paul Möbius who in 1889 wondered if the success of electrotherapeutics was due to "suggestion" initiated by the elaborate electrical apparatus, which features so prominently in all of the presentations of electrotherapy of the age (Schiller 1982). The American psychiatrist Morton Prince advocated the use of electrotherapy for hysteria but also noted "as is likewise the case when a cure is effected by other means, there is a tendency for it to return" (Prince 1902, D-124). For him there is a differentiation between hysterical aphonia and other diseases of the voice, as the hysteric cannot phonate but can cough or even sing. The tension was between hysteria as a somatic disease treatable by mechanical means and as a psychological disease, which needed psychotherapy.

It was the neurologists of the time who saw the psychological dimension of electrotherapy most clearly. By the 1930s even the electrotherapists who claimed a somatic effect argued that "sparks from a static machine are effective [in the treatment of hysteria] and have an additional psychic effect" (Cumberbatch 1939, 426). The psychiatrists, on the other hand, continued to use electrotherapy through World War I. One of the great scandals was the accusation that Freud's colleague at the University of Vienna, the psychiatrist Julius Wagner-Jauregg, director of the First Psychiatric Clinic in Vienna, winner of the Nobel Prize (1927) for the malaria therapy of general paralysis of the insane (tertiary syphilis), had used "electrotherapy" on "war neurotics" (shell shock) which had led to suicides and deaths. Freud testified for him on 14 and 16 October 1920 and he was eventually acquitted of all charges (Eissler 1979, 55). Freud wrote to Sándor Ferenczi: "Next Thursday I will have the pleasure all morning of functioning as an expert witness in the trial of the Commission for Military Violations of Duty against Wagner-Jauregg and others. It has to do with the war neuroses. I will naturally treat him with the most distinct benevolence. It also isn't his fault" (Brabant-Gerö et al. 2000, 3: 34–36). It was not, of course. It was electrotherapy's fault.

In 1895 Freud in *The Studies in Hysteria* had reported on Frau Emmy von N.'s (actually Fanny Moser) "spastic inhibition of speech, her peculiar stammer" (SE 2, 93) was the result of "convulsive inhibition of the organs of speech" due to the underlying motivation of her hysteria. They are "linked up with so many traumas, had so much reason for being reproduced in memory, that they perpetually interrupted the patient's speech for no particular cause, in the manner of a meaningless *tic*" (SE 2, 93). The stammering is "a simple conversion of psychical excitation into motor activity" (SE 2, 95). Freud treats Frau Emmy von N. as the first of his patients with the "talking cure." Thereafter electrotherapy is seen as less and less effective. Freud dismisses "faradizations of the sensitive muscles" and even the use of "high tension electric current" to cure another one of his hysterics, Fräulein Elisabeth von R.'s inability to walk, as a "pretence treatment" (SE 2, 138). Freud understands that the more powerful the shocks he administered to her the more she "seemed to take quite a liking to the painful shocks produced by the high tension apparatus, and the stronger these were the more they seemed to push her own pains into the background" (SE 2, 138). Freud understands the psychological rather than the neurological impact of the treatment. Freud turns again to the talking cure to intervene, as the electrotherapy seemed rather to reward the patient's hysteria. In this case study Freud again turns to the classic hysterical symptoms of the *globus hystericus*, in the case of two professional singers. One twenty-three year old "had a good voice, but she complained that in certain parts of its compass it was not under her control. She had a feeling of choking and constriction in her throat so that her voice sounded tight.... Although this imperfection affected only her middle register, it could not be attributed to a defect in the organ itself." The other was "a case of a singer under my observation in which a contracture of the masseters made it impossible to practice her art.... She was singing at a rehearsal in Rome at a time when she was in a state of great emotional excitement, and suddenly had a feeling that she could not close her open mouth and fell to the floor in a faint" (SE 2, 169–70). In both cases, with reference to the case of Frau Emmy, these were shown to have been psychological responses to traumatic events of a sexual nature. What is so remarkable is Freud's dealing with such professional users of the voice, who clearly were for him exemplary cases for his new model of intervention as they were inappropriate for electrotherapy. He woos these patients away from the electrotherapists who would have intervened into their vocal problems through faradic treatments. Yet Freud's was a dissenting voice in the treatment of neurosis and attendant vocal problems. Thus the debate shifted from physiological or somatoform to psychological or psychogenic categories, but it still continues (Lehtinen and Puhakka 1976; Mace, Ron, Deahl 1989; Puhakka and Kirveskari 1989).

By the oft discussed "Fragments of an Analysis of a Case of Hysteria" (1901, published 1905) Freud had abandoned electrotherapy in the treatment of his hysterical patients. The eighteen-year-old "Dora" (Ida Bauer) had been brought to Freud by her father Philip Bauer suffering from aphonia, depression, and fits of coughing, and who had threatened suicide. Diagnosed as early as 1894, as a twelve-year-old, Dora would have been subjected to intensive sessions of electrotherapy by her physicians (Decker 1992, 10–14). Her larynx would have appeared normal to them. Yet her adductor muscles were partially paralyzed, causing the vocal cords to remain separated. However, when she coughed the adductors were able to come together. This would have been seen through the use of the laryngoscope. To treat her they would have applied current directly to the larynx, but, as was clear when Freud she examined her, without any long-term success. Electrotherapy simply did not work as it should have. Dora's physicians were expecting a lesion; Freud came to understand the psychogenetic nature of her illness. (There are a number of "problems" with Freud's interpretation of the case of Dora; his choice of therapy is not among them [Bernheimer and Kahane 1985].) Freud saw in this case of failed electrotherapy a return to early childhood patterns, not a lesion of the nervous system. "Many of my women patients who suffer from disturbances of eating, *globus hystericus*, constriction of the throat and vomiting, have indulged energetically in sucking during their childhood" (SE 7, 182). This is his new reading of the loss of voice, a core symptom in the case of Dora. Freud's complicated account of this case stressed the sexual fantasy that lies at its core. But his treatment is the talking cure. Electrotherapy is never considered.

Yet there is a variable quite missing from Freud's public rejection of electrotherapy. It is the question of the central "biological" category of nineteenth century medicine: race. Freud's early patients were almost exclusively Jewish women and they (as well as all Jews) were deemed to be extraordinarily predisposed to hysteria. One might add that many of the Viennese neurologists were also Jews, as was the case with many of the Central European electrotherapists, such as Robert Remak (Killen 2006, 63). Access to medical specialties went in reverse of their social status: thus few Jews in the 1880s were academic surgeons. Freud's most startling exposure to such views may well have come during his stay in Paris during 1885 and 1886 when he studied with Jean Martin Charcot. Charcot represented the cutting edge of contemporary somatic medicine dealing with hysteria. In Charcot's *Tuesday Lessons*, such as the one for October 27, 1888, there is the stated presumption that "nervous illnesses of all types are innumerably more frequent among Jews than among other groups" (Charcot 1889, 2: 11–12). Charcot attributed this fact to inbreeding (Lagneau

1891). Charcot saw "the Jews as being the best source of material for nervous illness" (Charcot 1889, 1: 131). (Charcot had a number of Russian male Jews suffering from hysteria and neurasthenia as his patients. Their case notes are among his unpublished papers in Paris.) Freud, who translated the first volume of these lectures into German in 1892 (and certainly knew both volumes intimately), was also lectured by Charcot about the predisposition of Jews for specific forms of illness, such as diabetes, where "the exploration is easy" because of the intermarriage of the Jews (Gelfand 1988, 574). In his letter to Freud, Charcot used the vulgar "juif" rather than the more polite "Israélite" or more scientific "sémite" (Gelfand 1989, 304). In an off-the-record remark "a French physician," most probably Charcot, commented, "In my practice in Paris, ... I have the occasion to notice that, with the Jew, the emotions seem to be more vivid, the sensibility more intense, the nervous reactions more rapid and profound." And this leads to the "vital sap ris[ing] from his limbs, or his trunk, to his head [and] ... his overstrained nervous system is often apt, in the end, to become disordered and to collapse entirely" (Leroy-Beaulieu 1895, 168). This view was certainly present within mainstream German medicine at the time. The anthropologist-physician Georg Buschan, whose first position had been as an asylum physician in Leubus in 1886, stressed the "extraordinary incidence" of hysteria among European Jews as a sign of their racial degeneration in an address to the Organization of German Psychiatrists in Dresden on September 21, 1894 (cited in E. Morpurgo 1903, 66–67).

When Freud returned to Vienna from Paris and when he began teaching in the Medical Faculty, he found such views simply stated as commonplaces the predisposition of Jews for specific forms of mental illness. The standard handbooks of the time repeated this view in various contexts, including those that associated the hidden taint of the Jew's potential mental illness with the visible signs of degeneracy. And the view was not limited to the Jews of fin-de-siècle Europe. Georges Wulfing-Luer published in 1907 a detailed study of the Jews' predisposition to nervous diseases in which he traced this predisposition back into Biblical times, attempting to counter the argument of the situational causation of the nervousness of the Jews (Wulfing-Luer 1907). Such views were espoused by noteworthy opponents to political anti–Semitism, such as the French historian Anatole Leroy-Beaulieu. He, too, agreed "the Jew is particularly liable to the disease of our age, neurosis." He sees the reason that "the Jew is the most nervous of men, perhaps, because he is the most 'cerebral,' because he has lived most by his brain." He is "the most nervous and, in so far, the most modern of men" (Leroy-Beaulieu 1895, 168–69). And the treatment of choice for Jewish nervousness was electrotherapy.

Certainly the major figure to deal with the mental illness of the Eastern Jews is the Jewish psychiatrist Hermann Oppenheim, the widely cited author of a standard psychiatric textbook of the period (Oppenheim 1894–1913). His essay on the psychopathology of the Russian Jews is without a doubt the most widely cited and authoritative work in the field. Published in a *Festschrift* for August Forel, he begins with the complaint that "from year to year the growing hoards of patients from Russia come to us for advice and cure" (Oppenheim 1908, 1–9). The "us" is the Western physician. Oppenheim states quite directly that it is "well-known that Jews have a predisposition for neurosis and psychosis." Oppenheim makes an unstated distinction between the collectivity of the Eastern Jews, whose social milieu triggers the innate predisposition for mental illness and the individual Western Jew, such as himself, who may bear the taint but has not been exposed to the circumstance which trigger the illnesses.

What is striking in Oppenheim's account is the role that the voice as a sign of the sensibility of the patient or nosology of the disease plays. He notes that even "with the simplest test for sensitivity with needle pricks the patient cries out: 'Gewalt, Gewalt!' Certainly cowardliness, the fear of pain may play a role, but more evidently this cry seems to me a statement of the horrid path of suffering of this people i.e. this race" (Oppenheim 1908, 4). In another case study he describes the visit of a Russian-Jewish singer who had imagined a change in the quality of her voice upon the death of her husband. She appeared to be a hysteric according to Oppenheim, as the only sign of her putative aphonia, was a slight nasality in her voice. This he notes "was in intimate relationship to her mental state" (Oppenheim 1908, 6). The image of the female seems to subsume the image of the Jew and yet, for Oppenheim, the voice of the Eastern Jew permeates even the veneer of high culture. The altered voice of the Jew was a sign of the Jew's pathological relationship to the discourse of high culture. "The hidden voice of the Jew" reveals the Jew within even though all external signs have changed. It is the voice, more than any other quality, the distinctive lilt that can never be truly masked, that is the most evident sign of the modern Jew. It is the result of the very nature of the Jew's body, according to a medical authority of the day, Jews speak differently because the "muscles, which are used for speaking and laughing, are used inherently differently from those of Christians, and this use can be traced ... to the great difference in their nose and chin" (Blechmann 1882, 11). In self-consciously attempting to repress it, the *globus hystericus* becomes the symptom of choice. Oppenheim's hysterical opera singer reverts to the primeval sounds of her *Mauscheln*, speaking with a Jewish intonation, in Freud's early case studies the sign of damaged discourse becomes a generalized and medicalized symptom.

The question of a Jewish predisposition to hysteria marked by a new version of the "hidden language of the Jews," the *globus hystericus*, lead Freud to abandon the notion of hysteria as an inherited disease that had a specific racial component. All of this took place as he was also abandoning electrotherapy as ineffectual because of the psychological make up of his patients. Leopold Löwenfeld, one of Freud's most assiduous supporters, confronted the question of the racial predisposition of the Jews in his textbook of 1894. In his discussion of the etiology of neurasthenia and hysteria he examined the role that "race and climate" might play in the origin of these diseases:

> Concerning the claimed predisposition of the Semitic race, one can only state the fact that among the Israelites today there is an unusually large number of neurasthenics and hysterics. Whether this is the result of a specific predisposition of the race seems very questionable. Historically, there is no trace of such as predisposition to be shown. The epidemics of mass hysteria observed in earlier centuries never affected members of the Semitic race. I believe it more likely that the great predisposition of the Israelites does not rest in racial qualities, but in their present quality of life. Among these would come into consideration — in East Europe, the physical poverty as well as the extraordinary moral pressure, the practice of early marriage, and the great number of children — in the West, the great number of Israelites who undertake intellectual activities [Löwenfeld 1894, 44–45].

Freud read Löwenfeld's textbook very carefully. The opening pages are full of debates about the inheritability of hysteria and its relationship to trauma. Thus Löwenfeld claims that "inheritance plays a major role in the origins of neurasthenia and hysteria through the existence of an abnormal constitution of the nervous system." Freud retorts: "From where?" in the margin. Tucked away in a footnote, Löwenfeld quotes a source that claimed that to have seen a large number of cases of hysteria "without a trace of hereditary neurosis" (Löwenfeld 1894, 16–20). Freud chuckles: "Bravo! Certainly acquired." These comments reflected Freud's preoccupation with the universal question of whether all human beings could be divided into the healthy and the degenerate, the mentally sound and the hysteric, those who were tainted by race and those who were not. Löwenfeld's rejection of the predisposition for hysteria for *all* Jews meant it was possible to focus on the universal rather than the racialist question. And yet Löwenfeld's distinction between Eastern Jews with their mix of social and sexual causes for their mental states and Western Jews with their (highly sought) intellectual status shows that even there a dichotomy between the religious and the secular Jew is sought. Freud seems never to reach this section of the book; his eye remains fixed on the universal questions about the meaning and cause of mental illness and does not seem to enter into the debate about the Jews and madness. Therapies that attempted to alter the body rather than the psyche could not work: they engaged only a fantasy of the body, one contaminated by the biological thinking of anti–Semites. For Freud the ineffectual nature of electrotherapy demanded new universals of the psyche for it could never be through an intervention in the body that the psyche could be changed, but well cure of the symptomatic body and *globus*, through the new psychotherapy.

By 1911, the Scots physician Samuel Sloan, head of the Electro-Therapeutical Section of the [British] Royal Society of Medicine (which existed from 1907–1931) could look back at the question of the success of the method. He is, of course, an advocate of the method, presenting successful case studies of psychic neurasthenia caused by an inflammation of the vulva, of thought disorder and insomnia treated by faradization of the brain. But even the claim of such remarkable successes is qualified by Sloan who concludes that "the best results will be obtained by utilizing to the full all the resources of the healing art — electrical, dietetic, physical, psychic; and he is the most successful physician who has his quiver full of such weapons and who, in cases of difficulty, is fertile in resource" (Sloan 1911, 17). The "psychic" clearly was a reference to the psychological theories of mental illness now growing in importance on the continent (and after World War I in the English-speaking world).

By 1897 Sigmund Freud, having abandoned his view that all of his hysterics suffered from sexual trauma, continued to treat voice and vocal symptoms with psychoanalytic interventions. By 1905 Freud was able to extrapolate this symptom not as a sign of Jewish racial degeneration but as a universal "error" of early childhood experience. He refutes, in the case of Dora the very notion of the inheritability of hysteria, seeing it very much as an acquired disease, as the sufferers are largely the children of syphilitics. (Even though he believes there may be some "hereditary predisposition" for the illness.) (SE 7: 20, n. 1) Yet Freud's dominant view as expressed in his essay on "Infant Sexuality" (1905) comes to be that the *globus hystericus* is the repression of the earliest stage sexual development, the child's oral gratification, the desire for which becomes pathological in adulthood.

By the 1950s such psychological explanations had become commonplace (Aronson 1969). Judd Marmor stated in 1953 "the question, therefore, is not whether oral mechanisms are prominent in hysteria. That is taken for granted. The problem, rather, is whether these [oral] mechanisms may not play a more *determining* role in the dynamics of hysteria than has been generally assumed" (Marmor 1953). By that point there is no question that "talk therapy" is the only approach to *globus*.

By 1969 electrotherapy has become an adjunct of physiotherapy and the standard handbook of the day while speaking of diathermy, electroshock, ultrasonic, and ultraviolet therapies avoids any discussion of the treatment of the larynx or the voice (Scott 1969). The "tingle" effect, the key to the psychological function of electrotherapy, had ceased to be associated with medical treatment, as electricity became a commonplace of Western cultural experience (Fishlock 1994).

When these forms of electrotherapy were proved ineffective by the beginning of the twentieth century, more radical approaches, such as Wagner-Jauregg's "malaria therapy" for general paralysis of the insane were introduced. They gave way to electroconvulsive therapy developed in the late 1930s, which then fell out of fashion after the 1960s (and Ken Kesey's 1962 *One Flew Over the Cuckoo's Nest*) only to be quietly reintroduced in the past decades (Kneeland and Warren 2002, Fulton 1956). When Hannah Decker wrote her brilliant book on Freud's case of Dora, she was clearly appalled by the very notion of treating disorders of hysteria with electrotherapy as if electrotherapy were identical with ECT (Decker 1992, 11). If one could characterize the view of the post–1960s within and beyond the medical world, it would be that electrotherapy of all types (typified by ECT) were brutal, ineffectual, and archaic.

Recently, vagal nerve stimulation has been popularly heralded as the newest break through in the electrotherapy of depression following its use for the treatment of epilepsy (Donovan 2005). This is very much parallel to the adaptation of anticonvulsive drugs for mood stimulation a decade prior. Such treatment seemed to have a high (40 percent) rate of effectiveness in chronic and treatment-resistant cases of depression (Rush et al. 2000). Ironically one of the most evident side effects is disruption of the voice, with hoarseness and coughing being evident. It has been claimed that the longer the pacemaker is present, the more effective the treatment becomes (Sackheim 2001). It must be stressed that such an approach is different from more conventional (and contested) forms of electroconvulsive therapy (ECT) as it is inherently non-convulsive.

The powerful view of psychoanalysis (from Freud to Eugen Bleuler) that had placed *language disturbances* of all types rather than voice at the center of the diagnosis of syndromes such as schizophrenia. Even this radical substitution diminished after the 1960s. As mental illness became redefined by the application of psychopharmacology as a "brain disease," the importance of all linguistic symptoms vanished. Today, the reintroduction of electrotherapy in the form of vagal nerve stimulation follows the pattern of the re-somaticization of mental illness. Freud's assumption that the response to electrotherapy had to do with suggestion, which now can be supported by the parallel understanding of the alteration of brain structures through experience, has been replaced with a mechanical claim of the brain as a computer.

The wide range of electrotherapies for psychiatric disorders that has been proposed now follows that somatic model (Penry and Dean 1990, Mayberg and Lorenzo 2002). The best that can be said of them is that "success has remained questionable" (Niedermeyer 2003, 27). The treatment of the voice remains quite discrete as psychogenic causes are rarely examined. The treatment of the voice and speech now quite independent of its function as a symptom of mental illness: transcranial electric stimulation has been used in cases of speech disorders relating to stroke and parkinsonism. It is now completely a treatment used by laryngologists rather than psychiatrists.

"Race" as a category of predisposition seems relatively lacking in this discussion, even with its reintroduction in the 1990s introduction into contemporary medicine, but this may be an artifact of the slow acceptance of such categories in fields that do not claim any genetic predisposition. Perhaps an echo of the older association of the highly stigmatized nature of mental illness and the association with the murder (euthanasia) of the mentally ill in Nazi Germany has made this remain an uncomfortable tale. But it is a tale still being unraveled.

References

Anzieu, Didier (1986). *Freud's Self-Analysis*, trans. Peter Graham. London: Hogarth and International Psycho-Analytic Library.

Aronson, E. (1969). "Speech Pathology and Symptom Therapy in the Interdisciplinary Treatment of Psychogenic Aphonia." *Journal of Speech and Hearing Disorders* 34: 321–41.

Bernheimer, Charles, and Claire Kahane, eds. (1985) *In Dora's Case: Freud-Hysteria-Feminism*. New York: Columbia University Press.

Beven, William (1842). "An Inquiry into the Truth of the Electrical Nature of the Nervous Principle." *London Medical Gazette* 29: 173–6.

Blechmann, Berhard (1882). *Ein Beitrag zur Anthropologie der Juden*. Dorpat: Wilhelm Just.

Brabant-Gerö, Eva, Ernst Falzeder and Patrizia Giampieri-Deutsch, eds. (1993–2000). *The Correspondence of Sigmund Freud and Sándor Ferenczi*. 3 vols. Cambridge, MA: Belknap Press of Harvard University.

Bryan, Bettina Alexandra (1966). "Wilhelm Erb (1840–1921): Electrotherapeutics and Scientific Medicine in 19th-century Germany." Diss., University College [London].

Charcot, J. M. (1889). *Leçons du Mardi a la Salpêtrière*, 2 vols. Paris: Progrés medical.

Cumberbatch, Elkin P. (1939). *Essentials of Medical Electricity*. London: Henry Kimpton.

Decker, Hannah (1992). *Freud, Dora and Vienna 1900*. New York: Free Press.

Donovan III, Charles E. (2005) *Out of the Black Hole: The Patient's Guide to Vagus Nerve Stimulation and Depression*. New York: Wellness.

Eissler, Kurt R. (1979) *Freud und Wagner Jauregg vor der Kommission zur Erhebung militärischer Pflichtverletzungen*. Vienna: Löcker.

Fishlock, David (1994). "The Tingle Factor." *New Scientist* 144: 58–59.

Freud, Sigmund (1955–74). *Standard Edition of the Complete Psychological Works of Sigmund Freud*, ed. and trans., J. Strachey, A. Freud, A. Strachey, and A. Tyson. 24 vols. London: Hogarth; referred to as SE.

Fulton, John F. (1956). "Origins of Electroshock Therapy." *Journal of the History of Medicine and Allied Sciences*. 11: 229–230.

Gelfand, Toby (1988). "'Mon Cher Docteur Freud': Charcot's Unpublished Correspondence to Freud, 1888–1893." *Bulletin of the History of Medicine* 62: 563–588.

——— (1989). "Charcot's Response to Freud's Rebellion." *Journal of the History of Ideas* 50: 293–307.

Hedley W.S. (1900). *Therapeutic Electricity and Practical Muscle Testing*. Philadelphia: P. Blakiston's Son and Co.

Henke, Gerd (1970). "75 Jahre Elektromedizin: Entwicklung — Fortschritt — Ausblick." In Dietrich Jahn, ed., *Festschrift zur 75. Tagung der Deutschen Gesellschaft für Innere Medizin, Wiesbaden 1969*. Stuttgart: F.K. Schattauer.

Hirschmüller, Albrecht (1989). *The Life and Work of Josef Breuer*. New York: New York University Press.

Killen, Andreas (2006). *Berlin Electropolis: Shock, Nerves, and German Modernity*. Berkeley: University of California Press.

Kneeland, Timothy W., and Carol A.B. Warren (2002). *Push Button Psychiatry: A History of Electroshock in America*. Westport, CT, and London: Praeger.

Lagneau, Gustav (1891). "Sur la race juive et sa pathologie." *Academie de médecine* (Paris): Bulletin 3, ser. 26: 287–309.

Lehtinen, V., and H. Puhakka (1976). "A Psychosomatic Approach to the Globus Hystericus Symptom." *Acta Psychiatrica Scandavia* 53: 21–28.

Leroy-Beaulieu, Anatole (1895). *Israel Among the Nations: A Study of the Jews and Antisemitism*, trans. Frances Hellman. New York: G.P. Putnam's Sons.

Löwenfeld, Leopold (1894). *Pathologie und Therapie der Neurasthenie und Hysterie*. Wiesbaden: J.F. Bergmann.

Lovett Richard (1756). *The subtil medium prov'd, or, That wonderful power of nature ... which they call'd sometimes æther, but oftener elementary fire, verify'd: shewing, that all the distinguishing and essential qualities ascrib'd to æther ... are to be found in electrical fire...: giving an account of the progress and several gradations of electricity, from those ancient times to the present ...* London: Printed for J. Hinton, W. Sandby and R. Lovett at Worcester.

Mace, C., M. Ron, and M. Deahl (1989). "Is Globus Hystericus?" *British Journal of Psychiatry* 154: 727.
Marmor, Judd (1953). "Orality in the Hysterical Personality." *Journal of the American Psychoanalytic Association* 1: 656–670.
Masson, Jeffrey M., trans. and ed. (1985). *The Complete Letters of Sigmund Freud to Wilhelm Fliess 1887–1904*. Cambridge, MA: Belknap Press of Harvard University Press.
Mayberg, H.S., and A.M. Lorenzo (2002). "Penfield Revisited? Understanding and Modifying Behavior by Deep Brain Stimulation for PD." *Neurology* 59: 1298–99.
Mitchell S. Wier (1898). *Fat and Blood*. Philadelphia: J. B. Lippincott.
Morpurgo, E. (1903). *Sulle Condizioni Somatiche e psichiche degli Israeliti in Europa*, Bibliotece dell'idea Sionisa, 2. Modena: Tip. Operai.
Morus, Iwan Rhys (1992). Marketing the Machine: The Construction of Electrotherapeutics as Viable Medicine in Early Victorian England. *Medical History* 36: 34–52.
―――― (1998). *Frankenstein's Children: Electricity, Exhibition, and Experiment In Early-Nineteenth-Century London*. Princeton, NJ: Princeton University Press.
―――― (1999). "The Measure of Man: Technologizing the Victorian Body." *History of Science* 37: 249–82.
Niedermeyer, E. (2003). "Benjamin Franklin and Static Electricity." *American Journal of Electroneurodiagnostic Technology* 43: 26–30.
Oppenheim, Hermann (1894–1913). *Lehrbuch der Nervenkrankheiten fur Ärzte und Studierende*, 2 vols. Berlin: Karger.
―――― (1908). "Zur Psychopathologie und Nosologie der russisch-jüdischen Bevölkerung." *Journal für Psychologie und Neurologie* 13: 1–9 [Festschrift Forel].
Penry, J. K., and J.C. Dean (1990). "Prevention of Intractable Partial Seizures by Intermittent Vagal Stimulation in Humans." *Epilepsia* 31 (supplement 2): S40–43.
Prince, Morton (1902). "Neuroses." In Horatio Bigelow and G. Betton Massey, ed., *An International System of Electro-Therapeutics*. London: Henry Kimpton, pp. D-106–150.
Puhakka, H., and P. Kirveskari (1988). "Globus Hystericus: Globus Syndrome." *Journal of Laryngology and Otology* 102: 231–34.
Rush A.J., M.S. George, H.A. Sackheim, L.B. Marengell, M.M. Husain, C. Giller, Z. Nahas, S. Haines, R.K. Simpson, R. Goodman (2000). "Vagus-Nerve Stimulation (VGS) for Treatment-Resistant Depressions: A Multicenter Study." *Biological Psychiatry* 47: 276–86.
Sackheim, H.A., A.J. Rush, M.S. George, L.B. Marengell, M.M. Husain, C. Giller, Z. Nahas, S. Haines, R.K. Simpson, R. Goodman (2001). "Vagus-Nerve Stimulation (VGS) for Treatment-Resistant Depressions: Efficacy, Side Effects, and Predictors of Outcome." *Neuropsychopharmacology* 25: 713–28.
Schiller, Francis (1982). *A Möbius Strip: Fin-de-siècle Neuropsychiatry and Paul Möbius*. Berkeley: University of California Press.
Scott, Pauline M., ed. (1969). *Clayton's Electrotherapy and Actinotherapy: A Textbook for Student Physiotherapists*. London: Baillière Tindall & Cassell.
Sloan, Samuel (1911). "Success or Failure in Electro-therapy: A Consideration of Some of the Causes." *The Lancet* 178: 15–17.
Wulfing-Luer, Georges (1907). *La Pathologie Nerveuse et Mentale chez les Anciens Hébreux et la Race juive*. Paris: Steinheil.

Anti-Semitism in the Freud Case Histories

Harold P. Blum

Rampant in Vienna during Freud's lifetime, the influence of anti–Semitism is present in all of his classic case histories, many other papers, and his personal correspondence. This essay traces the influence of anti–Semitism and related conflicts in each of the case histories. Though not addressed or analyzed, conflicts and ambivalence about Jewish identity are evident in Freud, his patients, and their treatment. Anti-Semitism does not appear in the minutes of the Vienna Psychoanalytic Society. Considerations of anti–Semitism contribute to an enhanced understanding of the case histories, the development of psychoanalysis, and Freud biography. Insights into the impact of anti–Semitism are crucially applicable to other forms of socio-cultural prejudices and persecution.

In order to understand the influence of their cultural milieu on Freud, his patients, and their treatment, one must consider the intra-psychic and interpersonal effects of anti–Semitism in Vienna. Many of the same considerations would be applicable to other forms of religious, racial, and social prejudice. I shall indicate how anti–Semitism and Jewish identity were significant in the Freud case histories, though usually silent and not addressed. Conflicts related to Jewish identity were defensively kept from conscious awareness, or were deliberately eliminated from psychoanalytic publication. Though not specified in an individual paper, these conflicts infiltrated Freud's correspondence and much of his published corpus (Frosch 2005). The universal application of the radically new psychoanalytic theory and therapy overshadowed Freud's Jewish world. Freud wanted psychoanalysis to achieve scientific and academic acceptance; "it was only by the Christian Jung's appearance that psychoanalysis escaped the danger of becoming a Jewish national affair" (Freud and Abraham 1965, Letter to K. Abraham, May 3, 1908). Moreover, influenced by the enlightenment and German romanticism, assimilated, cultured Jewish intellectuals commonly held humanitarian ideals and a cosmopolitan outlook regarded as above and beyond their Jewish ethnicity.

Prior to 1848, most Jews were forbidden to reside in Vienna, paid special fees to be allowed brief temporary residence, and had to wear identifying garb.

There were special police to enforce edicts against Jews; official notices were addressed to "the Jew so and so" (Beller 1989; Decker 1991). In 1867 the Jews were granted full political rights and advanced rapidly in the professions parallel with their increasingly secular education. But in many other areas of life, Jews were restricted; emancipation was never fully realized. Anti-Semitism was an obvious impediment but also a goad to competitive and creative achievement. The Jewish population had dramatically increased in size and prominence, and had rapidly advanced in the business and cultural life of Vienna. Despite legal rights, there were limits; e.g., there was not a single Jewish full professor or judge in Vienna. A new kind of racial anti–Semitism appeared. Previously denigrated as infidels, and apostates, the Jews were now considered as an inferior, despised race. Wilhelm Marr, coined the term "anti–Semitism," promulgated in an infamous pamphlet, "The Conquest of the Jews Over the Germans" (1879). The son of a baptized Jew and exemplifying Jewish anti–Semitism, Marr introduced the pseudo scientific discourse of race. Jews were considered a perverse breed apart from Christian Germans. Jews were regarded as racial contaminants, which could damage the Christian population. Jews had an inherited disease like syphilis, a disease that could not be cured through re-education, indoctrination, or religious conversion (Gilman 1986). There were anti–Semitic myths, jokes and slurs about Jews, their deformed, effeminate person and personality, with images of Jews with horns, predatory teeth, and long curved hooked noses. Stereotyped vilification of Jews was internalized, contributing to Jewish anti–Semitism (Ostow 1995). Freud, in the meeting of the Vienna Psychoanalytic Society, December 9, 1908, connected a Jewish patient's persecutory delusions about his nose to conflicts about being Jewish and wanting to be baptized in opposition to his Zionist father. Conflict about Jewishness was, in effect, recognized as displaced oedipal conflict. There was, however, no further elaboration by the group about conflict concerning conversion to Christianity or becoming a closet Jew (Nunberg and Federn 1967).

The discussion was affectively charged for the entirely Jewish membership of Freud's group. That Freud was a scion of an Eastern European Jewish family and later an intellectual of the enlightenment does not do justice to his internal ambivalence and his conscious and unconscious conflicts about his Jewish identity. Though marginalized at the borders of converging, clashing cultures Freud belonged to the first generation of Viennese Jews who entertained hopes of no longer being disadvantaged, second class citizens. In *The Interpretation of Dreams* (1900), he stated that in the 1860s and 1870s, "every industrious Jewish schoolboy carried a cabinet minister's portfolio in his satchel." Freud also noted the rising tide of anti–Semitism in his home city. In 1878, Freud joined a pan German nationalist student society, but only ten years later German and Austrian nationalist societies excluded Jews. While many Jews avidly wanted to become assimilated Austrians and Germans, the culture was insidiously and perniciously prejudiced against them. Paradoxically, their prejudiced society potentiated the secular education of male Jews who then importantly contributed to cultural development.

No one can completely escape his/her historical time and place; this was true of Freud himself. Freud wrote to Fliess (Freud, S., 1985; 5 November 1897, p. 277): "One always remains a child of one's age." He wrote "of the increasing importance of the effects of the anti–Semitic movement upon our emotional life," (Freud 1900, p. 196). Emerging from adolescence with pride in his Jewish heritage, he unconsciously internalized anti–Semitic attitudes that he simultaneously fought against and ultimately analyzed. He joined Bnai Brith after his father's death in 1896 where he gave pioneer lectures on psychoanalysis to his Jewish "brothers." Jews were frequently slandered at city council meetings and Carl Lueger, Mayor of Vienna, was rabidly anti–Semitic. Freud had, after a previous election, celebrated the emperor's refusal to confirm Lueger as Mayor by lighting a cigar. It was Lueger who vilified any opponent as a Jew and proudly stated, "I determine who is a Jew." Anti-Semitism was overdetermined, with multiple meanings and functions in external reality and in fantasy life (Young-Bruehl 1996, Knafo, 1999).

When Freud finally escaped from Vienna in 1938 to England, one of his first acts was to join the British branch of the Bnai Brith. His final work on *Moses and Monotheism* (1939) was written during the escalating Nazi persecution of the Jews and while Freud was gradually succumbing to cancer. Freud attempted to understand the origins of anti–Semitism and the character of the Jews, which he thought contributed to anti–Semitism. Here Freud ambivalently implied that the Jews were partly to blame for their own persecution, indicative of negative splitting from the largely philo–Semitic attitudes expressed in the work.

Freud's concerns with anti-Semitism for the most part, however, do not appear in his published scientific writings. Breuer and Freud wrote (Breuer and Freud 1895, p. 18), that psychoanalysts "were obliged to pay as much attention in their case histories to the purely human and social circumstances of their patient as to the somatic data and the symptoms of the disorder," but the discussion of anti-Semitism which would then have been expected in the case histories were either absent, obscured or disguised. Anti-Semitism does not appear in the index of "Studies on Hysteria" (Breuer and Freud 1895), in the minutes of the Vienna Psychoanalytic Society, or directly in the case histories, except for a crucial footnote in Little Hans (1909). What was silent or spoken, hinted or implied were all significant considerations. Through unconscious defense, preconscious silent collusion, and conscious avoidance, anti-Semitism for a long time was a neglected topic in the psychoanalytic literature.

Anna O. (Bertha Pappenheim)

The Jewish background of the prototypical case history of Anna O. is nearly invisible and inaudible, and serves as a prelude to the submerged Jewish issues in Freud's later cases. Anna O., now identified as Bertha Pappenheim, was treated by Joseph Breuer between 1880 and 1882. Freud's mentor and senior colleague, Breuer later discussed this now famous patient with Freud, resulting in their joint publication of the case report in *Studies on Hysteria* (1895). In 1880, when Anna O. was 21 years old, she was delegated to be the nurse of her father, who was very ill with tuberculosis. She was Jewish, very bright, imaginative, and poetic, with penetrating intuition and fluency in many languages. She herself became ill, weak, easily fatigued, with a panoply of motor, sensory, and perceptual symptoms. She fell into somnolent states in the afternoon and her severe widespread symptomatology forced her to give up nursing her father. She would sometimes awaken from this state finding it difficult to speak; she gradually lost the ability to speak and was completely mute for two weeks. After her father died in 1881 her symptoms worsened and her spoken German deteriorated. Able to read French and Italian, she then spoke and responded to English with Breuer, and prayed in English. Breuer, one of the most eminent Jewish Viennese physicians of the day, physician to Brahms and other celebrities, observed that Anna O. was without religion, despite having heard her pray in English. Neither Breuer nor Anna O. questioned her prayer being recited in English. Ordinarily she would have been praying in Hebrew; Hebrew prayers were doubtless said after her father died, and when he was buried in a Jewish cemetery. Anna O. coined the term "talking cure" in a foreign tongue, English, avoiding German, and Yiddish.

Later in Anna O.'s life her suppressed and repressed Jewish identity returned with extraordinary intensity. She traveled widely on behalf of Jewish interests, particularly devoted to saving Jewish women who had been forced into sexual slavery. In 1904 she formed the Federation of Jewish Women. She established a shelter for unmarried Jewish mothers and visited the Henry Street Settlement in New York in 1909. At approximately the same time that Freud was lecturing at Clark University, citing the case of Anna O., Bertha Pappenheim was lecturing in America on problems of prostitution. She later translated Jewish folklore from Yiddish into German and wrote a book, *The Jewish Woman*, strongly supporting their education and equal rights (Ahsen 1974).

A decade after the end of Anna O.'s treatment, in 1882, Freud urged Breuer to write up her case for the collaborative work, *Studies on Hysteria* (1895). Following her gradual recovery, Jewish issues occupied the remainder of her life but do not appear in the comments or interpretations in the case history. The emancipated Jews largely rejected the Orthodox religion in which many had been reared. Paradoxically, emancipation, which might have promoted expression of their religious and ethnic backgrounds, contributed to the denial and avoidance of Jewish language, culture and customs. Yiddish was considered the inferior embarrassing language of the Eastern European Jews who lacked acculturation and classical education. Breuer, Freud and young Anna O. avoided the Yiddish that was very likely the mother tongue for all three. Nor did they indicate an appreciation of psychological and social conflicts involved in the typical celebration of Christmas by Viennese Jews.

It was during Christmas 1881 that Anna O. re-experienced scenes from the previous Christmas. She had at that time relinquished her nursing her father (which would have aroused her own fears of contracting TB). She was symptomatically improved after she recounted the scenes of the prior Christmas, during the subsequent Christmas. Christmas was an unnoticed stimulus and spur to their joint therapeutic efforts but not to recognition of her intense conflicts concerning Christian and Jewish observance. Bertha Pappenheim died in 1936 after dedicating her life to Jewish and feminist causes. In recognition of Bertha Pappenheim's outstanding accomplishments, the West German government in 1955 issued a postage stamp in her honor as a "helper of humanity."

Dora

The treatment of Dora was published by Freud (1905), "Fragment of an Analysis of a Case of Hysteria." He had "analyzed" her for hysterical symptoms, e.g. aphonia, dyspnea, tussis nervosa, for the last three months of 1900. Anti-Semitism figures in disguised form in the Dora case, which I regard as a contribution to the literature on the pre-history of the Holocaust (Blum 1994). During Freud's lifetime and until after World War II and the Holocaust, the social, cultural and historical framework of Freud's case histories were little explored. Dora's adolescent phase of life, her female gender, her family's relative affluence and their being Jewish, are all significant to multidimensional understanding of Dora's conflicts and symptoms. The influences of her Jewish and anti–Jewish milieu were important unexplored issues in Dora's personality development and disorder (Decker 1991). In September 1900, just before Dora started treatment with him, Freud learned that his coveted promotion to Associate Professor from his previous status as a lecturer (privatdozent) had been denied. Freud had regarded his not being promoted as an act of anti–Semitic prejudice.

"Dora," Freud's pseudonym for Ida Bauer, was analyzed for three months from October through December 1900, in turn of the century Vienna. This eighteen-year-old girl could not have anticipated that she would become an historical figure in psychoanalytic and feminist literature. Preceding and during Dora's treatment with Freud anti–Semitism was rampant in Europe. Many Jewish establishments were boycotted and vandalized. Blood libel against Jews resulted in the infamous Hilsner case. Hilsner had been convicted of child murder to obtain blood for Passover matzah, and his death sentence was commuted only after worldwide protests. The ongoing Dreyfus case in France added fuel to the fire of European anti–Semitism.

When Philip Bauer brought his daughter Ida for treatment, she could hardly have regarded the world as her oyster. She was denied the opportunity for higher education provided for her brother, Otto, who later became the Foreign Minister of Austria. Worldly and bright, with many cultural interests, Dora was oppressed by a society, which limited opportunities for Jews and for women. Dora's loss of voice and her other hysterical symptoms could not have been unrelated to her not having a voice for self-realization with equal opportunity. Culturally her aphonia represented the subjugation, and the silent protest of the disadvantaged and disenfranchised. The body language of her conversion hysteria had a Jewish dialect and her symptoms had determinants that included the invectives and innuendos to which Jews and women were subject. Dora's family and friends included Herr and Frau K (Mr. and Mrs. Hans Zellenka). They were all Jewish, as were Freud's family, friends and the initial members of the Wednesday Night Psychoanalytic Society. Dora's parents moved to the South Austrian town of Merano, now in Northern Italy, where she lived from 6 until 16. Although the town was popular as a summer spa resort among Viennese Jews, Dora's childhood experience and education were not within a Jewish community. She was sent to a convent school and exposed to the prevailing disparaging attitudes towards Jews. Christian texts at the time commonly depicted the Jews as villains, betrayers like Judas, Christ killers destined for punishment in this world and the next. Her convent schooling, not reported in the published case, must have had great psychological and social significance for Dora and for her Jewish parents, who sent her to the convent school. Choosing a Catholic school for their daughter could well have had significance for their daughter's later enactment of the parents' unconscious fantasies and conscious ambivalence regarding Jewish identity.

Freud wanted to demonstrate the clinical use of dreams in psychoanalytic treatment, and the Dora case revolves around two dreams. The first dream that Freud subjected to extensive analysis (Freud 1905, p. 64), was "A house was on fire. My father was standing beside my bed and woke me up. I dressed quickly. My mother wanted to stop and save her jewel case; but father said: 'I refuse to let myself and my two children be burnt for the sake of your jewel case.' We hurried downstairs, and as soon as I was outside I woke up." Freud's interpretations of this dream have been elaborated, revised and challenged by a host of authors. My comments about this dream will be largely restricted to the hidden issues of Jewish identity. Jewish issues were denied, evaded and avoided by analysts, consistent with the denial practiced by Dora's family. Her mother denied the affair between her husband and Frau K.; Herr K. denied the affair between Dora's father and Frau K., Dora's parents were in denial about the sexual advances of Herr K. toward their daughter. Dora both denied and affirmed that she was being sacrificed for the secret motives and agendas of her parents and the K.'s. Her father would swap his daughter, a bartered bride, for Herr K.'s wife. The jewel case represented not only Dora's virginity, but also her pride, honor, self-esteem, and the ideals and values which were being compromised by the adult authority figures in her life. The burning house in the first dream described is also the burning house of Jewish factories set afire in the periodic rioting since 1897 in Bohemia where her father's factories were located. (Bauer, Breuer, and Freud had roots in Bohemia.) The Jews were victimized by both sides in the nationalist antagonisms between Czechs and Germans. Dora's fleeing a burning house in the dream was over-determined. She was in flight from the burning homes and factories of the Jews that pre-figured the burning of books, synagogues, and Jews in the Holocaust (Blum 1994). Dora abruptly fled from treatment on December 31, 1900, when she informed Freud that that day was to be their last session. She married three years later in December 1903 at a reformed temple in Vienna. In 1905, her son was born and two months after his birth, Dora fled the house of Israel and left the Jewish community. She was formally baptized with her husband and son into Christianity. She attempted to erase the shame, humiliation and racial stigma of being Jewish, probably hoping to provide more advantages and opportunities for her family.

There were harbingers of the same conscious and unconscious conflicts and compromise formations in the second dream. In the second dream, Dora reported: "I was walking in a strange town ... I came into a house where I lived, went to my room, and found a letter from my mother lying there. She wrote saying that as I had left home without my parents' knowledge she did not wish to write to me to say that father was ill. Now he is dead and if you like you can come home.... Then I was at home.... I walked into the porter's lodge, and inquired for our flat. The maid opened the door to me and replied that mother and the others were already at the cemetery." The second dream occurred during Christmas, and the maid might well have been Christian. There were only two or three hours left of analysis before Dora's departure; Father Freud and her analysis were about to be buried. There is no mention in the case report that all the main characters were Jews, that Jews were buried in Jewish cemeteries with Jewish ritual.

There is an addendum to the second dream, which Dora initially forgot (Freud 1905, pp. 133–134). She had received a Christmas present, a photograph album sent by a young man, with a picture of the town square that Dora dreamt about. Her dream of being in a strange town reminded Dora of a previous visit to Dresden, when a cousin offered to show her around the famed museum. Dora declined the offer and went alone to the museum where she stood for two hours before Raphael's Madonna. The significance of Christmas, standing before the Madonna for an awesome two hours, did not elicit further comments or questions. What so possessed her about the picture of the Madonna that she was transfixed? How did this behavior relate to her ten years in a convent school? Who can stand before any picture for hours, and why did not Freud question her reaction? The idealized mother of Christ replaced Dora's denigrated Jewish mother and her own denigrated Jewish self-representation (Blum 1994, Billig 1999). Freud noted that identification with the Virgin Mother allowed the teenager to fantasize motherhood without guilt over unacceptable sexual fantasy. Freud remarked on her maternal longings but was apparently silent about her conflicts about being Jewish and idealizing the Madonna. Dora acted out the second dream by becoming the Christian mother of her baptized infant son. In retrospect Dora may well have been considering conversion to Christianity and burying her Jewish heritage when she reported the second dream.

Conversion had been the subject of discourse of Viennese Jews, but was not popular and deserters from the faith were recorded in "lists of shame." The reaction of Dora's parents to her conversion to Christianity is unknown. It is of interest that Dora's brother, Otto Bauer, who became the foreign minister of Austria, always remained a member of the Jewish community. Yet Otto Bauer later espoused gradual assimilation, advising Jews to marry Christians and to change their speech and manners so as not to alienate Christians. Identifying with the racist attitudes of the aggressor, he proposed that the undesirable features of the Jews had been inherited and could be modified and diluted through generations of intermarriage. Theodore Herzl, the founder of the Zionist state, contemplated Dora's solution before championing an independent Jewish state. Herzl proposed leading the Jews of Austria, except himself and other leaders, in a mass conversion to Christianity. The conversion would take place at high noon on a Sunday in solemn procession at Vienna's St. Stefan's Cathedral. Not wanting to his son to be disadvantaged, Herzl did not have his son circumcised and wanted the Jews to disappear into the crowd. Disillusioned by the Dreyfus case, Theodore Herzl later thought that anti-Semitism could be eliminated only by removing Jews to a separate homeland (Loewenberg 1983). In his letter to Fliess of May 7, 1900, just months before Dora's analysis began, Freud described himself as "an old, somewhat shabby Jew" (Masson 1985, p. 412). Internalizing the insults and denigration of the surround, many Jews harbored self-images of being shabby, seedy, and inferior. Social prejudice contributed to narcissistic injury, shame and humiliation. Dora's Christian identity was revoked after passage of the persecutory, dehumanizing racial laws in Nazi Germany. Both Dora and Sigmund Freud had to flee from Vienna just before emigration was foreclosed.

Little Hans

The case of Little Hans, entitled " The Analysis of a Phobia in a 5 Year Old Boy," (Freud 1909), may be regarded as the precursor of child psychoanalysis. Freud (1909, p. 6) wanted to use the case to confirm his findings about the importance of infantile sexuality and the Oedipus complex, which he had discovered in the analysis of adults. Freud stated (1909, p. 6), "surely there must be a possibility of observing in children at firsthand and with all the freshness of life the sexual impulses and wishes which we dig out so laboriously in adults from among their own debris." The Oedipus complex was considered crucial to the understanding of neurosis, and Little Hans, with persistent habitual masturbation, directly illustrated childhood sexuality. Little Hans was treated by his father, with Freud's "supervision," from January through May of 1908. Raised by affectionate, and supposedly permissive parents, the case report indicates that his parents could be quite seductive, coercive and punitive. He was threatened by his mother with abandonment, and castration. When he was 3½ his mother found him masturbating and warned, "if you do that, I shall send for Dr. A. to cut off your widler" (Freud 1909, p. 8). Little Hans and his parents were focused on his "widdler" (penis), parallel to Hans' preoccupation with the "widdlers" of his parents, children, horses, and other animals.

There was also silence about Little Hans' widdler in relation to his Jewish identity. Concerns of his parents about being Jewish, about raising their son as a Jew, and the xenophobia encountered by the Jewish minority in Vienna, were not discussed in the case history. In the paper that Max Graf, the father of Little Hans, wrote about his early experience in Freud's Wednesday Night Study Group, Max Graf (1942) referred to this very question. He had asked Sigmund Freud about raising his son as a Christian, and "wondered whether I should not remove him from the prevailing anti-Semitic hatred..." Freud had pointedly counseled his father, "if you do not let your son grow up as a Jew, you will deprive him of the little sources of energy which cannot be replaced by anything else. He will have to struggle as a Jew, and you ought to develop in him all the energy that he will need for that struggle" (Graf 1942, p. 473). Max Graf, whose father had converted to Christianity, had remained a member of the Jewish community and had married a Jewish woman, Olga Honig, who had been Freud's patient. The caring, hesitant parents of Little Hans must have been willing to follow Freud's advice as it resonated with their own inclinations. Freud had many times been to dinner at the apartment of Max and Olga Graf, and had probably known Little Hans from birth. In the case report there is no reference to parental concern about Jewish identity, ethnicity, or the Jewish male's stamp of circumcision. Freud's counter-transference and ambivalence contributed to the avoidance of Jewish issues, while he was possibly a symbolic mohel of little Hans (Rudnytski 1999). However, close reading of Little Hans, reveals that anti-Semitism appears in an almost casual, impersonal footnote. It is an extraordinary footnote, that bridges body and mind, individual and group psychology, unconscious fantasy and cultural attitudes. Freud (1909, p. 36) stated, "I cannot interrupt the discussion so far as to demonstrate the typical character of the unconscious train of thought which I think there is here reason for attributing to Little Hans. The castration complex is the deepest unconscious root of anti-Semitism; for even in the nursery little boys hear that a Jew has something cut off his penis—a piece of his penis, they think—this gives them a right to despise Jews. And there is no stronger unconscious root for the sense of superiority over women ... what is common to Jews and women is their relation to the castration complex." Freud presented an entirely new interpretation of circumcision (considered apart from his inaccurate propositions on femininity). Freud (1913, p. 153) later stated, "When our Jewish children come to hear of ritual circumcision they equate it with castration." Circumcision thus elicits castration anxiety in both Jews and Gentiles.

This was the first psychoanalysis of a socio-cultural prejudice and the first psychoanalytic contribution to an understanding of a very important unconscious determinant of anti–Semitism. Before Freud no one related circumcision to castration anxiety and then castration anxiety to anti–Semitism. In the case of a boy, avoidance of circumcision could be avoidance of a stigmatizing bodily sign. Pertinently, the girl's clitoris was called "the Jew" in idiomatic slang in Vienna (Gilman 1993). Although other religions also practiced circumcision, in Vienna at that time, circumcision identified the male as a Jew. This became particularly dangerous when the Nazis came to power.

We know that Freud was circumcised. Sigmund Freud's father wrote in the family bible, "my son Shlomo Sigismund long may he live, was born the third day of the week, the first day of the month of Iyaar, 5616, on the 6th of May 1856 and entered into the covenant ... on the 8th day of Iysaar, the 13th of May 1856. The mohel was Reb Samson Frankl" (Rice 1990). Questions have been raised, however, about whether Freud circumcised his own sons. Their not being circumcised is particularly hard to believe considering Freud's own Jewish identity, the traditions of his Jewish family who still observed Jewish holidays, and the relatively orthodox Jewish background of his wife, Martha Bernays Freud. Family and friends would visit after the birth of Freud's sons. Little Hans was born in 1903, not long after the birth of Freud's sons in the early 1890's. Could Freud have hypocritically urged Max Graf to raise his own son as a Jew, to not baptize Little Hans, having failed to raise his own sons as Jews beginning with their circumcision? Some of Freud's dreams and associations refer to his concerns that because of anti–Semitism his children would be deprived of the security of a homeland and the opportunity for successful careers. His dreams indicated that his children would be considered Jewish.

The circumcised-castrated Jew was represented through the opposite of having a long phallic nose. The Jewish phallus was associated with the social stereotype of the predatory and perverse character of the Jews. The conflicts associated with Jewish identity must have been present in Little Hans, as they had influenced the lives of his parents and grandparents. Though admired in Europe as an operatic prodigy, Herbert Graf went though a mock baptism in the hope that a baptismal certificate would be helpful with the Nazis. He actually had a Christian funeral, probably as a consequence of his much happier second marriage to a younger woman of Christian extraction.

During the years of the case histories, Freud had continued to be concerned with the problems of Jewish identity and anti–Semitism. Detecting anti-Semitism in Jung and other Swiss psychiatrists, he indicated to Abraham that their anti-Semitism had been directed away from himself and toward Abraham. On December 26, 1908, anticipating the publication of "Little Hans," creating an outcry, he wrote to Abraham (Freud and Abraham 1965), "German ideals threatened again! Our Aryan comrades are really completely indispensable to us, otherwise psychoanalysis would succumb to anti-Semitism."

Between Little Hans and the Wolf-Man cases, Jung had confessed to Freud in March 1909, about a scandalous relationship with a patient who soon identified herself to Freud as Sabina Spielrein. She fantasized having a child named Siegfried, representing a harmonious merger of Aryan and Jew, Freud and Jung, as well as the symbolic marriage and child of herself and Jung. During the Wolf-Man's analysis on August 20, 1912, Freud wrote to Spielrein, "My wish is for you to be cured completely. I must confess, after the event, that your fantasy about the birth of the savior to a mixed union, did not appeal to me at all. The law, in that anti-Jewish period, had him born from the superior Jewish race. But I know these are my prejudices." He later wrote to the pregnant Sabina Spielrein that he was cured of his predilection for the Aryan cause and hoped if the child turned out to be a boy, he would develop into a stalwart Zionist (Carotenuto 1984, pp. 116, 120).

The Rat-Man

Ernst Lanzer, tormented by obsessive fantasies, began his analysis with Freud on October 1, 1907. The analysis lasted approximately one year and was thus concurrent with the treatment of Little Hans. Because of the dramatic effect of his fantasy of a lethal torture consisting of a starved rat penetrating the rectum of his father and his future bride, he became known to posterity with the pseudonym of "The Rat-Man." Lanzer used many words with the stem of "rat," such as heirat, hofrat, errat, spielrat, etc. He spoke a "rat language" infused with obsessive thinking and a compulsion to talk. After hearing of the rat torture while in military service, in August 1907, he thought he saw the ground heave, as though there were a rat under it. Seeing a rat while visiting his father's grave, he assumed that the rat had had a meal from his father. As a child he used to bite. The rat had multiple meanings, e.g., feed and greed, lust, aggression, money, feces, penis, and baby.

The meanings of the rat, however, have negative denigrating connotations pertaining to Jews, and thus to the Rat-Man's conflicts about his Jewish identity. Freud's notes on the Rat-Man are the only surviving summary notes of the analytic process of any of his patients. The original record of the case, rather than the published case, has referents to the Jewish world and words of this patient and Freud. The Rat-Man thought "twenty kronen are enough for the parch," translated in a footnote, as a Jewish term for "a futile person" (p. 298). Strachey used the term "Jewish" rather than "Yiddish," and "parch" is now better translated as frugal or penurious. The Rat-man's overt preoccupations regarding the anus, odor, disease, and money were those attributed to Jews by the anti–Semitic culture. The Rat-Man was identified with a miserly mother, a father who was a gambler from a poor family, and he struggled with a family plan to have him marry a wealthy relative for money. He began treatment with a thought about the fee: "for each florin a rat." He reacted compulsively as though trivial debts to a fellow army officer and a post-office lady were matters of life and death. He fantasized that the money lender must be paid or the rat torture will be invoked, an unnoticed analogy to Shylock in "The Merchant of Venice" (Shakespeare 1595). Freud (1909, p. 288), noted that "rats have a special connection with money ... 'ratten' (rats) meant to him 'raten' (installments); rates ... money and syphilis converge in rats. He pays in rats—rat currency ... Syphilis gnawing and eating reminded him of rats." He thought his father and soldiers were syphilitic. The association of Jews with vermin, and with buying and lending on installments were social stereotypes.

On December 23, 1907, preceding Christmas, the Rat-Man recalled the suicide of a rejected dressmaker, sleeping through the night of his father's death, and thoughts of immortality. Just after Christmas, on December 27, the Rat-Man recalled a detail from Spring 1903 (Freud 1909, pp. 301–302). Entering a church "he suddenly fell on his knees, conjured up pious feelings and determined to believe in the next world and immortality. This involved Christianity and going to church in Unterach after he had called his cousin a whore. His father had never consented to be baptized, but much regretted that his forefathers had not relieved him of this unpleasant business. He had often told the patient he would make no objections if he wanted to become a Christian." Freud remarked that the Rat-Man's kneeling in church must have been against the scheme to marry him into a wealthy family of observant Jews. But neither Freud nor the Rat-Man wondered about the meaning of Christmas, his kneeling in church, and conflict about Jewishness. Freud's notes record the Rat-Man's use of the Yiddish word for whore, which he expected Freud to understand. The rat-man had a pious period of frequent prayers in his teens. He used prayers, magical incantations, and compulsive acts to ward off and undo his murderous, torturing fantasies and his incestuous behavior. The meaning of his religious bent and his conflicts about Jewish identity were not explored though Freud (1907) had already published "Obsessive actions and religious practices." The Rat-Man was inconsistently described as having become a free thinker, yet "he made up prayers for himself, which took up more and more time, and eventually lasted for an hour and a half" (Freud 1909, p. 193). His pious phrases, such as "May God protect him" could turn into their opposite — may God *not* protect him. He gave up these prayers and replaced them with a short formula, which he quickly recited so nothing could slip into it." Jewish prayers were eclipsed, and there was no reference to the rapid recitation of Hebrew prayers by observant Jews.

On December 28, 1907, the next day in Freud's notes of the same Christmas holidays, the Rat-Man recalled a story about a military officer's father who had been his own father's commander. The Rat-Man's father had provided Jews with spades to clear snow from a market station, a market that Jews were ordinarily forbidden to enter. The commander praised his father, whereupon his father retorted (Freud 1909 p. 305), "You rotter! You call me old comrade now ... but you treated me very differently in the past." Jews were simultaneously prohibited and exploited. The associations are replete with transference-counter-transference implications concerning Jewishness. But in the original case publication Jewish ethnicity and anti–Semitism were not explored and did not have free access to the market place of ideas.

The Wolf-Man

Serge Pankejeff, known to psychoanalytic posterity as The Wolf-Man, is also pertinent to both overt and covert anti–Semitism. Freud's four-year analysis of the Wolf-Man began in February 1910, and lasted four years. Their first meeting, a suggestive sadomasochistic primal scene, anticipated the major conflicts and personality disturbance described in the Wolf-Man's case history. Freud rather casually reported this patient's initial treatment reaction in a letter to Ferenczi, February 13, (Freud and Ferenczi 1993, 1910, p. 138), "A rich young Russian, whom I took on because of compulsive tendencies, admitted the following transferences to me after the first session: Jewish swindler, he would like to use me from behind and shit on my head.... When he saw three piles of feces on the street, he became uncomfortable because of the Holy Trinity and anxiously saw a fourth in order to destroy the association." Money and privilege were important to the Wolf-Man who encountered Freud with socially acceptable contemptuous anti–Semitic epithets. Even if exaggerated for shock effect, a Russian aristocrat could readily greet a Jew with insult and invective. He had arrived in Vienna with a retinue of servants and a personal physician. Born on Christmas Eve, the Wolf-Man expected to be regularly rewarded with a double set of gifts, birthday gifts, and Christmas gifts. He was entitled, elite, and identified with Christ in a form of narcissistic splitting, he was superior to the inferior, lowly Jews on whom he projected and displaced his own unacceptable homosexual and hostile impulses. Having led a dissolute life of the idle rich, he abruptly lost his fortune after the Communist revolution in Russia. Freud then arranged to take up a collection for him, so that Freud in effect gratified his wish to receive bountiful gifts. The Wolf-Man was in retrospect a borderline personality with multiple symptoms including constipation and derealization (Blum 1973). His feeling isolated from the world, was experienced as being enveloped in a veil. Prior to his analysis, this veil and his constipation were relieved by an enema usually administered by a male attendant. This was the relationship he proposed to repeat with Freud when he offered to have anal intercourse and defecate on the Jewish doctor in a fantasized homosexual rape and robbery. After his analysis with Freud, who had promised him a cure of his constipation, the constipation recurred. Freud re-analyzed him for four months, in 1919, without payment. In 1926 the Wolf-Man was referred for treatment to one of Freud's other patients, Ruth Mack, then in her mid-twenties. This very gifted young woman from an affluent Jewish family was nevertheless a psychoanalytic novice without prior training. Having concealed some funds and jewels that he retained, the Wolf-Man was essentially treated by Ruth Mack without fee. This fortified his expectation of monetary gifts and narcissistic entitlement. He was however, narcissistically injured because he was being treated by the young pupil rather than by the master. Contemptuous of the pupil, he rationalized that he was getting the benefit of Freud's knowledge since he was sure that she discussed him with her analyst, Freud. Despite the fact that she must have discussed the case in her free associations, she told the Wolf-Man that she barely mentioned him nor had Freud inquired about him. The Wolf-Man became enraged at Freud and at her. He subsequently reported the following dream (Mack-Brunswick 1928, p. 286): "the patient's father, in the dream a professor, resembling, however, a begging musician known to the patient, sits at a table and warns the others present not to talk about financial matters before the patient, because of his tendency to speculate. His father's nose is long and hooked, causing the patient to wonder at its change." In the Wolf-Man's associations the musician had tried to sell old music, which the patient refused to buy. The musician looked like Christ and the Wolf-Man's father; the Wolf-Man recalled that his father had been incorrectly called a "sale juif," a dirty Jew. In Russia (and the rest of Europe) Jews were regarded as mercenary and avaricious. The professor-father, that is Freud, is the dirty Jewish psychoanalyst, the swindler, trying to sell him psychoanalysis. His ascribing an avaricious motive to Freud was clearly a social stereotype of the Jews, as well as a projection of his own conflicts. Through the period of the Wolf-Man's childhood obsessional neurosis he was compelled to exhale when he saw beggars or cripples, exorcising the evil spirits causing his blasphemous thoughts. Jews were often depicted as evil sprits and predators, and exorcism was analogous to an enema. The beggars and thieves were Jews, like his analysts, after his fecal money. The Wolf-Man felt that Freud had overcharged him when he was rich and not protected him, as God the father did not protect his son from the crucifixion God ordained. The divine Christ was also a human who needed to defecate. He resolved this paradox by reasoning that if Christ ate nothing Christ would not have to defecate (no meal, no payment). These conflicts of incorporation, retention, and expulsion also represented his extraordinary ambivalence and splitting of representations. Money was the root of evil, yet worshipped as "holy shit."

The long, hooked nose in his dream invoked the stereotype of the perverse Jew-swindler. He had not relinquished his anti–Semitism in the service of his narcissistic entitlement and rage. The Wolf-Man was preoccupied with his own nose, symbolizing his penis, before and during his analysis. In adolescence he had severe acne and a sebaceous gland infection, which left a tiny hole in his nose. He would study his nose in the mirror, became reclusive and afraid of people, particularly his peers teasing him in school. At 17 he developed gonorrhea, which intensified his castration conflicts displaced onto the stereotyped Jewish nose. Considering the Wolf-Man's desiring gifts, as if it was always Christmas, Freud suggested instead that the Wolf-Man present a gift to Freud at termination. Reversing roles and requesting a gift, Freud believed this would relieve the Wolf-Man of excessive feelings of obligation toward his analyst. The Wolf-Man chose an Egyptian artifact, which Freud placed on his desk where it remains today. The Wolf-Man was now delegated to donate to Freud, resonating with his initial fantasy of the exploitative Jewish analyst. The gift exchanges did not then halt, extending from their initial transference–counter-transference reactions. When the Wolf-Man visited Freud at the end of World War I, Freud (1918) presented him with a book with a dedication written to the Wolf-Man and containing his own case report "From the History of an Infantile Neurosis."

In conclusion, for Freud, especially in the pioneer era of psychoanalytic discovery it was important to present scientific findings and hypotheses not "tainted" by data that might be considered to be uniquely Jewish. He considered psychoanalytic findings and formulations to have universal application, not limited to any ethnic group, race, society, or culture. It was important to have scientific and academic acknowledgement of Freud's revolutionary theories in the history of Western thought. However, the affective influence of internalized Jewish anti–Semitism, self-effacement, and craving for acceptance and recognition persisted in Freud, as well as in his Jewish patients. While anti–Semitism was overt or covert in each case history, it was not explored in the case reports and was presumably not analyzed. Similar issues surfaced a half-century later, when the editors of the original edition of Freud's letters to Fliess expunged Yiddish expressions.

For cross-cultural verification and illustration. Freud chose the Greek myths of Oedipus and Narcissus to describe crucial developmental phases and universal fantasies. However, his related writings on the mythical Moses are far more intimate, personal, and painfully ambivalent. Freud's insights are invaluable for the understanding of individual and group anti–Semitism as well as other forms and targets of irrational social and cultural denigration and discrimination. His oversights can retrospectively be utilized with current analytic concepts to enlarge understanding of unconscious conflicts and fantasies which are joined in silent avoidance of painful issues shared by analyst and patient. A transference–countertransference collusion may provide a barrier to analytic recognition of bias and conflicts that are crucially involved in socially sanctioned devaluation and hatred. Finally, these ever fascinating case reports represent the burgeoning early evolution of psychoanalytic theory and therapy in the context of a bygone era.

Footnote or Addendum to Anti-Semitism in the Freud Case Histories

Freud's (1911) "Psychoanalytic Notes on an Autobiographical Case of Paranoia" can now also be understood in an expanded context of cultural prejudice and racism. Schreber apparently suffered from paranoid schizophrenia with delusions, hallucinations, and suicidal behavior. He believed that God, colluding with the director of the mental hospital, Dr. Paul Flechsig, had emasculated him, that he was an object of their persecution. He was castrated, given a woman's breast and genitals, and would be impregnated by God, giving birth in identification with the Virgin Mary and Christ.

What Freud did not choose to comment upon was the red thread of racism and anti–Semitism in Schreber's delusional system. Freud (1911, p. 24) noted that Schreber divided God into anterior and posterior realms. "The posterior realms of God were, and still are, divided in a strange manner into two parts, so that a lower God (Ahriman) was differentiated from an upper god (Ormuzd) ... Schreber can tell us no more than that the lower God was more especially attached to the peoples of a dark race (the Semites) and the upper God to those of a fair race (the Aryans)." Freud did not choose to analyze or comment upon the red thread of racial anti–Semitism in Schreber's delusional system.

But Schreber (1955, orig. published 1903) told us much more about abusive prejudice in his memoir than Freud reported (Gilman 1993). He related that the lower Semitic god, Ahriman had rays that miraculously emasculate, whereas the rays of the Aryan upper god (Ormuzd) could restore manhood. Castrated by the Semitic-Jewish God, he additionally imagined that he was miraculously deprived of his healthy natural stomach and instead given an inferior Jew's stomach. He had split his identity between a superior Aryan male and an inferior Jewish female.

Schreber's God could not learn and misunderstood human beings. Freud (1911, p. 25) observed "God was quite incapable of dealing with living men, and was only accustomed to communicate with corpses." Schreber's delusional system foreshadowed Nazi ideology and the Holocaust (Blum 1986). The Nazi God (Hitler) preferred corpses. The Nazi division of people into the Aryan superior race and the inferior Semitic race is literally a page out of Schreber. Schreber identified with the emasculated Jew as a woman. As a megalomanic female redeemer, Schreber would give birth to a new race consonant with the order of things. The homologous Nazi "new order" with the goal of achieving an exalted Aryan racial purity is virtually transparent. Cultural and familial attitudes about Aryans and Jews had infiltrated Schreber's psychic reality and his delusions. How could it be otherwise? In his paranoia he was not only a victim of physical abuse, sexual abuse, and "soul murder" but probably also attuned to real environmental, external threats of abuse and persecution. That Flechsig had at that time practiced castration to treat hysteria, and the probable childhood abuse of Schreber by his physician father (Niederland 1984) is beyond the scope of this brief discussion. The anti–Semitism and racism in the Schreber autobiography and Freud's case report, so long overlooked by psychoanalysts, are important analytic, historical, and cultural considerations.

Addendum References

Blum, H. (1986). "On Identification and Its Vicissitudes." *International Journal of* Psychoanalysis 67: 267–276.
Freud, S. (1911). "Psychoanalytic Notes on an Autobiographical Account of a Case of Paranoia (Dementia Paranoids). " *Standard Edition 12.*
Gilman, S. (1993). *Freud, Race, and Gender.* Princeton, NJ: Princeton University Press.
Niederland, W. (1984). *The Schreber Case.* Hillsdale, NJ: Analytic.
Schreber, D. (1955). *Memoirs of My Nervous Illness.* Ed. I. Macalpine and R. Hunter. Cambridge, MA: Harvard University Press.

References

Ahsen, A. (1974). "Anna O — Patient or Therapist? An Eidetic View." In *Women in Therapy,* ed. V. Franks and V. Burtle, New York: Brunner/Mazel, pp. 263–283.
Beller, S. (1989). *Vienna and the Jews, 1867–1938.* New York: Cambridge University Press.
Billig, M. (1999). *Freudian Repression.* New York: Cambridge University Press.
Blum, H. (1974). "The Borderline Childhood of the Wolf Man." *Journal of the American Psychoanalytic Association* 22: 721–742.
_____ (1994). "Dora's Conversion Syndrome: A Contribution to the Prehistory of the Holocaust." *Psychoanalytic Quarterly* 63: 518–525.
Breuer, J., and S. Freud. (1895). *Studies on Hysteria.* S.E. 2.
Carontenuto, A. (1984). *A Secret Symmetry.* New York: Pantheon.
Decker, H. (1991). *Freud, Dora, and Vienna.* New York: Free Press.
Freud, S. (1900). "The Interpretation of Dreams." *Standard Edition* 4, 5.
_____ (1905). "Fragment of an Analysis of a Case of Hysteria." *Standard Edition* 7: 1–122.
_____ (1909a). "Analysis of a Phobia in a Five-Year-Old Boy." *Standard Edition* 10-:3–149.
_____ (1909b). "Notes Upon a Case of Obsessional Neurosis." *Standard Edition* 10: 153–318.
_____ (1913). "Totem and Taboo." *Standard Edition* 13: 1–162.
_____ (1918). "From the History of an Infantile Neurosis." *Standard Edition* 17: 3–122.
_____ (1939). "Moses and Monotheism." *Standard Edition* 23: 1–137.
_____ (1985). *The Complete Letters of Sigmund Freud to Wilhelm Fliess, 1887–1904.* Trans. J. Masson. Cambridge, MA: Harvard University Press.
Freud, S., and K. Abraham (1965). *A Psychoanalytic Dialogue: The Letters of Sigmund Freud and Karl Abraham.* Ed. H. Abraham and E. Freud. New York: Basic.
Freud, S., and S. Ferenczi. (1993). *The Correspondance of Sigmund Freud and Sandor Ferenczi, Vol. 1.* Ed. E. Falzeder and E. Brabant. Cambridge, MA: Harvard University Press.
Frosch, S. (2005). *Anti-Semitism, Nazism, and Psychoanalysis.* Basingstroke: Palgrave Macmillan.

Gilman, S. (1986). *Jewish Self-Hatred*. Baltimore, MD: Johns Hopkins University Press.
____ (1993). *Freud, Race, and Gender*. Princeton, NJ: Princeton University Press.
Graf, M. (1942). "Reminiscences of Professor Sigmund Freud." *Psychoanalytic Quarterly* 11: 465–476.
Knafo, D. (1999). "Anti-Semitism in the Clinical Setting." *Journal of the American Psychoanalytic Association* 47: 35–64.
Loewenberg, P. (1983). *Decoding the Past*. New York: A. Knopf.
Mack Brunswick, R. (1928). In Gardner, M. ed. (1971). *The Wolf Man. With the Case of the Wolf Man* by Sigmund Freud and a supplement by Ruth Mack Brunswick. New York: Basic.
Nunberg, H., and E. Federn, eds. (1964). *Minutes of the Vienna Psychoanalytic Society, vol. 2: 1908–1910*. New York: International Universities Press.
Ostow, M. (1995). *Myth and Madness: The Psychodynamics of Anti-Semitism*. New Brunswick, NJ: Transaction.
Rice, E. (1990). *Freud and Moses*. Albany: State University of New York Press.
Rudnytski, P. (1999). "Does the Professor Talk to God? Counter-Transference and Jewish Identity in the Case of Little Hans." *Psychoanalysis and History* 1: 175–194.
Young-Bruehl, E. (1996). *The Anatomy of Prejudices*. Cambridge, MA: Harvard University Press.

Freud's Theory of Jewishness
For Better and for Worse
Eliza Slavet

On September 30, 1934, Freud wrote a letter to his friend Arnold Zweig, in which he announced that he had begun a new work: "Faced with the new persecutions," he wrote, "one asks oneself again how the Jews have come to be what they are and why they have attracted this undying hatred [*unsterbliche haß*]. I soon discovered the formula: Moses created the Jews."[1] In this letter, Freud alludes to a provocative thesis at the heart of his final book, *Moses and Monotheism*: the origins and persistent survival of the Jewish people, he suggests, may be inextricably linked to the origins of the "undying hatred" of Jews and Judaism. According to Freud, these phenomena are neither divine nor predetermined, but rather a matter of choices made by humans living in historical time. In *Moses and Monotheism*, Freud developed a theory of Jewishness that was both racial and cultural, both hereditary and historical. Within this complicated narrative, he implies that regardless of any attempts to repress, suppress or repudiate Jewishness, the Jewish tradition will survive, for better or for worse.

Central to Freud's theory is the idea that Jewishness is constituted by the biological inheritance of an archaic memory that Jewish people are inexorably compelled to transmit to future generations, whether consciously or unconsciously. According to his version of the story, the Jewish tradition originated when an Egyptian named Moses chose a band of Semites upon whom he imposed a strict monotheism based on the abstract ideals of *Geistigkeit* (or as it is variably translated, intellectual spirituality or intellectuality). Freud was well aware of the historic specificity of this term within German Idealist philosophy, and he took special care to note the range of meaning which *Geist* could suggest—from "spirit" to "ghost" to "breath" which in Hebrew is the same word (*ruach*) as "soul"[2]—but he refashions the term to fit his definition of Jewish tradition.[3] According to Freud, by rejecting the most material and magical elements of "primitive" religions, Mosaic monotheism became supremely spiritual [*geistig*]: it condemned "magical ceremonies," denied the existence of an afterlife and prohibited material representations of the deity.[4] Whereas "primitive" religions proved their power through material evidence (such as magical ceremonies and iconic representations of the deity), the power of Mosaic monotheism was always a "hypothesis," for it existed in a realm *beyond sensory perception*.⁵ Unable to tolerate "such a highly spiritualized [*Vergeistigte*] religion,"⁶ the band of Semites killed Moses (repeating the murder of the primal father described in *Totem and Taboo*). The reason these events were not recorded in the Bible, Freud explains, is that the people repressed the memory of the murder. However, the memory-traces of Moses and his tradition continued to exert their influence. Ultimately, Freud insists that the memory-traces have been inherited "independently of direct communication and of the influence of education." Explicitly engaging with contemporary theories of evolution and race, Freud insists that this "acquired characteristic" (of Jewishness) has been biologically transmitted from one generation to the next.⁷ According to Freud, then, the biologically inherited memory of Moses constitutes Jewish tradition and compels Jews to be Jewish.

Surprisingly, this racial definition of Jewishness does not detract from Freud's emphasis on the spiritual-intellectual ideals of the tradition. Precisely because the Jewish tradition had reached the heights of ideal abstraction, its survival could not be explained solely by the usual cultural media — not "direct communication" nor "the influence of education by the setting of an example,"⁸ not rituals and not texts. The survival and transmission of Jewish tradition *required* a medium beyond sensory perception and this medium was biological heredity. While the Nazis also made claims about both their superior spirituality and the purity of their own biological material, in Freud's theory of Jewishness these two elements do not simply coexist; they are inseparable: the genealogical transmission both confirms the supreme *Geistigkeit* of the tradition and guarantees its survival. The inextricability of these terms also illuminates the troubled relationship between the persistent survival of Jewish tradition and the "undying hatred" that it persistently elicits.

Since Freud had explored the nature and origins of religious traditions in *Totem and Taboo*, he defensively asserted that *Moses and Monotheism* contained nothing that he had not already explained twenty-plus years before.⁹ Nonetheless, his final book obviously contains a great deal more — and more specific — than the earlier one. In *Totem*, Freud explored the nature and origins of a wide range of religious traditions, but he almost entirely skipped over the Jewish tradition. In *Moses and Monotheism*, he notes that he intends to explore

> what the real nature of a tradition resides in, and what its special power rests on ... what sacrilege [*Frevel*] one commits against the splendid diversity of human life if one recognizes only those motives which arise from *material* needs, from what sources some ideas (and particularly religious ones) derive their power to subject both men and peoples to their yoke [*unterjochen*] — to study all this in the *special case* [*Spezialfall*] *of Jewish history* would be an alluring task.¹⁰

While he begins this passage by referring to "the real nature of tradition" as if it were something universal, he concludes that the present work was driven by his desire to explore the "special case of Jewish history"—how it was that Jewish tradition had "subjected" generations to its "yoke," not only through material needs but through something else. In the shift from the universal case of "tradition" to the particular case of Jewish tradition, Freud strangely distinguishes his own work from all others that study tradition. Indeed, the distinction could apply to his life's work, for psychoanalysis focuses not on how people satisfy their "material needs"—food, water, shelter—but on how and why they are driven to satisfy non-material needs, how they are "subjected" to powers which do not necessarily have any political or legal currency, or ramifications in the material world. The question that Freud addresses in *Moses and Monotheism*, then, is how and why individuals have been regularly convinced that they are Jewish and that they should practice Jewish traditions even as the "Jewish tradition" does not itself satisfy any "material needs." The transmission and power of Jewish tradition, Freud suggests, rises beyond the realm of material needs, physical satisfactions and manifest powers; it subjects its people to its yoke through its spiritually-intellectual [*geistig*] ideals.

The Jewish tradition has survived at least in part because it has been genealogically transmitted from generation to generation. Since the formulation of Rabbinic Judaism in the Babylonian Talmud, Jewishness has been defined genealogically. Indeed, according to the Rabbis, "one cannot cease to be a Jew even via apostasy,"[11] or as Theodor Reik put it in his book on *Jewish Wit*, "once a Jew always a Jew."[12] Unlike children of Christians or Muslims who may choose to no longer be "counted" as Christian or Muslim, children of Jewish parents are "counted" as Jewish by both Jews and non–Jews, regardless of individual experiences, beliefs or choices. Even when parents attempt to reject or "repress" their Jewishness by not practicing Jewish rituals or by converting and raising their children as non–Jews, such children may still be considered as Jewish: by themselves, by their contemporaries and by history.[13] A person is Jewish *not* because he believes in a monotheistic god, keeps kosher, circumcises his sons, or any other number of supposedly singularly Jewish beliefs, practices or proclivities. According to Freud, a person is Jewish simply because he inherits the "memory-traces of the experience of our ancestors."[14] Freud's theory of Jewishness is compelling precisely because it articulates the racial aspects of culture; it suggests that culture derives from race rather than the other way around. Only when a person has inherited Jewishness does his belief (or disbelief) in a monotheistic God—or his circumcision of his sons, or his affection for Jewish authors and filmmakers, or his support of Israel—represent part of his "Jewish culture."[15] Otherwise, these are simply affections for things that historically (but not exclusively) have been associated with people who have inherited Jewishness.

In the ongoing debate about Freud's relationship to *Judentum*, one of the major questions has been whether he felt positively or negatively about it, and whether he saw it as a religion based on spiritual-intellectual ideals, or as a racial-ethnic identity based on internalized anti–Semitism. It has even been suggested that the racialization of Jewishness is a sort of a psychological problem along the lines of self-hatred, a "temptation" which Freud may have (or should have) resisted.[16] Most scholars who have addressed these aspects of Freud's final book have focused on either his insistence on the biological transmission of memory or his emphasis on Jewish *Geistigkeit*. While their projects are very different, Jan Assmann and Daniel Boyarin both read Freud's spiritualization [*Vergeisterung*] of Judaism as an ironic and defensive inversion of Christian anti–Jewish images of the Jewish people as mired in the materiality of text and flesh.[17]

By contrast, Yerushalmi and Gilman have each attend to Freud's peculiar insistence upon a "Lamarckian" notion of heredity, and hence, upon a racial definition of Jewishness—the idea that a person inherits Jewishness, for better and for worse, and regardless of her own feelings, beliefs or practices.[18] In his seminal 1991 work, *Freud's Moses: Judaism Terminable and Interminable*, Yerushalmi interprets Freud's insistence on this idea as a dangerous separation of "Jewishness" (the ethnic-racial condition of being Jewish) and "Judaism" (the religion sometimes practiced by Jewish people). If Jewishness can be transmitted "independently of direct communication and education by example," he writes (quoting Freud), "then that means that 'Jewishness' can be transmitted independently of 'Judaism,' that the former is interminable even if the latter is terminated."[19] For Yerushalmi, the emphasis on the (often discomforting) bodily definitions of Jewishness seems to detract from the more "noble and precious" ideals of Judaism. Whereas Yerushalmi and Gilman each concentrate on Freud's ethnic-racial definition of Jewishness, Assmann and Boyarin focus on his construction of the intellectual-spiritual ideals of Judaism. I argue that in his final book, Freud attempts to make sense of the counter-intuitive connections between Jewishness and Judaism and suggests that the *geistig* ideals of Judaism are inseparable from the bodily survival of the Jewish people. Freud insists on an idiosyncratic version of *Geistigkeit* not to deny the body (as Boyarin claims), but to make sense of the "special case" of bodily definition within Judaism.

It is impossible to determine whether Freud's theory of Jewishness should be read as a positive affirmation or an uncomfortable apprehension of the Jewish tradition.[20] It is also impossible to determine whether Freud's sense that Jewishness was "ineffaceable" was the result of his Jewish education[21] or whether it was the result of his "education" in anti–Semitic racism. Lou Andreas-Salomé and many others have wanted to believe that in his last book, Freud presented a positive testimony to the Jewish tradition. In January 1935, she wrote to Freud, responding to his description of his burgeoning work: "What particularly fascinated *me*," she writes, "is a specific characteristic of the 'return of the repressed,' namely, the way in which *noble and precious* elements return despite long intermixture with every conceivable kind of material."[22] While this sentence has been repeatedly quoted as evidence that Freud's last book can be read as an affirmation of the better elements of Jewish tradition, it seems instead to raise the question as to why an individual or a people would repress elements which were so "noble and precious." Freud did not solve the problem of whether *Judentum* is a religion or an ethnic-racial identity, but he did explore some of its most perplexing elements without determining whether their survival would be noble or otherwise.

Like many Jewish scholars before and since, Freud re-interprets what has often been regarded as a problematic particularity of the Jewish people: the fact that Jews are Jewish not because of religious beliefs, cultural practices, linguistic abilities or citizenship in a particular land, but because they have apparently inherited Jewishness in their bodies. While the bodily definition of Jewishness has been a source of racist anti–Semitism since at least the fifteenth century,[23] it can be traced to Jewish and Christian texts from the first century C.E.. Since Paul, Christian anti–Judaism has often centered around the idea that while Christianity has apparently ascended to the heights of abstract spirituality [*Geistigkeit*], the Jewish people remain mired in the materiality of the flesh and of the text. Freud seems to appropriate and invert the Christian trope of *Geistigkeit* to define what is most remarkable about the Jews,[24] but he ironically uses it to make sense of the most material and bodily element of Jewish definition, namely its genealogical transmission.

Freud's insistence on the biological transmission of Jewishness may seem incompatible with his emphasis on the abstract *geistig* ideals of Jewish tradition, but he develops idiosyncratic versions of the notions of both Jewish genealogy and *Geistigkeit* such that one confirms the other. While he mentions *Geistigkeit* throughout *Moses and Monotheism*, he explores this concept in detail in an oft-discussed section entitled "The Advance in Intellectuality [*Fortschritt in der Geistigkeit*]."[25] According to Freud, the most important element of Mosaic monotheism was the "prohibition against making an image of God."[26] This single precept had such a "profound effect" that a "new realm of intellectuality [*Geistigkeit*] was opened up," in which "ideas, memories and inferences became decisive in contrast to the lower psychical activity which had direct perceptions by the sense-organs as its content."[27] Whereas less *geistig* religions and traditions could be transmitted through material media such as texts, objects, rituals or lands, Jewish tradition was different. (Indeed, such material things can be transformed into idols of worship, thereby displacing the emphasis on pure *Geistigkeit*.) As Assmann has noted, Freud's *Moses* (and psychoanalysis more generally) can be seen as an affirmation of the Jewish aspiration to free the soul from the captivity of compulsive idolatry of the material world.[28] What is most remarkable about Freud's *Moses*, however, is that it allows us to think through the racial aspects of Jewishness without becoming mired in the materiality associated with race (i.e., particular physical or phenotypical characteristics).

Yet Freud still needed to contend with the obvious fact that genealogy *is* a matter of sensuality and sensory perception: (until recently) human reproduction required two bodies engaged in highly sensory activity, and genealogy could be guaranteed by witnessing the baby emerge from the mother's body. This "genealogical guarantee" is precisely what Freud transforms in his theory of Jewishness. Part of the "advance in *Geistigkeit*," he explains, was the transition from matriarchy to patriarchy:

> this turning from the mother to the father points in addition to a victory of intellectuality [*Geistigkeit*] over sensuality [*Sinnlichkeit*]—that is, an advance in civilization [*Kulturfortschritt*] since maternity [*Mutterschaft*] is proved by the evidence of the senses while paternity [*Vaterschaft*] is a hypothesis, based on an inference and a premiss. Taking sides in this way with a thought-process in preference to a sense [*sinnliche*] perception has proved to be a momentous step.[29]

Here Freud knowingly and ironically inverts[30] the "matrilineal principle" of Jewish definition in order to establish a masculine *Geistigkeit*[31] which nonetheless *incorporates* the body. According to the "matrilineal principle," if the mother is Jewish, the child is also Jewish, whereas if she is non–Jewish (even if the *father* is Jewish), the child is regarded as non–Jewish.[32] Though Rabbinic family law is almost entirely patrilineal, in determining the status of the offspring of mixed marriages it is *matrilineal*.[33] There are many explanations for this particular legal aspect of Jewish definition,[34] but the most common — and the most common sense — explanation is that the mother's identity can be "proved by the evidence of the senses" while the father's identity is always "a hypothesis, based on an inference and a premiss."[35] Freud "masculinizes"[36] the most "feminine" aspect of Jewish bodily definition so that it can remain in a realm beyond sensory perception. He does this not to "rewrite" Jewishness as Aryan (as Assmann suggests) or to reject carnality (as Daniel Boyarin argues),[37] but to make sense of the particularity of the bodily definition of Jewishness. Thus, while Freud insists that Jewish tradition is biologically transmitted, he masculinizes the materiality of biology so that it can remain in a realm beyond sensory perception.

By inverting the "matrilineal principle" of Jewish genealogy, Freud produces a particular kind of scientific theory of Jewishness, one which is not bound by the criteria of scientific evidence and proof that were becoming standard in the 1930s. Throughout his career, Freud drew ideas and materials from biological and evolutionary theories, and he regularly expressed an aspiration that psychoanalysis would be regarded as a "science," based on "actual" observations.[38] However, with the development of new technologies for documenting observations and for controlling experimental conditions, scientific standards began to be defined by the quality of material evidence (such as photographs) and controlled experimentation.[39] If psychoanalysis was a "science," it was one that had almost no access to *material* evidence and whose theories could not be "proved by the evidence of the senses." Psychoanalytic theory was always "a hypothesis, based on an inference and a premiss." Nonetheless, Freud could see — or at least was convinced he could see — that psychoanalysis "subjected" people to its power by presenting its hypotheses to its patients rather than by working with physical materials or by fulfilling "material needs."

So too, Freud observed that Jewish tradition is defined first and foremost by the fact that it does not require material "evidence" in order to "subject" the people to its "yoke." Rather, what "subjects" them is the "inference" that they have inherited *something*—Jewishness—defined not by "sensory perceptions" but by "abstract ideas," "memories and inferences."[40] Freud's theory of Jewishness could be considered "scientific" in the sense that it is a "hypothesis" based on observations of the "special case" of Jewish history. However, it is in a different—more *geistig*—realm than those "scientific" attempts to "prove" the genetic unity of all Jews (or at least all priestly males) using material evidence which, though microscopic, depends upon "sensory perception."[41] According to Freud's theory, the biological inheritance of Jewishness does not detract from its abstract *geistig* ideals as long as it remains a "hypothesis." Thus, Freud refigures the materiality of Jewish genealogy as a purely spiritual-intellectual [*geistig*] matter.

In insisting upon both the non-material idealism of *Geistigkeit* and the materiality of biological inheritance, Freud addresses long-standing questions of Jewish embodiment. As Howard Eilberg-Schwartz has suggested, throughout history, "Jewish bodies" have been "doubly damned." On the one hand, Jews were "inadequately embodied"—pictured as weak feminine men with small or foreshortened penises,[42] excessively interested in "feminine" concerns such as books, study and the family.[43] On the other hand, they were considered overly embodied—pictured as grotesque, hairy, smelly women—and too mired in the flesh—clinging to bodily rituals such as circumcision, *mikvah* (ritual immersion) and genealogical (rather than spiritual) definitions of the group. Over time, two general "strategies" for countering these charges emerged. The first was to "pursue embodiment,"[44] exemplified most clearly by certain Zionists such as Max Nordau in his fantasy of the "Muscle Jew" but anticipated by the Maccabees' pursuit of Greek ideals of fitness and bodily perfection. The second strategy was to "flee embodiment through the spiritualization of the tradition," which was exemplified by various Jewish scholars' attempts to redefine Judaism as the most *geistig* of religions along Kantian lines.[45] So too, the popular designation of the Jewish people as the "People of the Book" has, until quite recently, privileged certain disembodied "dimensions of Jewish experience at the expense of others."[46] While Freud's emphasis on the Jews' "Advance in Spirituality [*Fortschritt in der Geistigkeit*]" seems to similarly privilege the textual and intellectual [*geistig*] aspects of Judaism, it is complicated by his insistence on the genealogical transmission of Jewishness. On the one hand, by refiguring the materiality of Jewish genealogy as proof of the particularity of Jewish *Geistigkeit*, he seems more like those Jewish scholars who would insist that Judaism is a spiritual tradition of ideals rather than a race, or as one Holocaust-museum website puts it, "Among all the things that Judaism is, the one thing it is not is a race."[47] On the other hand, his insistence on the genealogical transmission of Jewishness seems more similar to the attempts of Jewish scientists—both in Freud's time and our own—to prove that the Jews are the most pure race rather than a parasitic mongrel group.[48] However, Freud refuses to make a choice between the two possibilities; he neither rejects the "racial" aspects of Jewish definition nor the "religious" ideals of Judaism. Instead, he develops a theory of Jewishness that incorporates both the racial materiality and the ideal intellectuality [*Geistigkeit*] of the Jewish people.

While Freud insists that the Jewish tradition has been genealogically transmitted, he attends to the image of the Jews as the "People of the Book" and to the ways in which texts transmit certain (if fallible) traces from the past. As he notes, the "pre-eminence given to intellectual labours [*geistigen Bestrebungen*] throughout some two thousand years in the life of the Jewish people has, of course, had its effect."[49] While this "effect" has been used to portray the Jews as pathetically feeble and overly bookish—that is, as "insufficiently embodied"—Freud inverts this portrayal. Boyarin proposes that Freud "spiritualizes" Judaism as part of a larger attempt to Aryanize and masculinize the Jewish man, but it is precisely in the realm of the body that Freud inverts the entire structure. Rather than "masculinizing" the Jewish man into an image of virile physical power, Freud presents a more complex and discordant image. As he explains, the "Holy Writ and the intellectual concern with it" has not only "held the scattered people together," it has also "helped to check the brutality and the tendency to violence which are apt to appear where the development of muscular strength is the popular ideal. Harmony in the cultivation of intellectual [*geistiger*] and physical [*körperlicher*] activity, such as was achieved by the Greek people, was denied to the Jews. In this dichotomy their decision was at least in favour of the worthier alternative [*Höherwertige*]."[50] Freud explicitly contrasts the violent brutality and muscular physiques of other peoples against the *Geistigkeit* of the Jews. Yet it is unclear whether either possibility is preferable.

If Moses' "dematerialization of God" was the initial advance in *Geistigkeit*, how have "the Jews *retained* their inclination to intellectual interests"? How have they preserved their "ideal factor"? The answer is that in killing Moses, the originator of the "ideal factor," the Jews acquired a memory that could never be completely repressed or erased and that would be inexorably transmitted from generation to generation. In *Totem and Taboo* and *Civilization and its Discontents*, Freud had explained that the sociality of (all) civilization was initiated by an originary act of violence.[51] As Jacqueline Rose writes, "monotheism, together with the 'advance in intellectuality' that is said to accompany it, takes hold only because of the bloody deed which presided over its birth." The "underlying thesis" is that "there is no sociality without violence, that people are most powerfully and effectively united by what they agree to hate. What binds the people to each other and to their God is that they killed him."⁵² It is this act of violence which ultimately makes the Jews Jewish, for it is the memory of this act that causes the Jewish people both to repress *and* to return to the Mosaic religion. After killing Moses, Freud explains,

> The Jewish people had abandoned the Aten religion brought to them by Moses and had turned to the worship of another god who differed little from the Baalim [local gods] of the neighboring peoples. All the tendentious efforts of later times failed to disguise this shameful fact. *But the Mosaic religion had not vanished without leaving a trace; some sort of memory of it had kept alive — a possibly obscured and distorted tradition.* And it was this tradition of a great past which continued to operate (from the background, as it were), which gradually acquired more and more power over people's minds and which in the end succeeded in changing the god Yahweh into the Mosaic god and in re-awakening into life the religion of Moses that had been introduced and then abandoned long centuries before.⁵³

Indeed, it is only through the complicated processes of the repression of the memory of murder and its re-awakening that the Jewish tradition ultimately ascends to the "heights of abstraction," initiated by Moses' aniconic prohibitions. While the Jewish people have not "harmonized" their *Geistigkeit* with physical activity (like the Greeks), their *Geistigkeit* originates from the transcending of a brutal and physical act of violence, and the eventual acceptance of the transcendent monotheism that drove them to commit the act of violence.

Oddly, while Freud builds his narrative around this originary murder, in "The Advance in Intellectuality [*Geistigkeit*]," he does not directly refer to this violent act or to its memory. Instead, he refers to the violence of *other people*, and explains that the Jews "retained their inclination to *geistig* interests" at least in part *because* of this violence. "The nation's political misfortune taught it to value at its true worth the one possession that remained to it — its literature."⁵⁴ Here Freud seems to argue that the *text* defines the Jewish people, though he has spent pages and pages speculating about how the Jewish tradition — the memory-traces of the murder of Moses — has survived over innumerable generations, *despite* and *beyond* the tendentious textual distortions, through some means *other than direct communication*. Has Freud momentarily repressed the originary brutal act of murder and replaced it with the brutal and violent tendencies of *others* who cause the Jews their "political misfortunes"? Though the *text* may have remained the most valuable "possession" of the Jewish people, it did not compel them to preserve their tradition, or to be Jewish. It is not the texts that make Jews Jewish, but rather the "permanent imprint" of the Mosaic tradition: distorted, repressed and returned such that Jews continue to feel compelled to *turn* to these texts, to "awaken" the memory-traces that (hypothetically) have been genealogically transmitted. (Nonetheless, one could argue that the genealogical definition of Jewishness was produced and perpetuated through texts such as the Talmud and later commentaries.)

While there are converts to Judaism,⁵⁵ for the majority of Jews, it is the genealogical inheritance of Jewishness that compels them to embrace this tradition, or to repress, repudiate or return to it. Indeed, according to Freud, repressions and repudiations are evidence of transmission, acknowledgements that there is a presence, that the tradition has been inherited. Why else "repudiate" Jewishness if it is not present?[56] On a lighter note, this sort of backward logic could be compared to that of the tobacco companies' argument that smoking does not cause lung cancer. Rather, the tobacco companies argue that it is the genetic predisposition to lung cancer that causes people to smoke.[57] In other words, an individual's beliefs do not necessarily cause him or her to feel Jewish and to turn to Judaism. Rather, it is the inheritance of Jewishness (and the subsequent identification of the person as Jewish) that can compel a person to *be* Jewish and to do, practice and have an affinity for particular things that are understood as Jewish. In this respect, we can repeat after Lacan and say that "there is no repression prior to the return of the repressed."[58]

At least since the Holocaust, there has been a wishful movement to repudiate the racial definition of Jewishness because it seems too close to externally imposed anti–Semitic definitions. Not surprisingly, then, a number of scholars have attempted to reduce or remove these aspects both from Freud's definition and from Jewish communities' self-definitions.[59] Scholars and community leaders have understandably shied away from discussions suggesting that the "racial" definition of Jewishness could be anything more than a historical relic, and with the scientific establishment's denial of "race" as a useful category since the 1950s, it seemed as if "race" may become a thing of the past.[60] (Nonetheless, in this first decade of the twenty-first century, there has been a surge of headlines announcing the biomedical usefulness of genetic definitions of racial groups, including the Jews.[61]) It may well be true that Jewishness will some day be defined through ritual practices or beliefs rather than through genealogy; as Shaye Cohen has convincingly noted, "the nexus of religion, ethnicity, and nationality [and I would include "race" in this list] was not revealed to the people of Israel by Moses at Mount Sinai but [was] created by historical Jews living in historical time."[62] By emphasizing that the genealogical definition of Jewishness was a historical invention rather than a divine act, Cohen implies that this problematic aspect of the Jewish tradition is in-essential to its divine nature and to the continued survival of the Jewish people. By contrast, Freud turns to history in order to understand the persistence — the *Unsterblichkeit* [immortality] — of the Jewish tradition, including the genealogical definition of the Jewish people.

This "racial" definition of Jewishness may indeed be something which is better forgotten and which will eventually slip away into the mists of oblivion. However, we should be careful what we wish for. As Freud notes, when a portion of the painful past "returns from oblivion," it "asserts itself with peculiar force, exercises an incomparably powerful influence on people in the mass, and raises an irresistible claim to truth against which logical objections remain powerless."⁶³ Throughout his life, Freud suggested that the return of the repressed is inevitable. In his final book, he extended this theory to suggest that the Jewish people will survive, despite all reforms, repudiations and repressions. As shocking as this may sound, such a guarantee of the future is not necessarily hopeful, for it could also suggest that the "fixity of identity"—and the violence that is so often legitimated by it—is inescapable.

Yet what is perhaps most radical about Freud's theory of Jewishness is not its racial element, but the historical and human origin of this element. Rather than making Jewish difference a matter of divine election, Freud insists that the Jews were chosen by the man Moses, that is, by a human living in historical time. According to Freud's version of the story, the most decisive historical act was not Moses' choice of the Jews, but their own violent act of murder as well as their subsequent efforts to make sense of these decisive acts.⁶⁴ The discomfort—and strength—of Freud's theory of Jewishness is the notion that the repressed *returns* and that we cannot predetermine whether the return will be for better or for worse. We can, however, take historical and human actions to work through these returns and to sustain the more "noble and precious" elements in the future.

Notes

1. Freud to Zweig, September 30, 1934, Sigmund Freud and Arnold Zweig, *The Letters of Sigmund Freud and Arnold Zweig*, trans. Elaine Robson-Scott and William Robson-Scott (New York: Harcourt Brace & World, 1970), 91.

2. See Sigmund Freud, *Moses and Monotheism*, S.E., vol. XXIII (1939), 99. In order to maintain consistency, I include the German whereever Freud uses the word *Geistigkeit* or *geistig(e)*. Unless otherwise noted, all quotations from Freud's work are from James Strachey, ed., *The Standard Edition of the Complete Psychological Works of Sigmund Freud (S.E.)*, trans. James Strachey and Anna Freud, 24 vols. (London: Hogarth and the Institute of Psycho-Analysis, 1953).

3. Michael Mack explores the relationship between Freud's thought and the German Idealist tradition in much more detail. Specifically, he suggests that Freud ironically inverted Kant's proposal that Christ was a revolutionary who inaugurated "an overthrow" of Jewish moral philosophy and thereby "turned the tables on Kant by shedding light on reason's irrationality." See Michael Mack, *German Idealism and the Jew: The Inner Anti-Semitism of Philosophy and German Jewish Responses* (2003), 152, 154.

4. See Jan Assmann, *Moses the Egyptian: The Memory of Egypt in Western Monotheism* (Cambridge, MA: Harvard University Press, 1997), 151.

5. "The new realm of intellectuality [*Geistigkeit*] was opened up, in which ideas, memories and inferences became decisive in contrast to the lower psychical activity which had direct perceptions by the sense-organs as its content." Freud, *Moses and Monotheism*, 113.

6. Ibid., 47.

7. Ibid., 99–100.

8. Ibid., 99.

9. As he explains in the March 1938 Prefatory note to the third essay of *Moses and Monotheism*, "Not that I should have anything to say that would be new or that I did not say clearly a quarter of a century ago." See Ibid., 55.

10. Ibid., 52–53, my emphasis.

11. Though the early Rabbis attempted to construct a Judaism based solely on practice and faith, Boyarin notes that in the Babylonian Talmud they rejected this option, "proposing instead the dis-

tinct ecclesiological principle: 'An Israelite, even if he sins, remains an Israelite.' Daniel Boyarin, "The Christian Invention of Judaism: The Theodosian Empire and the Rabbinic Refusal of Religion" *Representations* 85 (2004): 22.

12. "The story is told in New York of the banker Otto Kahn and the humorist Marshall P. Wilder who was a hunchback. Strolling along Fifth Avenue, Kahn pointed to a church and said: 'Marshall, that's the church I belong to. Did you know that I once was a Jew?' Wilder answered: 'Yes, Otto, and once I was a hunchback.'" Theodor Reik, *Jewish Wit* (New York: Gamut, 1962), 90.

13. This was true for a number of Freud's contemporaries, including his own sons, not to mention Disraeli, who is generally regarded as the first Jewish prime minister of England though he was raised as a Christian. When Max Graf (the father of "Little Hans") asked Freud whether he should raise his son as a Jew or have him baptized, Freud responded, "If you do not let your son grow up as a Jew, you will deprive him of those sources of energy which cannot be replaced by anything else. He will have to struggle as a Jew, and you ought to develop in him all the energy he will need for that struggle. Do not deprive him of that advantage." In other words, even if you do not raise him as a Jew, he will be regarded as such. Since he has inherited Jewishness, you should let him know what it means to "be" a Jew from an insider's perspective. See Max Graf, "Reminiscences of Professor Sigmund Freud," *The Psychoanalytic Quarterly* 11 (1942): 473. See also Jay Geller, "The Godfather of Psychoanalysis: Circumcision, Antisemitism, Homosexuality, and Freud's 'Fighting Jew,'" *Journal of the American Academy of Religion* 67.2 (1999).

14. Freud, *Moses and Monotheism*, 99.

15. On this point, Michael Kramer has argued that all definitions of Jewish literature proceed from a racial definition of Jewishness. His essay in *Prooftexts* elicited a heated debate in which the respondents seemed to protest a bit too much against Kramer's argument. See Michael P. Kramer, "Race, Literary History, and the 'Jewish Question.'" *Prooftexts* 21.3 (2001).

16. Jacques Le Rider goes so far as to suggest that a racial definition of Jewishness is a psychological problem that "Freud radically overcame," forgoing the "temptation of falling back into 'biological,' 'hereditary,' and 'racial' representations of the Jewish identity." Jacques Le Rider, "Jewish Identity in *Moses and Monotheism*," *The Psychohistory Review* 25 (1997): 247. Similarly, Richard Bernstein argues that the racialization of Jewishness is incompatible with its noble and precious ideals: "Freud explicitly denies the importance of biological transmission and *positively* asserts the importance of an 'ideal factor' in Jewish survival." Richard J. Bernstein, *Freud and the Legacy of Moses* (New York: Cambridge University Press, 1998), 113.

17. See Assmann, *Moses the Egyptian: The Memory of Egypt in Western Monotheism*; "Der Fortschritt in der Geistigkeit. Sigmund Freuds Konstruktion des Judentums," *Psyche* 2.56 (2002); Daniel Boyarin, *Unheroic Conduct: The Rise of Heterosexuality and the Invention of the Jewish Man* (Berkeley: University of California Press, 1997).

18. See Sander L. Gilman, *Freud, Race, and Gender* (Princeton, NJ: Princeton University Press, 1993); Larry Stewart, "Freud Before Oedipus: Race and Heredity in the Origins of Psychoanalysis." *Journal of the History of Biology* 9 (1976); Yosef Hayim Yerushalmi, *Freud's Moses: Judaism Terminable and Interminable* (New Haven, CT: Yale University Press, 1991).

19. Yerushalmi, *Freud's Moses: Judaism Terminable and Interminable*, 90.

20. As Yerushalmi has noted, "the sense that Jewishness is both inherited and indelible" is "shared equally by Jews who ... would discard their Jewish identity if they could, as well as by Jews who passionately affirm[ ] that identity." Ibid., 32.

21. Yerushalmi amply demonstrates that Freud's knowledge of Judaism was much broader than Freud liked to publicly proclaim. See Ibid.

22. Lou Andreas-Salomé to Freud, January 1935, Sigmund Freud and Andreas-Salomé, *Letters*, trans. William and Elaine Robson-Scott, ed. Ernst Pfeiffer (New York: Harcourt, Brace, Jovanovich, 1972 [1966]), 206. Bernstein, *Freud and the Legacy of Moses*, 119; Yerushalmi, *Freud's Moses: Judaism Terminable and Interminable*, 78.

23. See Yosef Hayim Yerushalmi, *Assimilation and Racial Anti-Semitism: The Iberian and the German Models*, Leo Baeck Memorial Lecture (New York: Leo Baeck Institute, 1982).

24. See Assmann, "Der Fortschritt in der Geistigkeit. Sigmund Freuds Konstruktion des Judentums," 166–167; "The Advance in Intellectuality: Freud's Construction of Judaism," *New Perspectives on Freud's Moses and Monotheism*, eds. Ruth Ginsburg and Ilana Pardes (Tübingen: Max Niemeyer Verlag, 2006), 16.

25. That Freud saw the "Advance in *Geistigkeit*" as the "quintessence" of his work is evidenced

by the fact that he had his daughter Anna read this section as a ventriloquized lecture at the 1938 Psychoanalytic Congress in Paris. Indeed, even as he thought he might not publish the work in its entirety, he published this section separately in the winter of 1939. See Assmann, "Der Fortschritt in der Geistigkeit. Sigmund Freuds Konstruktion des Judentums," 157; Bernstein, *Freud and the Legacy of Moses*, 82–89.

26. Freud, *Moses and Monotheism*, 113.
27. Ibid.
28. Assmann, "Der Fortschritt in der Geistigkeit. Sigmund Freuds Konstruktion des Judentums," 169.
29. Freud, *Moses and Monotheism*, 114.
30. See Jan Assmann, *Die Mosaische Unterscheidung: oder der Preis des Monotheismus* (Wien: Carl Hanser Verlag, 2003), 166–167.
31. Boyarin calls this a "masculine *Geistigkeit*." See Boyarin, *Unheroic Conduct: The Rise of Heterosexuality and the Invention of the Jewish Man*, 260.
32. It is possible, though unlikely, that Freud did not know that Jewishness is transmitted through the mother's rather than the father's genealogy. However, he probably would not make such a big point — insisting on it twice — about the "preference for paternity" if he did not know that the rabbis generally "prefer" maternity over paternity in determining whether a child is Jewish.
33. Shaye J. D. Cohen, *The Beginnings of Jewishness: Boundaries, Varieties, Uncertainties* (Berkeley: University of California Press, 1999), 264.
34. See Ibid., 263ff.
35. Freud, *Moses and Monotheism*, 114.
36. Boyarin, *Unheroic Conduct: The Rise of Heterosexuality and the Invention of the Jewish Man*.
37. More explicitly, Boyarin argues that by rejecting the carnality of the Jews, Freud masculinizes them: "Where the Jews have been accused of carnality and, therefore, of being like women, Freud ... would demonstrate that they are more spiritual, and more rational, than the Others, and therefore more masculine than the accusers themselves.... Freud set out to counter antisemitic charges that Jews are not spiritual but carnal, female and not male." Ibid., 246, 253.
38. Sigmund Freud, "Recommendations to Physicians Practising Psycho-Analysis," *S.E.*, vol. XII (1912); "Lines of Advance in Psycho-Analytic Therapy," *S.E.*, vol. XVII (1919); *The Future of an Illusion*, *S.E.*, vol. XXI (1927).
39. See Léon Chertok and Isabelle Stengers, *A Critique of Psychoanalytic Reason: Hypnosis as a Scientific Problem from Lavoisier to Lacan*, trans. Martha Noel Evans, in collaboration with the authors (Stanford, CA: Stanford University Press, 1992).
40. Freud, *Moses and Monotheism*, 113.
41. See Nadia Abu El-Haj, "'Bearing the Mark of Israel?' Genetics and the Quest for Jewish Origins," Unpublished draft [personal communication] (2004). See also John M. Efron, *Defenders of the Race: Jewish Doctors and Race Science in Fin-de-Siécle Europe* (New Haven, CT: Yale University Press, 1994); Raphael Falk, "Zionism and the Biology of the Jews," *Science in Context* 11.3–4 (1998).
42. Sander Gilman has thoroughly explored the ways in which Jewish bodies and bodily parts have been portrayed, specifically in terms of penises, feet, noses, smells and hair. See Sander L. Gilman, *The Jew's Body* (New York: Routledge, 1991); *Creating Beauty to Cure the Soul: Race and Psychology in the Shaping of Aesthetic Surgery* (Durham, NC: Duke University Press, 1998).
43. See Boyarin, *Unheroic Conduct: The Rise of Heterosexuality and the Invention of the Jewish Man*, 244ff.
44. Howard Eilberg-Schwartz, *People of the Body: Jews and Judaism from an Embodied Perspective* (Albany: State University of New York Press, 1992), 5. See also Boyarin, *Unheroic Conduct: The Rise of Heterosexuality and the Invention of the Jewish Man*, 246–248. More recent revivals of the "Tough Jew" can be found in the revival of the Maccabees' "heroic" story, the delight in Alan Dershowitz's "tough" *chutzpah*, and the romanticization of Jewish gangsters in two books titled, *Tough Jews*. See Paul Breines, *Tough Jews: Political Fantasies and the Moral Dilemma of American Jewry* (New York: HarperCollins, 1990); Rich Cohen, *Tough Jews: Fathers, Sons and Gangster Dreams* (New York: Simon and Schuster, 1998).
45. See for example, Boyarin, *Unheroic Conduct: The Rise of Heterosexuality and the Invention of the Jewish Man*, 246ff; Hermann Cohen, *Religion of Reason: Out of the Sources of Judaism*, trans. Simon Kaplan (New York: Frederick Ungar, 1972).
46. Eilberg-Schwartz, *People of the Body: Jews and Judaism from an Embodied Perspective*, 1. For

the recent return to matters of the (Jewish) body, see the recent essay by Kirshenblatt-Gimblet which documents the emerging split in Jewish Studies between the new "Berkeley (or California) school" of studies of the "People of the Body" and the older (east coast-based) school of studies of the "People of the Book." Barbara Kirshenblatt-Gimblett, "The Corporeal Turn." *Jewish Quarterly Review* 95.3 (2005).

47. Florida Holocaust Museum, *What Is Judaism?* 2003, Available: http://www.flholocaustmuseum.org/history_wing/antisemitism/related_topics/judaism.cfm, September 26, 2005.

48. To counter William Z. Ripley's claims that the Jews were not a race, Joseph Jacobs argued that they were the most pure race. Joseph Jacobs, "Are Jews Jews?" *Popular Science Monthly* 55 (1899); *The Jewish Race: A Study in National Character* (London: Privately printed, 1899); William Z. Ripley, "The Racial Geography of Europe: A Sociological Study, Supplement: The Jews." *Popular Science Monthly* 54 (1899). By contrast, Maurice Fishberg went to anthropological lengths to demonstrate that the Jews were not a distinct racial group. Maurice Fishberg, *The Jews: A Study of Race and Environment* (New York: Walter Scott, 1911). See also Abu El-Haj, "'Bearing the Mark of Israel?' Genetics and the Quest for Jewish Origins."; Efron, *Defenders of the Race: Jewish Doctors and Race Science in Fin-de-Siécle Europe*; Falk, "Zionism and the Biology of the Jews"; Eric L. Goldstein, "'Different Blood Flows in Our Veins': Race and Jewish Self-Definition in Late Nineteenth Century America." *American Jewish History* 85.1 (1997).

49. Freud, *Moses and Monotheism*, 115.

50. Ibid.

51. In *Civilization and its Discontents* Freud reiterates that he had come to this conclusion by analyzing *Chritianity* specifically. "From the manner in which, in Christianity, this redemption is achieved — by the sacrificial death of a single person, who in this manner takes upon himself a guilt that is common to everyone — we have been able to infer what the first occasion may have been on which this primal guilt, which was also the beginning of civilization, was acquired." Sigmund Freud, *Civilization and its Discontents*, S.E., vol. XXI (1930), 136. See also Sigmund Freud, *Totem and Taboo*, S.E., vol. XIII (1913), 153–155.

52. Jacqueline Rose, "Response to Edward Said," *Freud and the Non-European* (New York: Verso, 2003), 75.

53. Freud, *Moses and Monotheism*, 69–70, my italics.

54. Ibid., 115.

55. While the possibility of conversion to Judaism might seem to disprove the purely genealogical injunction to "be" Jewish, in fact, the process of conversion emphasizes this logic: the "convert is adopted into the [Jewish] family and assigned a new 'genealogical' identity," by receiving a new Jewish name whose ending is "ben Avraham" or "bas Avraham" (son or daughter of Abraham). See Daniel Boyarin, *A Radical Jew: Paul and the Politics of Identity* (Berkeley: University of California Press, 1994), 240–241.

56. Following Jan Assmann's argument about the mnemohistory of Egypt, one could argue that for a person to "successfully" convert (away from Judaism, in this case), she must continue to remember her past. As Assman writes, "Conversion defines itself as the result of an overcoming and a liberation from one's own past which is no longer one's own. Remembering their disowned past is obligatory for converts in order not to relapse." Assmann, *Moses the Egyptian: The Memory of Egypt in Western Monotheism*, 7.

57. I thank Geoffrey Bowker for suggesting this comparison.

58. Slavoj Žižek, *Enjoy Your Symptom! Jacques Lacan in Hollywood and Out* (New York: Routledge, 1992), 14.

59. See, for example, Bernstein, *Freud and the Legacy of Moses*.

60. Of course, in America and elsewhere, "race" is not a thing of the past and it is not simply "genealogical": skin color continues to function as a way of ascertaining whether a person is likely to have experienced racism.

61. See Jenny Reardon, "Race and Human Difference in a Genomic Age," *differences: A Journal of Feminist Cultural Studies* 15.3 (2004).

62. Cohen, *The Beginnings of Jewishness: Boundaries, Varieties, Uncertainties*, 348.

63. Freud, *Moses and Monotheism*, 85.

64. Ruth Ginsburg's essay compliments my point here: The primary trauma is "the experience of being aggressive perpetrators. Only in the second place is it the trauma of a persecuted victim." See Ruth Ginsburg, "Whose Trauma Is It Anyway? Some Reflections on Freud's Traumatic His-

tory," *New Perspectives on Freud's Moses and Monotheism*, eds. Ruth Ginsburg and Ilana Pardes (Tübingen: Niemeyer, 2006), 80.

References

Abu El-Haj, Nadia. "'Bearing the Mark of Israel?' Genetics and the Quest for Jewish Origins." Unpublished draft (personal communication), 2004.
Assmann, Jan (1997). *Moses the Egyptian: The Memory of Egypt in Western Monotheism*. Cambridge, MA: Harvard University Press.
_____ (2002). "Der Fortschritt in der Geistigkeit: Sigmund Freuds Konstruktion des Judentums." *Psyche* 2 (56): 154–171.
_____ (2003). *Die Mosaische Unterscheidung: oder der Preis des Monotheismus*. Wien: Carl Hanser Verlag.
_____ (2006). "The Advance in Intellectuality: Freud's Construction of Judaism." *New Perspectives on Freud's Moses and Monotheism*. Ed. Ruth Ginsburg and Ilana Pardes. Tübingen: Max Niemeyer Verlag.
Bernstein, Richard J. (1998). *Freud and the Legacy of Moses*. New York: Cambridge University Press.
Boyarin, Daniel (1994). *A Radical Jew: Paul and the Politics of Identity*. Berkeley: University of California Press.
_____ (1997). *Unheroic Conduct: The Rise of Heterosexuality and the Invention of the Jewish Man*. Berkeley: University of California Press.
_____ (2004). "The Christian Invention of Judaism: The Theodosian Empire and the Rabbinic Refusal of Religion." *Representations* 85: 21–57.
Breines, Paul (1990). *Tough Jews: Political Fantasies and the Moral Dilemma of American Jewry*. New York: Harper Collins.
Chertok, Léon, and Isabelle Stengers (1992). *A Critique of Psychoanalytic Reason: Hypnosis as a Scientific Problem from Lavoisier to Lacan*. Trans. Martha Noel Evans, in collaboration with the authors. Stanford, CA: Stanford University Press.
Cohen, Hermann (1919 [1972]). *Religion of Reason: Out of the Sources of Judaism*. Trans. Simon Kaplan. New York: Frederick Ungar.
Cohen, Rich (1998). *Tough Jews: Fathers, Sons and Gangster Dreams*. New York: Simon and Schuster.
Cohen, Shaye J.D. (1998). *The Beginnings of Jewishness: Boundaries, Varieties, Uncertainties*. Berkeley: University of California Press.
Efron, John M. (1994). *Defenders of the Race: Jewish Doctors and Race Science in Fin-de-Siécle Europe*. New Haven, CT: Yale University Press.
Eilberg-Schwartz, Howard (1992). *People of the Body: Jews and Judaism from an Embodied Perspective*. Albany: State University of New York Press.
Falk, Raphael (1998). "Zionism and the Biology of the Jews." *Science in Context* 11 (3–4): 587–607
Fishberg, Maurice (1911). *The Jews: A Study of Race and Environment*. New York: Walter Scott.
Florida Holocaust Museum (2003). "What Is Judaism?" http://www.flholocaustmuseum.org/history_wing/antisemitism/related_topics/judaism.cfm. September 26, 2005.
Freud, Sigmund (1912). "Recommendations to Physicians Practising Psycho-Analysis." *Standard Edition* Vol. XII.
_____ (1913). *Totem and Taboo*. [1912–1913]. *Standard Edition* Vol. XIII.
_____ (1919). "Lines of Advance in Psycho-Analytic Therapy." *Standard Edition* [1918]. Vol. XVII.
_____ (1927). *The Future of an Illusion*. *Standard Edition* Vol. XXI.
_____ (1930). *Civilization and its Discontents*. *Standard Edition* Vol. XXI.
_____ (1939). *Moses and Monotheism*. [1934–1938]. *Standard Edition* Vol. XXIII.
Freud, Sigmund, and Andreas-Salomé (1972 [1966]). *Letters*. Trans. William and Elaine Robson-Scott. Ed. Ernst Pfeiffer. New York: Harcourt, Brace, Jovanovich
Freud, Sigmund, and Arnold Zweig (1970). *The Letters of Sigmund Freud and Arnold Zweig*. Trans. Elaine Robson-Scott and William Robson-Scott. New York: Harcourt Brace & World.
Geller, Jay (1999). "The Godfather of Psychoanalysis: Circumcision, Antisemitism, Homosexuality, and Freud's 'Fighting Jew.'" *Journal of the American Academy of Religion* 67 (2): 355–385.

Gilman, Sander L. (1991). *The Jew's Body*. New York: Routledge.
_____ (1993). *Freud, Race, and Gender*. Princeton, NJ: Princeton University Press.
_____ (1998). *Creating Beauty to Cure the Soul: Race and Psychology in the Shaping of Aesthetic Surgery*. Durham, NC: Duke University Press.
Ginsburg, Ruth (2006). "Whose Trauma Is It Anyway? Some Reflections on Freud's Traumatic History." *New Perspectives on Freud's Moses and Monotheism*. Ed. Ruth Ginsburg and Ilana Pardes. Tübingen: Niemeyer, 77–91.
Goldstein, Eric L. (1997). "'Different Blood Flows in Our Veins': Race and Jewish Self-Definition in Late Nineteenth Century America." *American Jewish History* 85 (1): 29–55.
Graf, Max (1942). "Reminiscences of Professor Sigmund Freud." *The Psychoanalytic Quarterly* 11.
Jacobs, Joseph (1899). "Are Jews Jews?" *Popular Science Monthly* 55: 502–511.
_____ (1899). *The Jewish Race: A Study in National Character*. London: Privately printed.
Kirshenblatt-Gimblett, Barbara (2005). "The Corporeal Turn." *Jewish Quarterly Review* 95 (3): 447–461. Available: http://muse.jhu.edu/journals/jewish_quarterly_review/v095/95.3kirshenblatt-gimblett.html.
Kramer, Michael P. (2001). "Race, Literary History, and the 'Jewish Question.'" *Prooftexts* 21 (3): 287–321.
Le Rider, Jacques (1997). "Jewish Identity in *Moses and Monotheism*." *The Psychohistory Review* 25: 245–254
Mack, Michael (2003). *German Idealism and the Jew: The Inner Anti-Semitism of Philosophy and German Jewish Responses*. Chicago: University of Chicago Press.
Reardon, Jenny (2004). "Race and Human Difference in a Genomic Age." *differences: A Journal of Feminist Cultural Studies* 15 (3): 38–65
Reik, Theodor (1962). *Jewish Wit*. New York: Gamut.
Ripley, William Z. (1899). "The Racial Geography of Europe: A Sociological Study. Supplement: The Jews." *Popular Science Monthly* 54: 163–175, 338–351
Rose, Jacqueline (2003). "Response to Edward Said." In *Freud and the Non-European*. New York: Verso, 2003.
Stewart, Larry (1976). "Freud Before Oedipus: Race and Heredity in the Origins of Psychoanalysis." *Journal of the History of Biology* 9: 215–228.
Strachey, James, ed. (1953). *The Standard Edition of the Complete Psychological Works of Sigmund Freud (S.E.)*. Trans. James Strachey and Anna Freud. 24 vols. London: Hogarth and the Institute of Psycho-Analysis.
Yerushalmi, Yosef Hayim (1982). *Assimilation and Racial Anti-Semitism: The Iberian and the German Models: Leo Baeck Memorial Lecture*. New York: Leo Baeck Institute.
_____ (1991). *Freud's Moses: Judaism Terminable and Interminable*. New Haven, CT: Yale University Press.
Žižek, Slavoj (1992). *Enjoy Your Symptom! Jacques Lacan in Hollywood and Out*. New York: Routledge.

Freud and Levinas
Talmud and Psychoanalysis Before the Letter
ETHAN KLEINBERG

The names Sigmund Freud and Emmanuel Levinas conjure up vastly different images of Jewish identity. In most tellings, Freud is identified with atheism, assimilation, science, and secular Jewish thought. By contrast, the Lithuanian born French philosopher Levinas is identified with ritual observance, the study of Talmud, and religious Jewish thought. Thus if one were to consider these two thinkers under the rubric of "God and Godlessness," the pairing of Sigmund Freud and Emmanuel Levinas seems justified if one assumes Levinas will provide the "God" and Freud the "Godlessness." But the pairing becomes more interesting if we allow the "God and Godlessness" to serve as a common formative issue in the upbringing and education of these two apparently disparate thinkers. I would like to suggest that for both Freud and Levinas this issue of God and Godlessness in relation to the question of what it means to be a Jew comes to a head in their respective use and application of the figure of Moses.

Freud's *The Man Moses and the Monotheistic Religion* is a strange book and one that has attracted serious attention from scholars including Richard Bernstein in *Freud and the Legacy of Moses* and I must confess that I owe a debt to Professor Bernstein's work in the formation of this essay as will become apparent. But it was Yosef Yerushalmi's discussion of the "Talmudic" nature of Freud's *Moses* coupled with Levinas's stated recourse to "psychoanalysis before the letter" in his Talmudic lecture from 1963, *Towards the Other*, that is the basis of this investigation.[1]

My first intuition was to search for the "Talmudic" in Freud and the "psychoanalytic" in Levinas but as I was reading *The Man Moses and the Monotheistic Religion* I was struck by another and apparently more controversial reading. The opening sentence of *Moses and Monotheism* has rightly been a lightning rod for religious, philosophical, and historical commentary. Freud states: "To deny a people the man whom it praises as the greatest of its sons is not a deed to be undertaken lightheartedly — especially by one belonging to that people."[2]

There are many ways to approach this sentence but I would like to do so using Amos Funkenstein's concept of "counter history." For Funkenstein, counterhistories form a specific genre of history "whose function is polemical. Their method consists of the systematic exploitation of the adversary's most trusted sources against their grain — 'die Geschichte gegen den Strich kämmen.' Their aim is the distortion of the adversary's self-image, of his identity, through the deconstruction of his memory."[3] Now the use of this term is complicated by whether one sees Freud as an adversary or advocate of "Judaism" but there is no doubt that Freud's reading employs the most trusted sources of Judaism read against the grain. If Moses was an Egyptian, as Freud argues in this work, and if the monotheistic religion is in fact the creation of the Egyptian Pharoah Akhenaten, then Freud has transposed the identities of the Hebrews and the Egyptian in a fashion that turns the oppressors (the Egyptians) into the saviors and further turns the oppressed (the Hebrews) into the oppressors through the murder of this Egyptian Moses at the hands of the Hebrew people. Thus Freud has provided a counter-historical account of the Exodus that subverts the meaning of the original narrative. But Freud's argument, and Funkenstein's interpretive category, assumes an immanent historical approach that subordinates or denies the possibility of transcendent meaning. To put it simply, it privileges historical understanding over divine revelation.

But there is another definition of "counter history" or to put it more accurately "counter historicism" that has been employed by Samuel Moyn and myself in the investigation of Emmanuel Levinas's work.[4] In this usage, "counter history" does not contain the same political connotations as in Funkenstein's variant and as are manifest in Freud's contentious claim about the origins of Jewish identity. Instead, "counterhistoricism" refers to the infinite nature of a thought or ideal that transcends time and space. Emmanuel Levinas's counterhistoricism asserts that certain lessons, ideas, and morals transcend time and are thus always accessible regardless of the specific historical context.

Thus in contrast to Freud's counter-historical Moses whose true identity is revealed by scientific, historical, and psychoanalytic analysis, Levinas's counterhistorical Moses is one whose teachings transcend time, space and historical context. Levinas tells a story about Moses who wants to know the future of the Talmud. Moses is transported to Rabbi Akiba's academy. When Moses enters the school he is disconsolate to discover that he doesn't understand anything of the lessons being taught. His mood is lifted, however, when at the end of the session Rabbi Akiba attributes his lesson to the teachings of Moses at Mt. Sinai. Here the eternal message is delivered within the context of temporal change and the authority of Rabbi Akiba is not questioned despite the incomprehensibility of his teachings to Moses. Thus Levinas places his emphasis on the transcendent communicability of God via the rule of Law as revealed to Moses.

In Freud and Levinas, the use of Moses highlights the issue of immanence and transcendence in relation to Judaism, Jewish thought, and Jewish history. The psychoanalytic investigation into Moses and the monotheistic religion provides an immanent historical understanding of the Jewish people whereas Levinas's investigation into revelation and the permanence/infinite nature of Torah and Talmud emphasize the transcendent nature of Judaism. I suppose this would also correlate to the Levinas/God, Freud/Godless distinction. But I would mislead you if I suggested that there was such a distinct divide between the two for traces of each can be found in the other. There is transcendence in Freud and immanence in Levinas.

It should come as no surprise to find the concepts or categories of immanence and transcendence wrapped around each other in any discussion of Jewish thought. And while the title of this paper is "Talmud and Psychoanalysis Before the Letter" I could have pushed things further and referred to Talmud and psychoanalysis before the law because for both Freud and Levinas, an essential moment in the history of the Jewish people (of the culture and religion) is the revelation and presentation of the Ten Commandments and the Torah: the books of Moses. Here we can also refer to the significance that Derrida affords this originary or arche moment of archivization in *Mal d'Archives* and there is much to be said about this relation as well.[5]

But I want to turn our focus to the character of the Torah, the books of Moses, which is in itself an imminent object that implies the transcendent. As such it is the embodiment of this conflict, this tension between a historical reality conditioned by material circumstance and the infinite, unconditional, and unrepresentable force that gives it its authority. The tension embodied in this work authored by, or revealed to, Moses is what both Freud and Levinas see as the key to understanding the longevity and future of the Jewish people.

Now it must be said that Freud and Levinas are the products of different milieus, educational trajectories, and even cultures, as we will discuss presently. But it is also important to note that Freud was composing his *Moses* in the 1930s at the same time that Levinas was looking to the concept of transcendence in order to break with his former teacher (and at the time Nazi party member) Martin Heidegger.[6] Thus the historical context of the mounting pressure of anti-Semitism in Austria and France provide the backdrop for our investigation into the specific uses, and perhaps abuses, of Moses in the service of some of the more peculiar assertions in the endeavors of both thinkers.

I will start with Freud. This serves our purposes well because Freud represents the enlightened Maskilim in the most canonical sense of the term. Yerushalmi's assertions not withstanding, Freud represents a familiar trajectory for German speaking cosmopolitan Jews. Whether or not Freud knew Hebrew or Yiddish, whether or not he was versed in the religion of his fathers, Freud chose to present himself as a secular Jew absolved of the burden of religious belief and instead shackled to the project of scientific investigation. His early work on Feuerbach, whom in 1875 he claimed "among all other philosophers I worship and admire this man the most," set the table for his future assessment of religion.⁷ Feuerbach's indefatigable mission to unmask theology as the outcome of purely human needs resonates in all of Freud's works. Indeed the language of Freuds's statement about Feuerbach highlights the transition from the "worship" of religion to the "worship" of one who sought to uncover the underlying, and entirely human, sources of religious belief. Freud's views were not outside the mainstream of enlightened German Jewish culture as annunciated by the project of the Science of Judaism (*Wissenschaft des Judentums*), itself a nineteenth century phenomenon announced by Immanuel Wolf in his 1822 essay *On the Concept of the Science of Judaism*. In this essay Wolf asserts "the fundamental principle of Judaism is again in a state of inner ferment, striving to assume a shape in harmony with the spirit of the time. But in accordance with the age, this development can only take place through the medium of science. For the scientific attitude is the characteristic of our time."⁸ By the early twentieth century, it was clear that this "scientific attitude" was antagonistic toward categories such as faith that could not be demonstrated through objective data and Freud's own rigorous science of psychoanalysis was clearly poised to expose the purely human aspects of religion and Freud makes this explicit in *Totem and Taboo* and *The Future of an Illusion*.

But this leads Freud to a problem that he articulates in his introduction to the 1930 Hebrew translation of *Totem and Taboo*.

> No reader of [the Hebrew version of] this book will find it easy to put himself in the emotional position of an author who is ignorant of the language of holy writ, who is completely estranged from the religion of his fathers— as well as from every other religion — who cannot take a share in nationalist ideals, but who has yet never repudiated his people, who feels that he is in his essential nature a Jew and who has no desire to alter that nature. If the question were put to him: "Since you have abandoned all these common characteristics of your countrymen, what is there left to you that is Jewish?" He could not now express that essence clearly in words; but some day, no doubt, it will become accessible to the scientific mind.⁹

The issue at hand is how to understand the essence of Judaism divorced from any religious pretenses. Freud was committed to the process of *bildung*, secularization and assimilation in his lifestyle and his work but this should not be equated with conversion or the sacrifice of his Jewish identity. Yerushalmi and Bernstein are both very instructive on this point. The commitment to a secular understanding of religion, thus Judaism, and the problems this raises in relation to any sort of "Jewish identity" seems to be the *raison d'être* of his Moses book. It is the basis for his counter historical claim that Moses was an Egyptian and that the origins of the Jewish people are the direct result of this "great man" and not divine revelation. Freud tells us that the Jews were not chosen by God but instead chosen by Moses. The question as to why Freud would make such a move at a time of mounting anti-Semitic persecution and on the eve of one of the darkest chapters in the history of the Jewish people is a source of great speculation. It is what makes Freud's *Moses* so strange. By removing the transcendent theological imperative as the basis of Judaism (God's choice) Freud opens onto an ontological and purely anthropological question about the essence of Judaism that he hopes to answer via the science of psychoanalysis.

Here I'd like to turn to an aspect of Freud's *Moses* that is discussed at length in the studies by Yerushalmi, Derrida and Bernstein. Freud's historical argument that Moses was an Egyptian follower of the monotheistic religion of Akhenaten, who in the face of persecution from the Egyptian authorities chose to bestow his religion on the Hebrew people, seems to lack substantial historical support.[10] But as it turns out the argument does not rest on historical evidence so much as psychoanalytic evidence as is revealed when Freud tells that there was not one Moses but two. The Egyptian Moses, the stern and strict father figure who was the tireless advocate of a monotheism that forbid graven images, was killed by the Hebrew people who incorporated these traits into their early conception of God based on their memory of Moses "for in truth it was not an invisible god but the man Moses who led them out of Egypt."[11] But if Moses was killed why wasn't the Jewish religion abandoned and how is it that two generations later (according to Freud) the second Moses came to found the religion of Judaism that fused the volcanic Jahve religion with the monotheistic religion of the Egyptian Moses? And how did the traits of the human Moses come to be ascribed to the former volcano God? For Yerushalmi this is a source of great consternation, as Freud's extrapolation from individual cases of trauma to the history of the Jewish people (or religion in general) appears to sit on very shaky ground that can only be supported by recourse to the discredited evolutionary theory of acquired characteristics espoused by Lamarck. Freud tells us that if "we accept the continued existence of such memory-traces in our archaic inheritance [heritage], then we have bridged the gap between individual and mass [group] psychology and can treat peoples as we do the individual neurotic."[12] This assertion requires the inheritance of memory traces independent of direct communication or education and thus some sort of "phylogenetic" transmission of traumatic memory from generation to generation.[13] It is this leap that Yerushalmi finds embarrassing. But Richard Bernstein has shown Freud's position to be more circumspect, more nuanced and more fruitful and I would like to follow his lead. Bernstein tells us that while Freud does have some Lamarckian proclivities, they are not "striking or radical in the way in which Yerushalmi (and others) indicate." Instead Bernstein offers the possibility that what Freud has discovered "is that there are certain basic psychological dispositions and characteristics" and that these must be factored into our understanding of biological evolution.[14] I would like to build on this based on work in the field of cultural evolutionary studies and evolutionary history.

In his work from 1976, *The Selfish Gene,* Richard Dawkins presents a construct he refers to as the meme.[15] The meme (a shortening of the Greek "mineme" meaning imitation) is precisely an acquired cultural trait that is passed down from generation to generation through natural selection: "Fashions in dress and diet, ceremonies and customs, art and architecture, all evolve in historical time in a way that looks like highly speeded up genetic evolution, but has really nothing to do with genetic evolution."[16] If we emphasize the transmission of ceremonies and customs, would it be too far a stretch to suggest that Freud is presenting the possibility that cultural traits are passed down from generation to generation through the interaction of parents and children but also predicated on cultural norms in a way that the response to a trauma long removed is re-enacted, encoded, and phylo-memetically transmitted so that the neurosis of the individual would precisely mimic, or at least be generated by, the neurosis of the group? Especially given Dawkins statement that "When you plant a fertile meme in my mind you literally parasitize my brain, turning it into a vehicle for the meme's propagation."[17] It is also the case that for Dawkins, the longer a meme survives the more fertile it is, and the more accurate its replications. One can't help but think of Freud's discussion of the longevity of the Jewish people. This may be too much so let us look to a separate instance of evolutionary history to provide an historical template that corresponds to Freud's own historical investigation in *Moses*.

In William McNeil's *Plagues and Peoples* from 1977, McNeil provides a macro narrative of human development based on Darwinian evolutionary theory and specifically the role that disease plays in the history of humankind.[18] In this book the parasite seems to be afforded far more agency than any individual but it is really evolution that dictates why and how historical events occur. One example of McNeil's methodology will serve us well.[19] In his analysis of the origins of the Black Plague in Europe, McNeil admits that he does not have sufficient historical evidence to recreate the conditions that led to the outbreak of bubonic plague. What he does have is evidence from more recent outbreaks and using an evolutionary framework he discerns the processes that lead from parasitic stasis to outbreak. Because the model is evolutionary and the process of natural selection is constant, McNeil can use his investigation into the plague outbreak in 1894 to give us an historically plausible account of the origins of the plague outbreak in the fourteenth century. Now this argument is based on scientific observation of verifiable data, it is immanent, but what is interesting is that it allows for a permanence of meaning based on a certain notion of the transcendent truth of natural selection. The mechanism used to analyze the modern case history is equally applicable to past events. But the longevity of this explanation comes at the expense of human agency.

I would like to argue that Freud follows the same scientific logic in his historical analysis of Moses which is not based on any hard evidence of what happened in the past but instead on the discoveries of psychoanalysis in the present. Like McNeil, Freud asserts that there is a permanent, in this case psychic, mechanism that is at play and given the correct conditions the archaic memory can be triggered. Thus the murder of the Egyptian Moses turns out to be the repetition of the killing of the primal father as enunciated in *Totem and Taboo*.

Bernstein tells us this acting out is the result of the psychic memory but triggered by specific historical events. "The great deed and misdeed of primeval times, the murder of the father, was brought home to the Jews, for fate decreed that they should repeat it on the person of Moses, an eminent father substitute."[20] But as with the first patricide this crime is also repressed and the memory lies latent until such historical conditions occur as to bring it forth again with the arrival of the second Moses and the transformation of the Yahweh religion. So again we see a scientific model that allows for historical understanding predicated on a certain notion of transcendence.[21] For Freud's analysis to hold, the primal trauma can never be overcome and must sit locked within our psychic make up waiting to be triggered. As with McNeil, Freud's analysis assumes a permanence that allows for explanation but at the expense of agency.

Perhaps more important, Freud uses this investigative strategy to conserve a permanent essence of Judaism that will always survive. It is an encoded trace memory that evolved into an advance in intellectuality (*Der Fortschritt in der Geistigkeit*).[22] Furthermore this explanation of an inherited Jewish character allows Freud to assert the permanent or transcendent essence of Jewishness. Here Freud takes the mantle from the great man Moses who gave Judaism its essence. Freud reveals the historical truth about Moses and Jewishness and in so doing revokes the divine Revelation at Sinai and removes the cloak of religion. This then allows Freud to place his own legacy as the next advance (*der Fortschritt*) in the intellectuality (*der Geistigkeit*) of the Jewish people.[23] One might argue that this is Freud the Talmudist who has uncovered the deepest secret of Judaism and has done so before the letter, by looking at the moment before the creation of the books of Moses. For Freud, Torah in and of itself is not the answer although it holds the clues to understand the importance of the man Moses. And yet it is still the Torah that provides the material for Freud's psychoanalytic investigation. And here we should be instructed by Derrida's discussion of Jacob Freud's gift to his son Sigmund: the bible of his youth but clothed in a new skin.[24] Indeed, the contents of the Torah do not change for Freud but the skin does. The stories and lessons of the Bible are to be conserved but now seen under the book cover of Freud's psychoanalytic understanding of religion. Thus Derrida's reference to a second circumcision, a second covenant, is made explicit in Freud's understanding of the essence of Judaism that conserves its transcendent quality but devoid of religion.

At the same time that Freud was working through the possibilities of a de-divinized Judaism, Emmanuel Levinas was performing a *Teshuvot* or return to the religion of his youth. Now it would be wrong to claim that Levinas was a Talmudic scholar in the traditional sense of the term. While he was raised in Vilna, Lithuania (the home of the famous Talmudic institutes of the Gaon of Vilna and Chaim of Volon) he did not study Talmud in his youth but came to it in the late 1940s and 1950s. Indeed he came to Talmud after the famous Talmudic institutes had been destroyed and the instructors killed in the Shoah.

There is a chasm between Levinas and the Talmudic traditions of Vilna that surrounded him in his youth but that he certainly did not embrace. Like Freud, Levinas was raised in an enlightened Jewish household. His parents owned a Russian bookstore and spoke Russian to him at home. Levinas went to Russian schools for as long as he could and then attended Moses Schwabes' *Gymnasium*. His parents did not intend him to become a rabbinic scholar but to attend a University and this is how Levinas came to study at the University of Strasbourg and then with Heidegger in Freiburg. There are certainly similarities between the assimilationist tendencies of the Freuds and the Levinases but here it is essential to stress that Maskilim in Vilna were not the Maskilim of Vienna. Levinas was not an assimilated Jew in the modern German, French or Austrian sense of the term. He was probably closer to Moses Mendelsohn than the more secular young Gershom Scholem or Raymond Aron and certainly less secular than Freud. Throughout his life Levinas was ritually observant but the belief that Levinas was trained as a Talmudic scholar overplays the importance of religious observance for Levinas. In contrast one must be careful not to overplay the importance of enlightenment or *Bildung* either. Any study of Levinas must take account of the importance of both Enlightenment and cultural assimilation as well as religious piety and ritual observance.

But here I want to point to a definitive moment in Levinas's philosophical career. Up until the second world-war, Levinas's emphasis was on the importance of philosophy in the service of understanding religion or the possibility of religion. After the war and the Shoah this relationship was inverted and from this point on Levinas presents religion as the necessary precondition for philosophy. This is evidenced by his turn to Talmud after the war but one can also read this in *Totality and Infinity* from 1961.

But the turn to Talmud and to Moses cannot be seen as a continuation of the Lithuanian Talmudic tradition. The debt to Torah of which Levinas speaks in the 1960s was not paid until after the war. Instead we must recognize Levinas's use of Talmud and Moses as indebted to extra talmudic sources such as phenomenology and perhaps most important the work of Søren Kierkegaard. I have argued elsewhere that the source of Levinas's counterhistoricism, his emphasis on meaning that transcends time, is the work of Søren Kierkegaard but while Levinas is not a traditional Talmudist he is not a protestant either.[25]

In Kierkegaard's presentation, a story such as that of Abraham and Isaac is as meaningful to us today as it was to the first Hebrews because: "no generation begins other than where its predecessors did, every generation begins from the beginning, the succeeding generation comes no further than the previous one, provided the latter was true to its task and didn't betray it."[26] This statement is a response to the Hegelian view of history that was popular in the mid–nineteenth century. The movement away from Hegel is not incidental as Levinas follows Kierkegaard in part to move away from the Hegelian variants that were popular in Levinas's France. But Levinas also wants to escape the rule of history, and perhaps the very real historical conditions that surrounded him in the 1940s (the Shoah). It is also this emphasis on the transcendent quality of the Torah and Talmud that allows Levinas to cross the "bridge of longing" between the destroyed Vilna of his youth and the Paris of his present. For Levinas the issue is Ethics and the turn to Talmud is a reversal of his pre-war emphasis on philosophy (an emphasis troubled throughout the thirties by Heidegger's political choices). After the Shoah, philosophy could not be trusted to provide an Ethics and because Levinas's focus is Ethics, the paradigmatic figure is not Abraham but Moses.

Levinas is not content to let Kierkegaard's "Knight of Faith" bask in personal salvation and instead looks to Moses who was given the daunting challenge of translating divine will into law. For Levinas it is essential that the Law be universal and communicable. But it must also be temporal, even if it is has recourse to the eternal, and this occurs via the study of Talmud. It is not the word of God in a miraculous sense but the word of God in our own context. Here the transcendent touches on the immanent and one cannot help but notice the way that the historical event of the Shoah serves as the impetus for Levinas's return to Talmud and his counterhistoricsm.

The use of Moses points to some striking affinities between Freud and Levinas, especially in regard to the relation between Judaism and Christianity and the role of anti–Semitism in understanding Jewish identity. Freud characterizes Christianity as a regression of the intellectual advance of the rigorous monotheism of the Jews insofar as it is a return to a polytheism of sorts.[27] In one of his earliest forays into Talmud, "Place and Utopia" from 1950, Levinas characterizes Christianity as a religion of myth, a story for children where the Father will take care of them and miracles supplant agency and responsibility. Levinas presents Judaism as a religion for adults attached to the here and now. For Levinas, Judaism has "chosen action and the divine word moves it only as Law [Mosaic Law]. This action does not tackle the Whole in a global and magical fashion, but grapples with the particular."[28] Both see Christianity as a regression from the more mature stance taken by Judaism and presented as an "advance in intellectuality" by Freud and a "religion for adults" by Levinas. Both also see this as one of the sources of anti–Semitism.

But there are serious differences between Levinas and Freud highlighted by their uses of Moses. In his 1964 Talmudic lecture on "The Temptation of Temptation," Levinas examines a text from the tractate *Shabbat* pp. 88a and 88b. The text itself is a discussion of the moment in Exodus when Moses brought the Torah to the Jewish people, Rav Abdima bar Hama bar Hasa instructs us that the Lord said "If you accept the Torah, all is well, if not here will be your grave."[29] The tract is about Moses but the emphasis is on the seemingly predetermined choice in response to the Lord's statement. The issue gets more interesting for Levinas as he tells us that the "temptation of temptation" of which he speaks "may well describe the condition of the west." This temptation of temptation is the temptation of philosophy, the seduction of reason as a tool by which humans can master and control the world around them. We must also be aware that this temptation is one that seduced Levinas in the years before World War Two and led him to Heidegger. "Philosophy, in any case, can be defined as the subordination of any act to the knowledge one may have of the act ... the act in its naiveté is made to lose its innocence. Now it will arise only after calculation, after a careful weighing of pros and cons. It will no longer leave the other in its otherness but will always include it in the whole ... from this stems the inability to recognize the other person as other person, as outside all calculation, as neighbor, as first come."[30] Make no mistake that Levinas is claiming that the love of, or quest for, knowledge in and of itself is the obfuscation or even obliteration of Ethics. It is the denial of the Other based on the hubris of the self that believes it can obtain the truth on its own. Freud would certainly have succumbed to the temptation of temptation in Levinas's eyes. But if knowledge, philosophical or scientific, is not the answer then what is? Here Levinas returns to Moses: "The revelation which is at stake in the following text will permit us to discover this order prior to the one in which a thought tempted by temptation is found."[31] This is a revelation conditioned by the threat of death: "The teaching, which the Torah is, cannot come to the human being as a result of a choice." I suppose one could think about the ways that Freud's definition of Jewishness is not the result of a choice either. But Levinas continues: "That which must be received in order to make freedom of choice possible cannot have been chosen, unless after the fact."[32] In Levinas's reading the consent to Torah is given before the revelation of the laws of Moses and is done so only when faced with the alternative of death. God chose the Jewish people. Thus for Levinas, Revelation is the condition for reason. This is why Levinas refers to the biblical response "we will do and we will hear." The doing precedes the hearing, the act of accepting comes before we hear the commandment.

But there is more at stake here for Levinas because even during times of crisis or turmoil, even when seemingly all of the Jewish people have strayed from the path, Revelation is still accessible. Thus even when the Hebrews chose to worship the golden calf and thus lost their adornments, Moses maintained the covenant and "kept his crowns." The connection is made more immanent when Levinas states "The text may be speaking of those times when Judaism is practiced or studied only by a small minority, perhaps only by one man, when it seems to be completely continued in treaties, immobilized between book bindings, and when living Jews have lost all influence as Jews."[33] Writing in 1964 one could imagine Levinas responding to the secularization of world Jewry or the historical conditions that annihilated over 6 million Jews. The key for Levinas is that even if only one man has access to the Torah, the meaning is still accessible to all because it transcends time, space and historical context even if it is relevant to all. But the onus is on that "one man."

Levinas recounts Chaim of Volozhin's interpretation of a passage from the *Saying of the Fathers*. In the passage the rabbinical scholars compare the Torah to glowing coals. And Levinas states: "Rabbi Chaim of Volozhin interpreted this remark approximately as follows: the coals light up by being blown on, the glow of the flame that thus comes alive depends on the interpreters breath."[34] For Levinas, meaning remains in the coals regardless of time or context and what seems to matter most is not the blowers training but his or her engagement with the coals. Here Levinas's counterhistoricism allows him to rekindle the coals through the force of his breath. And here the Levinasian interpretation encounters difficulties. Despite the pretensions to universalism, it appears that any one individual can access the transcendent meaning of Torah. But what is to keep this from proliferating into multiple potentially conflicting interpretations and ultimately into relativism? Levinas tells us that the relation between God and the individual is expressed in obedience to the Law through the reading and study of Talmud but that this reading cannot be solipsistic. It must be communicable to others in your time. But from where does Levinas obtain the authority to read and teach Talmud? And why is he not "the great man" whose intellectual interpretation and innovation is actually the most important factor, as in Freud's description of Moses or a description of Freud himself.

The issue of authority and authorization is essential to our understanding of both of these thinkers and to our understanding of their use and identification with Moses. Where does authority, intellectual or religious, come from and who grants it? For Freud, it is his faith in scientific investigation and his confidence in his own "scientific mind." The essence of Judaism is revealed through the science of psychoanalysis and thus the understanding of Judaism is revealed in his interpretation of Moses: Freud the atheist becomes the conduit of revelation. This is a revelation based on the immanent conditions of the human psyche but that conserves the transcendent permanence of Jewishness. For Levinas, it is his belief in divine revelation and his confidence in his own ability to read, interpret, and teach Talmud. Levinas's use of Moses reveals the transcendent nature of the Torah and Talmud that is always accessible and always relevant. But we must also take account of the immanent historical conditions of the Shoah that gave rise to Levinas's particular reading. Thus both thinkers claim to define, explain, and instruct us about the tradition of Judaism but both of their positions are self-authorized. Freud has granted himself authority to provide a scientific definition of the essence of Jewishness via his invention of psychoanalysis. Levinas has granted himself the authority to read, interpret and teach Talmud based on his own philosophical strategies and devoid of traditional rabbinic instruction or oversight. In a sense both are Moses. They are each the father/author of a school of thought with disciples and doctrines, acolytes and heretics. And as with their respective interpretations of the man Moses, their legitimacy can be interpreted as either self generated or divinely inspired. In the end, both use Moses to construct a rapprochement between the categories of immanence and transcendence that presents an understanding of the essence of Judaism that is derived, be it through Talmud or psychoanalysis, "before the letter."

Notes

1. Sigmund Freud, *Der Mann Moses und die monotheistische Religion: Drei Abhandlungen* (Amsterdam: Verlag Albert de Lange, 1939); *Moses and Monotheism* trans. Katherine Jones (New York: Vintage, 1967). Richard Bernstein, *Freud and the Legacy of Moses* (Cambridge: Cambridge University Press, 1998); Yosef Yerushalmi, *Freud's Moses: Judaism Terminable and Interminable* (New Haven, CT, and London: Yale University Press, 1991); Paul Schwaber, "Scientific Art: The Interpretation of Dreams," *The Psychoanalytic Study of the Child*, Volume 31/1976. Emmanuel Levinas, *Nine Talmudic Readings* trans. Annette Aronowicz (Bloomington: Indiana University Press, 1990), 24. This lecture was originally published in *La Conscience juive face à l'histoire: le pardon*, eds. Éliane Amado Lévy-Halensi and Jean Halperin (Paris: PUF, 1965) and republished in Levinas, *Quatre lectures talmudiques* (Paris: Éditions de Minuit, 1968).
2. Freud, *Moses and Monotheism*, 3.
3. Amos Funkenstein, "History, Counterhistory, and Narrative" in *Perceptions of Jewish History* (Berkeley and Los Angeles: University of California Press, 1993), 36.
4. See Samuel Moyn, "Emmanuel Levinas's Talmudic Readings: Between Tradition and Invention," *Prooftexts* 23, no. 3 (Fall/Winter 2003), 42–68, and Ethan Kleinberg, "The Myth of Emmanuel Levinas" in *After the Deluge: New Perspectives on the Intellectual and Cultural History of Postwar France* (Lanham, MD: Lexington, 2004).
5. Jacques Derrida, *Mal d'Archive: une impression freudienne* (Paris: Éditions Galilée, 1995), *Archive Fever* trans. Eric Prenowitz (Chicago: University of Chicago Press, 1996).
6. See Ethan Kleinberg, *Generation Existential: Heidegger's Philosophy in France, 1927–1961* (Ithaca, NY: Cornell University Press, 2005), chapter 7; and also Samuel Moyn, *Origins of the Other* (Ithaca, NY: Cornell University Press, 2005), chapter 3.
7. Peter Gay, *Freud: A Life for out Time* (New York: W.W. Norton, 1998), 28.
8. Immanuel Wolf (Wohlwill), "Über den Begriff einer Wisssenschaft des Judentums" in *Zeitschrift für die Wissenschaft des Judentums*, 1 (Berlin 1822), translated into English as "On the Concepts of a Science of Judaism" in *Leo Baeck Institute Yearbook*, 2 (1957).
9. Sigmund Freud, *The Standard Edition of the Complete Psychological Works of Sigmund Freud*, 24 volumes, trans. and ed. James Strachey (London: Hogart, 1953–74), vol. XIII, xv.
10. Freud, *Moses and Monotheism*, 31.
11. Freud, *Moses and Monotheism*, 37.
12. Freud, *Moses and Monotheism*, 128.
13. Freud, *Moses and Monotheism*, 125. See also Sigmund Freud, *A Phylogenetic Fantasy: Overview of the Transference Neuroses*, ed. with an essay by Ilse Grubrich-Simitis, trans. Axel Hoffer and Peter T. Hoffer (Cambridge, MA: Harvard University Press, 1987).
14. Bernstein, *Freud and the Legacy of Moses*, 57.
15. Richard Dawkins, *The Selfish Gene* (New York: Oxford University Press, 1976).
16. Dawkins, *The Selfish Gene*, 204.
17. Dawkins, *The Selfish Gene*, 207.
18. William H. McNeil, *Plagues and Peoples* (New York: Anchor, 1976).
19. McNeil, *Plagues and Peoples*, chapter 4.
20. Freud, *Moses and Monotheism*, 113. Bernstein, *Freud and the Legacy of Moses*, 40–41. Bernstein uses the Strachey translation: "Fate had brought the great deed and misdeed of primeval days, the killing of the father, closer to the Jewish people by causing them to repeat it on the person of Moses, an outstanding father figure."
21. Joel Whitebook has suggested that the model presented by Freud, and McNeil as well, is transhistorical rather than transcendent. I would argue that belief in the transhistorical nature of these models requires the same sort of "leap of faith" that is necessary in religious belief but now

applied to the infallibility of scientific (modern secular) thought. Thus even the seemingly neutral term "transhistorical" assumes that the model itself is able to transcend time and place to be universally applicable. See Brad S. Gregory, "The Other Confessional History: On Secular Bias in the Study of Religion," *History and Theory*, Theme Issue 45 (2006).

22. Freud, *Moses and Montheism*, 142–146. See Bernstein, *Freud and the Legacy of Moses*, 82–83.

23. The term *Fortschritt* (progress, step forward) is far more Hegelian than the Darwinian term *Entwicklung* (development, evolution) and this Hegelian connotation is heightened by the coupling with *Geistigkeit*. It would be interesting to examine the Hegelian overtones of Freud's "*der Fortschritt in der Geistigkeit*" especially in relation to Hegel's lectures on the "Philosophy of History" where he states that "*Weltgesgichte ist der Fortschritt im Bewusstsein der Freiheit*." Here one might ponder the possibility that, for Freud, the Jewish people are the people of *Geist* and that as the embodiment of reason they are the principle of history according to the Hegelian use of "*Geist*" and "*Weltgeschicte*." This too would be a sort of "counterhistory" where Freud inverts Hegel's claims about Christianity and Judaism.

24. Derrida, *Archive Fever*, 22.

25. Kleinberg, "The Myth of Emmanuel Levinas" in *After the Deluge: New Perspectives on the Intellectual and Cultural History of Postwar France* 2004). See also Moyn, "Emmanuel Levinas's Talmudic Readings: Between Tradition and Invention," *Prooftexts* 23, no. 3 (Fall/Winter 2003), 42–68 and Moyn, *Origins of the Other*, 164–207.

26. Soren Kierkegaard, *Fear and Trembling*, trans. Alastair Hannay (New York: Penguin Putnam), 146–147.

27. Freud, *Moses and Monotheism*, 112.

28. Emmanuel Levins, *Difficile Liberté* (Paris: Albin Michel, 1976), 145.

29. Emmanuel Levinas, *Nine Talmudic Readings*, trans. Annette Aronowicz (Bloomington: Indiana University Press), 30.

30. Levinas, *Nine Talmudic Readings*, 35.

31. Levinas, *Nine Talmudic Readings*, 36.

32. Levinas, *Nine Talmudic Readings*, 37.

33. Levinas, *Nine Talmudic Readings*, 44.

34. Emmanuel Levinas, *Beyond the Verse: Talmudic Readings and Lectures*, trans. Gary D. Mole (Bloomington: Indiana University Press, 1994), 109, 210 n. 8.

References

Bernstein, R. (1998). *Freud and the Legacy of Moses*. Cambridge: Cambridge University Press.
Dawkins, R. (1976). *The Selfish Gene*. New York: Oxford University Press.
Derrida, J. (1995). *Mal d'Archive: une impression freudienne*. Paris: Éditions Galilée. *Archive Fever*, trans. Eric Prenowitz. Chicago: University of Chicago Press, 1996.
Freud, S. (1913). "Totem and Taboo." *Standard Edition*. London: Hogart, XIII: 1–161.
_____ (1939). "Moses and Monotheism." Standard Edition. Volume XXIII: 7–140.
_____ (1987). *A Phylogenetic Fantasy: Overview of the Transference Neuroses*, ed. with an essay by Ilse Grubrich-Simitis, trans. Axel Hoffer and Peter T. Hoffer. Cambridge, MA: Harvard University Press.
Funkenstein, A. (1993). *Perceptions of Jewish History*. Berkeley and Los Angeles: University of California Press.
Gay, P. (1998). *Freud: A Life for Our Time*. New York: W.W. Norton and Co.
Gregory, B.S. (2006). "The Other Confessional History: On Secular Bias in the Study of Religion." *History and Theory*, Theme Issue 45.
Kierkegaard, S. (1843). *Fear and Trembling*, trans. Alastair Hannay. New York: Penguin Putnam, 1987.
Kleinberg, E. (2004). "The Myth of Emmanuel Levinas." In *After the Deluge: New Perspectives on the Intellectual and Cultural History of Postwar France*, ed. Julian Bourge. Lanham, MD: Lexington Books.
_____ (2005). *Generation Existential: Heidegger's Philosophy in France, 1927–1961*. Ithaca, NY: Cornell University Press.

Levins, E. (1976). *Difficile Liberté*. Paris: Albin Michel.
Levinas, E. (1990). *Nine Talmudic Readings,* trans. Annette Aronowicz. Bloomington: Indiana University Press.
____ (1994). *Beyond the Verse: Talmudic Readings and Lectures*, trans. Gary D. Mole. Bloomington: Indiana University Press.
La Conscience juive face à l'histoire: le pardon, eds. Éliane Amado Lévy-Halensi and Jean Halperin. Paris: PUF, 1965, and republished in Levinas, *Quatre lectures talmudiques*. Paris: Éditions de Minuit, 1968.
McNeil, W.H. (1976). *Plagues and Peoples*. New York: Anchor.
Moyn, S. (Fall/Winter 2003). "Emmanuel Levinas' Talmudic Readings: Between Tradition and Invention." *Prooftexts* 23 (3): 42–68.
____ (2005). *Origins of the Other*. Ithaca: Cornell University Press.
Schwaber, P. (1976). Scientific Art: The Interpretation of Dreams. *The Psychoanalytic Study of the Child* 31: 515–533.
Wolf (Wohlwill), I. "Über den Begriff einer Wisssenschaft des Judentums." In *Zeitschrift für die Wissenschaft des Judentums* 1 (Berlin 1822), trans. into English as "On the Concepts of a Science of Judaism" in *Leo Baeck Institute Yearbook* 2, 1957.
Yerushalmi, Y. (1991). *Freud's Moses: Judaism Terminable and Interminable*. New Haven, CT, and London: Yale University Press.

Freud's Moses and Viennese Jewish Modernism

ABIGAIL GILLMAN

To add to the rich discussion of Freud's Moses, I shall not begin with the questions: who is Freud's Moses, and why did Freud identify with him? My starting point is the "how" of the two Moses texts: the rhetorical strategies by which Freud arrives at his highly experimental interpretations of the great man in "The Moses of Michelangelo" (1914) and in the essays comprising *Moses and Monotheism* (1933–38). These interpretive methods get to the heart of what Freud sought to accomplish by refiguring the biblical Moses; they also confirm a series of important connections between Freud's cultural poetics and the literary practices of Viennese Jewish modernism.

Viennese modernism, die Wiener Moderne, is narrowly defined as the avant-garde, cosmopolitan literary movement that peaked in the years 1880 to 1910, years which saw revolutionary changes in philosophy, plastic and visual arts, music, literature, and last but not least, in the political realm. Freud would not have regarded himself as a modernist. He was a realist and a rationalist. His personal artistic tastes were conservative, Victorian; he disapproved of the radical experimentation in literature and the arts taking place all around him, and by and large ignored the aesthetics of his contemporaries Kokoschka, Schiele, Klimt. Yet, as Peter Gay notes, Freud's "analysis of art was far more radical than his taste in beauty" (Gay 1988, p. 166); the same can be said of his cultural poetics. In his unorthodox approach to the biblical Moses, it was the artist even more than the scientist who served as Freud's ally. Freud's expressions of ambivalence towards Jewish modernists in turn-of-the-century Vienna are well-known. In 1926, Freud wrote to Arthur Schnitzler that he had long been aware of the "wide-reaching correspondences [Übereinstimmungen] that exist between our conceptions of some psychological and erotic problems," and that this awareness led him to avoid direct contact with the distinguished writer (Freud to Schnitzler 1955, p. 100). This doppelgängerscheu presumably also caused Freud to avoid direct communication with another central figure, the poet and dramatist Richard Beer-Hofmann, until the latter's seventieth birthday; in a letter dated July 10, 1936, Freud wrote of "many meaningful correspondences [Übereinstimmungen] between you and me" (Freud to Beer-

Hofmann 1936). I shall take this opportunity to explore the correspondences between Freud and the Viennese Jewish modernists on a number of levels—as a shared ambivalence about Judaism and Jewish identification, as a shared concern with memory, and as a shared practice of writers seeking to create new genres of cultural memory.

Before turning to the Moses essays, I want to revisit the preface to the Hebrew translation of *Totem and Taboo* which Freud composed, ostensibly, to establish his pedigree as a Hebrew (and Jewish) author. In this preface, Freud describes himself as one "who is ignorant of the holy writ, who is completely estranged from the religion of his fathers—as well as from every other religion—and who cannot take a share in nationalist ideals, but who has yet never repudiated his people, who feels that he is in his essential nature a Jew and who has no desire to alter that nature" (Freud 1934b [1930], p. XV). Still speaking of himself in the third person, Freud continues:

> If the question were put to him: "Since you have abandoned all of these common characteristics of your countrymen, what is there left to you that is Jewish?" he would reply: "A very great deal, and probably its very essence." He could not now express that essence clearly in words; but some day, no doubt, it will become accessible to the scholarly mind [Freud 1934b (1930), *SE* 13: XV].
>
> These lines vivify the dilemma of Jewish memory at the turn of the century and the exact challenge Freud takes up when he turns to the tradition of Moses. Freud begins by noting the inadequacy of the available forms of Jewish identity—religion, scripture, nationalism. This sentiment was widespread among European Jewish intellectuals in the early twentieth century. Franz Kafka lamented that the Jewish legacy he inherited from his father amounted to "little souvenirs of early times" [Kafka 1966 (1919), p. 81]. Hugo von Hofmannsthal, not Jewish but of partial Jewish heritage, described his generation's inheritance as consisting of "pretty furniture and oversensitive nerves" (Hofmannsthal 1979 [1893] p. 174). Martin Buber, in describing the purpose of a Jewish cultural Renaissance, wrote: "I shall try to extricate the unique character of Jewish religiosity from the rubble with which rabbinism and rationalism have covered it" [Buber 1987 (1967) p. 81].

Freud goes on to insist that his "essential nature" is unalterably Jewish. To the question, Was ist an dir noch jüdisch? (What is still Jewish about you?) he responds, the main thing, the principle thing. But there is a catch: the principle thing cannot be put into words. It is tempting to connect Freud's disclaimer with the modernist crisis of language, wherein all that is essential eludes direct representation, but this type of asymbolia also played an important role in the discourse of Jewish identity in Freud's day. There were no straightforward answers to the many Jewish Questions facing German and Austrian Jews in the early twentieth century—no solution to anti-Semitism, no obvious way to sustain one's individuality as a Viennese Jew, and no language in which to express these dilemmas. My cognate passage is a 1908 diary entry from Arthur Schnitzler: "Another person need only defend his individuality—one of our own must first overcome the prejudice against Vienna, then that against Jewishness, and then that against himself. And it is the same with the Jew as with the Viennese: it is not simply the 'others' who are against him, no, it is above all the Jew, the Viennese" (Schnitzler 1987–1999 [1908], Entry of 13.1.1908.)

Lastly: Freud is confident that his Jewish nature will become accessible to scholars in some future time and place. How is this to be explained? Might Freud have been so wise as to foresee a conference titled "Freud's Jewish World?" Let me suggest a psychoanalytic explanation for Freud's belief that his hidden Jewish self, like all our most important selves, was only temporarily inaccessible. The logic behind this thought is not Jewish per se; it extends rather from Freud's understanding of human memory. I refer to in particular to two of Freud's most important and long-held theories about human memory. In "Beyond the Pleasure Principle," Freud repeated his observation that the memory-traces of excitatory processes "which form the foundation of memory ... have nothing to do with the fact of becoming conscious; indeed they are often most powerful and most enduring when the process which left them behind was one which never entered consciousness" (Freud 1920, *SE* 18: 25). The idea was first formulated in the letter to Wilhelm Fliess of December 6, 1896, and it was developed in *The Interpretation of Dreams* (1900), "The Unconscious" (1915), and in "A Note on the Mystic Writing Pad" (1925). The second, related idea has to do with the stratified structure of the memory apparatus itself. I cite from the famous letter to Fliess: "As you know, I am working on the assumption that our psychic mechanism has come into being by a process of stratification: the material present in the form of memory traces being subjected from time to time to a rearrangement in accordance with fresh circumstances—to a retranscription. Thus what is essentially new about my theory is the thesis that memory is present not once, but several times over" (Masson 1985, p. 207).

Though the model becomes more sophisticated over the years, the basic assumption remains. Memories are not fixed entities, akin to mental photographs. Memories are stored as traces or transcriptions in several layers of the mind. "Progressive" or healthy recollection describes a process whereby the memories move from more primitive to more advanced strata, and ultimately into language; repression is tantamount to the conscious mind's refusal to put memories into words. In the course of a lifetime, the process should occur automatically: the registrations or memory traces are "rearranged," "retranscribed," translated in later strata, as our understanding of our past develops and memories acquire different significance. When such a development would generate unpleasure, and the memory is repressed rather than re-translated, the result is what Freud calls "survivals" or "anachronisms." Rather than enter the more advanced strata, the uncomfortable memories emerge in pictorial form in dreams, or they take the form of a neurotic or psychotic symptom. Freud later applies the term "fixation" to describe a relationship or attachment that persists in a primitive, immature form, dictated by the rules of a less mature self. Even in healthy recollection, the memory-traces only enter language at a relatively "late stage," only once they have become accessible to the pre-conscious mind. These two fundamental ideas—that our most potent, formative memories may never have entered consciousness, and that the process of knowing our memories, of expressing them "clearly in words," is no simple achievement—have relevance in every sphere of Freudian thought.

I propose that we interpret the comments about Jewishness in the preface to *Totem and Taboo* as follows. There is no such thing as a Jewish "essence." Like all of our most potent memories, my Jewish character emerges in different forms at different stages in life. My reluctance to fix its meaning, or to give it a univocal formulation in the here and now, is not a matter of suppression or ambivalence, but rather a testimony to its powerful and enduring character. Any communication would have to take into account the ways in which it accrues and evolves over time and in time.

The belief that human memory is present "not once, but many times over" shapes the grammar and form of Freud's essays on Moses, no less than it does the evolution of psychoanalytic technique. But what further links these two domains—Freud's writings on art and culture, and his theory of memory—is the stratified character of art. I do not have time to spell out Freud's discussions of the artistic imagination and the analysis of art and the artist in the essay "A Childhood Memory of Leonardo da Vinci." The important point is that Freud interprets the work of art, the product of the imagination, as a direct extension of the human memory apparatus, and as such, as a kind of memory-text or memory-narrative in its own right. What Freud sees when he looks at the painting *La Gioconda*, at Michelangelo's Moses statue, or, for that matter, at the biblical Moses, are multiple transcriptions of a single memory-trace. Freud aspired to incorporate these various temporal layers into his own essays. When writing about Moses, one might say, Freud puts an unspoken truth into words for the sake of overcoming the Jewish fixation of, and on, Moses. In "The Moses of Michelangelo," the superior Moses whom Freud retrieves is the invention of an artist; in *Moses and Monotheism*, one might argue, Freud himself writes like an artist, when, after "depriv[ing] a people of the man whom they take pride in as the greatest of their sons," he pieces together a new account of Moses' composite identity, of what he calls the "tradition" of Moses (Freud 1939 [1934–38], *SE* 23: 7).

As in the case of the Hebrew preface to *Totem and Taboo*, the rhetorical starting point in "The Moses of Michelangelo" is a gesture of negation. What Freud must this time oppose is the widely held view that Michelangelo's statue depicts an actual historical episode — Moses sees the Israelites prostrating themselves before the golden calf, and is on the verge of rising up to shatter the tablets of the law. Freud stages his opposition to the canonical view through elaborate citation and dismissal of the art historians, the end result of which is to establish that Michelangelo's statue depicts an imagined episode — not the anticipation of an act (i.e., the shattering of the tablets), but the afterimage, the "testimony" of a movement (i.e., the not-shattering of the tablets). In other words, what Freud sees is not an act about to occur, but the remains of an action and a reaction.

> In his first transport of fury, Moses desired to act, to spring up and take vengeance and forget the Tables; but he has overcome the temptation, and he will now remain seated and still in his frozen wrath and in his pain mingled with contempt. Nor will he throw away the Tables so that they will break on the stones, for it is on their especial account that he has controlled his anger; it was to preserve them that he kept his passion in check [Freud 1914, *SE* 13: 229–230].

Freud sees in Michelangelo's Moses the incipient identities of the two Moses characters he describes in *Moses and Monotheism*: the Egyptian Moses, who is impulsive, passionate, capable of breaking the tablets; and the Midianite Moses who resembles Michelangelo's Moses in that he is "capable of the highest mental achievement that is possible in a man," namely, of struggling successfully "against an inward passion for the sake of a cause to which he has devoted himself" (Freud 1914, *SE* 13: 233). By claiming that Michelangelo immortalized Moses not for his deed, but rather for his mental and psychological power, Freud does indeed universalize Moses; he removes him from the national drama, and justifies this move both in artistic and psychoanalytic terms.

Now I return to the question of "how": How does Freud locate the evidence to support his image of the internally divided hero? He does so by recasting the statue as a complex icon with three distinct temporal layers. "As our eyes travel down it the figure exhibits three distinct emotional strata. The lines of the face reflect the feelings which have won ascendancy; the middle of the figure shows the traces of suppressed movement; and the foot still retains the attitude of the projected action" (Freud 1914, *SE* 13: 230). The section below registers passion, and the section above, restraint. But these are ultimately not where the action is for Freud. Freud is primarily intrigued with the middle section, and above all with the right hand and arm. Moses' hand encapsulates in miniature the compromise that the statue as a whole embodies: the hand "violently" pressing into the beard, with only one finger still entangled in the left-sided strands of the beard, is the physical trace of the tension between passion and restraint that Moses as a whole embodies. The rhetorical function of the hand as a trace or mark of compromise corresponds to role of the circumcision in *Moses and Monotheism*.

Freud's larger agenda involves using the evidence found on the statue itself to contradict, and to supplement, the Hebrew Bible. The approach to scripture in this essay is in many ways quintessentially modernist. As the Israelites do in worshipping the golden calf, one might argue, Freud's essay deposes the biblical Moses in favor of a graven image that preserves a tradition of Moses that is "superior"—at least in Freud's reading—to the biblical story. In normative

Judaism, replacing text with image is the idolatrous act par excellence. But for Jewish modernists, the terms have become reversed: Hebrew scripture had become the idol, a "distorted" text incapable of retaining the truth about Moses. In "The Moses of Michelangelo," Freud does not attack scripture outright. He cites the bible only in the third and final chapter of the essay, apologizing for citing "anachronistically" from the Luther Bible (Freud 1914, SE 13: 231). It is of course scripture per se that Freud transforms into an anachronism in the course of this third chapter. Freud proceeds to cite Exodus 32 almost in its entirety (he omits verses 1–6, 12–13, and 21–29), beginning at the point when God tells Moses to go down from the mountain. Too much scripture is included to convey, not simply too little correspondence with the statue, but the total absence of correspondence between text and image. After noting that the scriptural text has been "clumsily put together from various sources" and contains "glaring incongruities and contradictions," Freud confirms that the moment depicted by the statue is not present in the biblical narrative (Freud 1914, SE 13: 231–232). But then why quote scripture in the first place? Even more puzzling, why does Freud preface this final section of the essay by saying that he will at last "reap the fruits of [his] endeavors" (Freud 1914, SE 13: 229)?

The citation from scripture is purely rhetorical; it functions not as a proof-text, but only to stage the disparity or contradiction between the biblical text (especially when viewed through the lens of higher criticism) and the sculpted text. This deposing of the Bible by way of art is exemplified by the inclusion, alongside the biblical passage, of four sketches or cartoons that Freud claims to have commissioned by an artist to illustrate the three stages Michelangelo's statue codifies. The cartoons support Freud's own alliance with the artist in the endeavor of commemorating Moses' heroism, but the series of gestures they illustrate also provide a metaphor for Freud's treatment of Hebrew scripture as such. In the first picture, Moses holds the tablets firmly in place with his hand. When he looks to the Israelites, Moses' grasp loosens, he turns his head and they slip from his grasp and rotate onto their head: the evidence of this is the tiny "protruberance" located on the bottom, which Freud postulates was originally on top. This accidental slippage is more convincing in the Freudian scheme than the claim that Moses rose and broke the tablets intentionally. This almost losing that to which he had devoted his life brings Moses to his senses and leads him to secure them (*fixieren*) them against his body. Finally, the arm swings back around, only one finger remains entangled in the beard, and the tablets are once again secured, even though upside down.

This improbable, almost laughable image of the rotating tablets is a gesture that exemplifies how Jewish modernists treat scripture. They don't "shatter" it — the Bible remains their most important interlocutor. They do turn it on its head. I think of the memorable title of Yehuda Amichai's poem: "I want to confound the Bible." *Ani kol cach rotzeh l'valbel et ha-Tanach!* I really want to confound the Bible, the poet declares. Appropriately enough, the Hebrew verb for "confound" or "baffle," *l'valbel*, is just what God in Genesis 11 does to the language of the tower builders to defeat their militant chauvinistic and potentially idolatrous intentions.

In lieu of a more detailed analysis of *Moses and Monotheism*, I shall call attention to five key strategies at work in that text.

First: Freud continues his demoting of scripture, the Jewish religious archive, into an unreliable and distorted source of Mosaic memory. Here, not only does Freud portray the Bible as full of contradictions and tendentious (nationalist) motives, he puts forth his most provocative term for biblical narratives thus far, likening them to mausoleums (*Grabbauten*): "The poetically embellished narrative which we attribute to the Yahwist, and to his later rival the Elohist, were like mausoleums beneath which, withdrawn from the knowledge of later generations, the true account of those early things—of the nature of the Mosaic religion and of the violent end of the great man—was, as it were, to find its eternal rest (Freud 1939 [1934–38], *SE* 23: 62). Like a decorative structure atop a tomb, scripture not only conceals, or lays to rest, the Mosaic religion, it attempts to beautify that rupture.

Second: as in the previous essay, Freud garners key evidence from two traces, or signs, that are shown to contain various layers: the Hebrew name Moshe, and the ritual of circumcision. He refers to circumcision as his *Leitfossil*, or "key-fossil." Like the Mona Lisa's smile or Michelangelo's hand, the bodily mark functions as a relic or memory-trace, a "survival" from earlier epochs which Freud translates in his narrative, to reveal its double-sided character. Circumcision is no longer the sign of the covenant between God, Abraham and Sarah. Like Moses himself, it turns out that the ritual of circumcision is not a Jewish original; it is a mark of the original identity between Egyptian and Jew.

A third strategy familiar from the 1914 essay that becomes even more pronounced in the later Moses texts is the splitting of the hero. The biblical Moses is revealed to be a trope: a combination of two completely different men, an Egyptian Moses and a Midianite Moses, and a long list of divisions and compromises follows. The first compromise pertains to "the dependence of Jewish monotheism on the monotheistic episode in Egyptian history" (Freud 1939 [1934–38], *SE* 23: 31). Others pertain to the fusion of two religions, two founders of religions, both who happened to be named Moses, and two peoples, only one of which underwent a traumatic experience.

Splitting the hero into two forms the crux of Freud's poetics. By representing the great man as divided against himself, Freud accomplishes in the domains of culture and religion that which he came to see as central to healthy remembering for his patients: he recasts heroism as the overcoming of resistance, and at the same time, he reveals a culture's own internal resistances to remembering. Moreover, though not a believer, Freud was deeply concerned with idolatry. In the Moses book, written during the National Socialist period, Freud writes not only against anti–Semitism, but also against Jewish nationalism. In an anti-nationalistic coup de grace, Freud deliberately embraces an Egyptian Moses as part of the "truth" of the Jewish people.

A fourth priority is to confront readers with Jewishness as a slippery reality rather than a fixation or anachronism. Freud's Moses was both too Jewish and not Jewish enough: He was Jewish enough to enrage his Jewish readership, not Jewish enough to provide the German-speaking Jewry with support in a time of crisis. In the words of the enlightened explorer in Franz Kafka's "In the Penal Colony," Freud's Moses declares: "I can neither help nor hinder you" (Kafka 1971, p. 157). For various reasons, Viennese Jewish modernists tried to keep alive the question of what is and is not Jewish. At the climax of Richard Beer-Hofmann's novella, *The Death of Georg*, the aesthete-protagonist Paul awakens for the first time to hear the voice of his own blood, the blood of a nameless Volk of wanderers. "He too was of their blood" (Beer-Hofmann 1980, p. 114). Critics have long been divided. Is this conclusion too Jewish (i.e. racialist), or unconvincing, given the unlikelihood of Paul's undergoing any kind of authentic conversion? Then there is Arthur Schnitzler's novel *The Road into the Open* (1908). Is it a Jewish novel, or isn't it? There are many Jewish characters, to be sure, but the central plot involves a Viennese aristocrat and his Catholic mistress, and Schnitzler intentionally leaves open the connection between the Jewish and the non–Jewish novel plots. Then there is the comedy *Professor Bernhardi* (1912). Is Bernhardi Schnitzler's idea of a Jewish hero? Yet he refuses to occupy the role of "medical Dreyfus," and what is more, he "only happens to be Jewish," as another character points out (Schnitzler 1999, p. 182).

Lastly, I want to emphasize the centrality of compromise in Freud's poetics. Just as Judaism is a compromise, so is the genre of *Moses and Monotheism*. Freud's approach to commemoration was modeled upon his understanding of the artistic imagination's ability, outlined in "The Creative Writer and Daydreaming," to thread past, present and future together "on the string of the wish that runs through them all," in the interest of producing a *Zukunftsbild*: an image of / for the future (Freud 1910, SE 9: 148). *Moses and Monotheism* is not only an amalgam of past and present concerns, memory and history; it is a composite of discourses, disciplines and genres. That Freud resists each one as an independent enterprise enables him to draw upon them all partially and imperfectly. The first principle of this new genre of Jewish memory is thus its commitment to compromise. Compromise understands itself as the mirror image of distortion, of the (less mature) crossbreed or hybrid work. Compromise is progressive, not regressive; it is the modus operandi of fathers, and of artists. Freud's essays take numerous distorted texts as their touchstones, texts that turn out to be, like dreams, distorted in fairly legible ways. However, Freud does not use the term distortion to describe what he sees as "the essential outcome, the momentous substance, of the history of the Jewish religion"; he uses the notion of compromise. Freud will claim to have tracked down the numerous compromises that yielded what came to be known as "the man Moses and the monotheistic religion," but as a practitioner of cultural memory writing in an artistic mode, he must invent compromises of his own.

The ultimate expression of Mosaic memory, which is also the genre that best captures the remembered-forgotten character of all that is most important in life, is "tradition." Freud describes tradition, as Richard Bernstein has shown, as operating in ways exactly parallel to unconscious memory in the case of the individual. The concept of tradition pays homage to the enigma of memory: the sheer force of characters who endure, and past ideas that resurface, and the wholly unpredictably ways in which they do so. Allying himself with the tradition of Moses enables Freud to approach not only Mosaic monotheism, but also all religion, from the perspective of unconscious memory rather than conscious transmission; most importantly, it legitimates his own counter-scriptural writing, even granting him a type of irrefutability that he refers to as "historical truth." Tradition, by definition, has a hybrid character: Freud provocatively describes it as "a supplement but at the same time contradiction" of the official record (Freud 1939, *SE* 23: 68). Traditions behave sometimes like poets and at other times like historians, combining truth and fiction in ways that perhaps only the artist would recognize.

Freud's technique in the Moses essays— both in "The Moses of Michelangelo" (1914) and in *Moses and Monotheism* (1933–38) derives in equal part from psychoanalytic experience and his own aesthetic vision. His goal in each case is to identify (or invent) *Lücke*, a lack or blank space, symbolizing forgotten or repressed chapters of the past. Next, he brings together various layers of the past, some known, some forgotten, into a meaningful new arrangement. Finally, his own text creates a double optic effect, one that allows the reader to observe the historical individual, the great man, alongside later representations of him (historical and legendary accounts, written and oral traces). Rather than collapsing the aspects or characteristics of his subjects into a monolithic image, Freud takes pains to emphasize their stratified character. Yet, whereas the artist corrects reality to fulfill a wish, Freud does not fulfill the wishful expectations of his readership. In the case of Moses to be sure, he is determined to fashion a controversial image of the founder of Judaism, one that is as provocative as anything he ever produced.

The writers of Viennese Jewish modernism viewed culture as a domain in which characters, authors, and their audiences could make the journey from amnesia to self-knowledge. In his psychoanalytic practice, Freud came to regard the therapeutic situation as a transitional space wherein repression might be undone and fixations worked through in the interest of achieving a healthy relationship to the past. Freud's essays on Moses allowed him to work through his resistance to received forms of collective memory. His essays became that transitional space wherein the identity of Moses could be questioned, redefined, and re-inscribed in a progressive fashion.

References

Beer-Hofmann, Richard (1980). *Der Tod Georgs*. Stuttgart: Reclam.
Buber, Martin (1987 [1916]). "Jewish Religiosity." In *On Judaism*, ed. Nahum M. Glatzer. New York: Schocken, 1987.
Freud, S. (1900). *The Interpretation of Dreams. Standard Edition* 4, 5: 1–626.
_____ (1908). The Creative Writer and Daydreaming. *Standard Edition* 9: 141–153.
_____ (1910). "A Childhood Memory of Leonardo da Vinci." *Standard Edition* 11: 57–137.
_____ (1914). "The Moses of Michelangelo." *Standard Edition* 13: 209–238.
_____ (1915). "The Unconscious." *Standard Edition* 14: 159–215.
_____ (1920). *Beyond the Pleasure Principle. Standard Edition* 18: 1–64.
_____ (1925). "Note on the Mystic Writing Pad." *Standard Edition* 19: 225–232.
_____ (1934b). "Hebrew Preface to *Totem and Taboo*." *Standard Edition* 13: 15.
_____ (1939 [1934–38]). *Moses and Monotheism: Three Essays. Standard Edition* 23: 7–137.
_____ (1955). Letter to Arthur Schnitzler, May 25, 1926. *Neue Rundschau* 66: 100.
_____ (1963). Letter to Richard Beer-Hofmann, July 10, 1936. Fischer Almanach, "Das siebenundsiebzigste Jahr": 64.
Gay, Peter (1988). *Sigmund Freud: A Life for Our Time*. New York: Norton.
Hofmannsthal, Hugo von (1979). *Reden und Aufsätze I, 1891–1913*. Frankfurt a. M.: Fischer Taschenbuch Verlag, 174–5.
Kafka, Franz (1966). Letter to His Father/Brief an den Vater. New York: Schocken.
_____ (1971). *The Complete Stories*, ed. Nahum N. Glatzer. New York: Schocken.
Masson, Jeffrey M., ed. and trans. (1985). *The Complete Letters of Sigmund Freud to Wilhelm Fliess, 1887–1904*. Cambridge, MA: Harvard University Press.
Schnitzler, Arthur (1987–1999). *Tagebuch*. Ed. Werner Welzig, unter Mitwirkung von Peter Michael Braunwirth, Susanne Pertlik und Reinhard Urbach. Wien: Österreichische Akademie der Wissenschaften.
Schnitzler, Arthur (1998). *Der Weg ins Freie*. Frankfurt am Main: Fischer Taschenbuch Verlag.
_____ (1999). *Das weite Land: Dramen 1909–1912*. Frankfurt am Main: Fischer Taschenbuch Verlag.

Freud's Michelangelo
The Sculptural Meditations of a Hellenized Jew
MARY BERGSTEIN

In his introduction to "The Moses of Michelangelo" Freud stated, "Works of art do exercise a powerful effect on me, especially those of literature and sculpture, less often of painting."[1] Sculpture, with all its ambivalence as a surrogate for the human body, and its uncanny potential for "coming to life," had a special place in Freud's intellectual formation—a place that was perplexing in terms of his Jewish identity.

Jewish law prohibits figurative art, particularly sculptured representations of the deity. The Hebrew tradition was fundamentally opposed to the institution of Greek athletic nudity and glorification of the naked body, whether in life (military events or athletic games) or in art.[2] This is proclaimed in Jubilees (first century A.D.) where the rabbis forbade the nudity and idolatry associated with Greek sport to the Jews: "They should cover their shame, and should not undress themselves as the Gentiles [Greeks] uncover themselves."[3]

In Freud's day scholars of Judaism, especially those writing in the Protestant cultures of England and the United States, emphasized the principle that Hellenic and Jewish cultures were mutually antagonistic. In 1901, for instance, Solomon J. Solomon declared that, "How far he can assimilate what is best of Hellenic influence without prejudice to his individuality is clearly one of the chief problems that beset the modern Jew."[4] Freud's love of ancient and Renaissance sculpture was partly motivated by his desire to be "Hellenized" or "westernized" in the Greco-Roman tradition.

Renaissance civilization, which flourished under the Church of Rome, created a highpoint of anthropomorphic, essentially Pagan art, the alluring forms of which (according to Heinrich Graetz) inspired "sumptuousness and perfidy."[5] This was opposed to Jewish monotheism, where the pursuit of pure spirit and intellect was considered counter to the cult of the saints, or to the Greek multiplicity of anthropomorphic gods with human-like passions.

Freud's personal library contained numerous photographs of the idealized heroic nude in Greco-Roman or Renaissance sculpture. The studying of such images in books, for the scientific purposes of archaeology and art history, seems to have trumped the Jewish prohibition on gazing at anthropomorphic representation of immortals or the aggrandized athletic nude. This was true not only for Freud, but also for archaeologists such as Emmanuel Löwy and Ludwig Pollak, among others.

Freud used Michelangelo's sculpture in his quest for self-identity, and his interest in the *Moses* was sparked by Giorgio Vasari's *Life of Michelangelo*, which he read in the late 1890s.[6] Vasari praised the *Moses* for the virtuoso handling of marble, especially the bravura technique of the beard. He added the famous remark that the Jews of Rome flocked to worship the statue on the Jewish Sabbath, and what they adored in the sculpture of God's favorite was a thing not human, but truly divine.[7] In the German edition of the *Lives* the editor contradicted Vasari, citing eighteenth-century clerics who claimed that Roman Jews never visited the churches. All of this must have been intriguing for Freud, who underlined Vasari's Jewish anecdote in his personal guidebook to Rome, *Rom und die Campagna* by Thomas Gsell Fells.[8]

In my view, Vasari's *Life of Michelangelo* clearly intersected with Freud's personal dilemma. His father, Jakob Freud, was an itinerant merchant who read Hebrew and Yiddish instead of Greek and Latin, and told his ten-year-old son that he had remained passive when an anti–Semite ordered him off the sidewalk and knocked his fur hat into the mud. It has long been assumed that a persistent awareness of his beloved father's status as *Ostjude* made Sigmund Freud feel simultaneously guilty (of parricide) and defensive (of his Jewish origins).[9]

Freud went to Italy whenever he could, and Rome had a special meaning in his psychological make-up, as a place that was at once intellectually sacred and erotically charged. He spoke of an extraordinary desire for Rome and Pompeii throughout his correspondence with Wilhelm Fliess, stating in December 1897 that, "My longing for Rome is, by the way, deeply neurotic."[10] The equation of Rome with sexual love as well as intellectual fecundity was not merely a personal idiosyncrasy on Freud's part: it was deeply embedded in culture, and the centuries-old play on words ROMA/AMOR was well known to him from Goethe's *Roman Elegies*, among other sources. As a Hellenized Jew, these fears (Papal Rome), and wishes (ROMA=AMOR), or love for Roma as the desired mother, fed into to his own theory of the Oedipus complex.[11]

Paradoxically, Freud also sought his ancient Jewish roots in Rome. Interwoven with Lamarckian assumptions about the evolution of the individual and his race (ontogeny recapitulating phylogeny), Freud persistently saw his own Jewish origins in the world of classical antiquity. In a letter of 1934 to Suzanne Cassirer Bernfeld he wrote, "none of us [Jews] has ever lost his longing for the Mediterranean."[12] And in his *Moses and Monotheism* of 1939 he proclaimed, that, "Jews are composed for the most part of remnants of the Mediterranean peoples and heirs of the Mediterranean civilization." He went on to claim that the "archaic heritage" of the Jews was present in innate phylogenic "memory traces."[13] This quest for retrievable memory traces is, of course, profoundly allied with the process of psychoanalysis itself.

Since Judaism was aniconic, and there were no Jewish representations of the prophets, Michelangelo's *Moses* personified the quintessential patriarch for Freud. It was the best image of the most powerful Jewish father. In terms of ethnographic authenticity, the hyper-serious, bearded *Moses* was in some ways a "real" Jew, like the *Ostjuden* (such as Freud's parents) who had settled in the Leopoldstadt section of Vienna. But Michelangelo had represented this Jewish father as a muscular, classicizing figure, as strong and beautiful as the pagan River Gods and the *Laocoön*.[14]

In "The Moses of Michelangelo" Freud created an essay that, in eclipsing the cultural world of his own father, was vindicated by the example of Michelangelo himself, who, as an elegant predecessor for Freud, had stood at the pinnacle of Western culture, and portrayed in the figure of *Moses* a tormented amalgam of his biological father (Lodovico Buonarroti), his symbolic father (Pope Julius II), and himself. All of this reflexive potential opened up an interminable commentary about fathers and sons, in which no fixed meaning can, or necessarily should, stand as truth.[15] Freud's complete classical education and his abiding obsession with Rome never let him down. In a letter to Ernest Jones of 4 June 1922 Freud referred to himself as the "Pontifex Maximus" of psychoanalysis, punning on the meanings of that title as "Major Bridge-Builder," "Emperor," and "Pope."[16]

In late summer of 1912 he visited the *Moses* on a daily basis. Freud described his inspired Roman solitude as an exquisite melancholy, under the enchantment of which he explored the ruins of the Palatine, the park of the Villa Borghese, and the *Moses*. His vivid narration of solitary pilgrimages to San Pietro in Vincoli describes the viewing of the statue in a dark church as evoking a response of uncertainty, anxiety, or even paralysis.

> How often have I mounted the steep steps from the unlovely Corso Cavour to the lonely piazza where the deserted church stands, and have essayed to support the angry scorn of the hero's glance! Sometimes I have crept cautiously out of the semi-gloom of the interior as though I myself belonged to the mob upon whom his eye is turned — the mob which can hold no fast conviction, which has neither faith nor patience, and which rejoices when it has regained its illusory idols.[17]

Freud, of course, *was* in Rome to look at Pagan and Christian sculpture. When he entered the church of San Pietro in Vincoli he effectively defied the Jewish stricture against graven images, engendered the anger of the Jewish patriarch's gaze, and returned that gaze in a single moment. The situation was charged with contradictions and conflict that perhaps only Vasari's ironic story could assuage.

Both Vasari and Freud focused upon the movements of the statue's beard. Freud, of course, contended that while rising and letting the tablets slip, *Moses* gained control of his rage; thus the right hand was retracted in the beard, pulling it along in the wake of his gesture, and clamping down on the slipping tablets with his inner right arm. Freud believed that Michelangelo's *Moses* was and always will be a figure in the act of restraining himself from rising in the anger of his own passion.

But the stupendous beard also served to complicate a number of Oedipal and Jewish concerns. First, it was a reference to Julius II, who let his own beard grow in defiance of canon law, as a symbol of mourning after a battle lost to the French. It also rendered the statue *terribile* in the likeness of Michelangelo himself.[18]

At the same time, it created a quality of ethnic authenticity that made Michelangelo's *Moses* look like a Jew, as mystical and uncompromising as those from the East who had sought refuge in cosmopolitan Vienna. Freud was aware of Johan Joachim Winckelmann's statement that Michelangelo's *Moses* wore his beard the way [eighteenth-century] Jews did, if they wanted to be "real" Jews.[19]

Freud's Philippson Bible showed "historical" beard styles with drawings of "real" Jews from Syria, Arabia, and Persia. And in the 1895 performance of Lessing's *Nathan the Wise*, Adolf von Sonnenthal, the so-called "Jewish Jupiter" of the Viennese stage, posed as Nathan. His right hand is brought to his imposing beard.

In modernity a long untrimmed beard immediately signaled an eastern Jew with all his propensities for servility, mysticism, and the precarious existence that designated him as a permanent refugee in any European country.[20] The "wandering Jews" treated by Jean-Martin Charcot for what was considered a "hypomanic travel syndrome," wore untrimmed beards.[21]

Freud was somewhat disparaging of Jewish men, such as his wife's relatives, who did not shave or cut their hair when in mourning. Nevertheless, it is notable that in his "close-the-eyes" dream he was late to his father's funeral because of being delayed at the barber. Tension between filial piety and parricidal wishes is represented by Freud's simultaneous intention and inability to close his father's eyes.[22] The beard of Michelangelo's *Moses* must have signaled similar ambivalence: wishes and fears.

But Freud was drawn to Michelangelo's sculpture long before he composed his essay on the *Moses*. In a letter to Wilhelm Fliess of December 1896 Freud remarked that, "I have now adorned my room with plaster casts of statues. It was a source of extraordinary invigoration for me."[23]

A photograph from 1913 portrays Freud seated on his veranda with a framed reproduction of *The Healing of the Cripple* and *Raising of Tabitha* from the fresco cycle of Saint Peter by Masolino and Masaccio (Florence, S.M. del Carmine, Brancacci Chapel). A reduced copy of Michelangelo's *Dying Slave* (one of the "invigorating" casts) stands at his side.

This photographic portrait, probably by Freud's brother, Alexander (nicknamed "Court Photographer" of the Freud household) was arranged casually, like a snapshot. But, like a classically inspired Renaissance portrait, it is meant to define the interior mind of the sitter by his association with certain venerable objects. It is in the tradition Titian's *Portrait of Jacopo Strada* where the Renaissance antiquarian holds a small sculptured nude Venus. This portrait, in the Kunsthistorisches Museum, Vienna, was well known to Freud and his cohort.

The reproductions of Masolino's frescos were relevant to Freud in his role as a healer. Ernest Jones was in Florence in November 1912 and promised Freud he would obtain photographs of works of art.[24] "I saw this morning a picture where cripples were healed even by touching the *shadow* of St. Peter as he walked by. I suppose you wished to avoid Christian topics in your articles, but if you would like photographs of any particular idea depicted in religious art, I could surely find them for you."[25] Jones evidently did bring Freud photographic reproductions of the Brancacci Chapel murals, one of which Freud had matted and framed, and installed on his veranda. Here, in the same scene, painted by Masolino, are two episodes: *St. Peter Healing the Cripple* and *The Raising of Tabitha* as narrated in the Acts of the Apostles (3: 1–10, 9: 36–41). These scenes deal with Peter as a miraculous physician, healing a begger who had been crippled from birth and actually dispelling the death of Tabitha.[26] His rewards were immense astonishment and gratitude. Acts has it that when St. Peter healed the crippled begger, people were astounded, utterly stupefied at the transformation. The story of Tabitha is more dramatic yet. Peter is called to the couch where Tabitha's washed and anointed body had been laid out. Insisting on being alone with the woman, he tells her to rise. "He gave her his hand and helped her to her feet. The next thing he did was to call in those who were believers and the widows to shown them that she was still alive."[27] In the fresco painting Tabitha sits up facing the commanding Peter with crossed arms, the typical Renaissance gesture of gratitude and humility; three bearded men express profound surprise.

From Freud's point of view, it is important to remember that St. Peter was an apostle of Christ with miraculous healing powers, but he was also the first pope, the bearded chief patriarch of the Church of Rome, Pontifex Maximus.

But Michelangelo's sleeping tomb figure, or *"Dying Slave"* as he has come to be nicknamed, has an even more provocative significance in this image. The photographic portrait of Freud with the idealized nude as an identifying attribute openly defies the Jewish prohibition against the lure of images, athletic beauty, and the anthropomorphism of divinity.[28]

Within the casually parallel syntax of the figures in the photograph (one living and the other plaster) the image speaks in terms of the rhetoric of the gaze. Freud's own gaze is outward, penetrating, and full of agency and observational power. This is juxtaposed with the mental state of the somnolent, epicene statue, which is drawn inward, as though pulled irresistibly toward unconscious realms.

Apropos the "lure of sumptuousness and perfidy," the so-called "*Dying Slave*" has been described as Michelangelo's most hedonistic and voluptuous homage to the male body — both heroic and insistently passive.[29] And perhaps it is the passivity of this "dying" figure that disturbs us the most here, as in the Hellenistic *Barberini Faun* (Munich) that was recarved by Bernini in the seventeenth century.

Freud's photographic self-alignment with a three-dimensional reproduction of Michelangelo's statue is defiant, in terms of Jewish aniconism, and self-defining, in terms of Freud's own work on sleep, dreams, and the unconscious mind.

In the art-historical literature read by Freud at this time, Michelangelo's *Slave* was described as an absent presence, asleep and probably dreaming, if not really "dying." Art scholars emphasized fluidity between the waking and dream states, and the fruitful conditions of sleep, death, and enchantment. They spoke of the figure's highest consciousness as being released, or unlocked, during his immersion in sleep. The nude ephebe was suspended in a state in which, "the sleeping mind of the immortal youth is musing upon solemn dreams."[30] This was the kind of heady psychological Neo-Platonic rhetoric that made for Renaissance art history in Freud's day. The appreciation of Renaissance *Geist* was most important to the German-speaking writers on Michelangelo at the end of the nineteenth century.

Such writings resonated with those of contemporary psychologists whose books were also in Freud's library, such as the volumes on adolescence by Stanley Hall. Hall's poetic ruminations upon the beneficial education of the beautiful, athletic young men by the ancient Greeks, and the developmental processes of sleeping and dreaming in adolescence, are startling. Hall might just as well have been talking about Michelangelo's nude *Slave*, when in his textbook on adolescent psychology, he wrote the following:

> The presentiments and previsions of love, which often first arise spontaneously and naturally in sleep, seem to illustrate the old trope that the stars of other and larger systems come out best when the sun of our own personal consciousness has set.
> Indeed in the reverie and daydreaming common at this stage [adolescence], when the soul transcends its individual limitations and expiates over the whole field of humanity, past, present, or future it is perhaps quite as near the world as our habitual, but generally unremembered dreams, as it is to the waking world of memory. In the new horizon now opening to the mind, unconscious cerebration generally has a larger role and for a time it is more uncontrolled by the consciousness, over into which it shades by imperceptible gradations.[31]

The accessibility of the unconscious to acute observation by an analyst was the crucial basis for psychoanalysis. The statue and its art-historical critique emphasized a psychological state that was well below (or beyond) the surface of awareness. Here, Michelangelo's *Slave*, clothed in the costume of heroic nudity, serves as a sort of *personification of the unconscious mind*. As such, it ennobles much of the seemingly enigmatic or arcane material of Freudian thought.

A venerable Renaissance *exemplum*, like this important sculpture by Michelangelo lent an historically retrospective seal of approval to Freud's most innovative work.

Michelangelo's cultural-philosophical system was, of course, vastly different from that of Freud, who looked back at the Renaissance from an interval of four centuries. But this photograph does not represent an anachronistic diversion of Michelangelo's sixteenth-century worldview.

Rather it portrays a poignant episode in the historiography of art, and in the history of psychoanalysis.

And let us turn back again to Giorgio Vasari, and Freud's "Moses of Michelangelo." At the end of his life Freud wrote arguing that the biblical Moses was not a Jew at all, but an Egyptian. Complex thoughts like these germinate in the psyche long before they manifest in prose, and his experiences with Michelangelo's *Moses* must have in some way formed the plot of that most surprising intellectual project, the *Moses and Monotheism* of 1939.

Notes

1. Freud 1914 *SE* 13: 211–238
2. Bonfante 1989, 545–6, 563.
3. Quoted in Poliakoff 1987, 146.
4. Solomon 1901, 554.
5. Graetz 1846, 88, 177.
6. Jones 1953–57 I, 346.
7. Vasari, ed. Barocchi, 1962, vol. 1, 30–31.
8. Gsell Fells 1912, 754.
9. Flem 2003, 51–52.
10. Masson 1985, 284–85.
11. Haddad 1996, Chapters 1, 2.
12. Bernfeld 1951, 112.
13. Freud 1939 *SE* 23: 91, 98–100.
14. Bergstein 2006, 60–61.
15. Bergstein 2006, 161.
16. Paskauskas 1995, 486–7. Freud, writing to Jones about Strachey: "Believe me, I am not fond of acting the Pontifex maximus and having to interfere between your people and yourself. I would prefer to see them more intensely attached to you than to me."
17. Freud 1914 *SE* vol. 13: 213.
18. Beck 155–56.
19. Thode 1908, 195.
20. Roth 1927, 29.
21. Meige 1893, 277–91; Gilman 1991, 72–76.
22. Rudnytsky 47, 334.
23. Masson 1985, 214.
24. Paskauskas 1995 169.
25. Paskauskas 1995, 170.
26. Baldini and Casazza 1991, 121–127.
27. Acts 9: 36–91.

28. See Bergstain 2003, 9–20.
29. Hibbard 1974, 152.
30. John Addington Symonds, quoted by Thode 1908, 211.
31. Hall 1904, vol. 2, 262–63.

References

Baldini, Umberto, and Ornella Casazza. *The Brancacci Chapel,* trans. Lysa Hochroth. New York: Abrams, 1992.
Beck, James. *Three Worlds of Michelangelo.* New York: W.W. Norton, 1999.
Bergstain, Mary. "The *Dying Slave* at Berggasse 19." *American Imago* 60 (Spring 2003): 9–20.
―――― "Freud's Moses of Michelangelo: Vasari, Photography, and Art Historical Practice." *Art Bulletin* 88 (March 2006): 158–176.
Bernfeld, Suzanne Cassirer. "Freud and Archaeology." *American Imago* 8 (June 1951): 107–128.
Bonfante, Larissa. "Nudity as a Costume in Classical Art." *American Journal of Archaeology* 93 (1989): 543–570.
Flem, Lydia. *Freud the Man: An Intellectual Biography,* trans. Susan Fairfield. New York: Other, 2003.
Freud, Sigmund. "*Moses and Monotheism.*" 1939. *Standard Edition* 23: 91, 98–100.
―――― "*The Moses of Michelangelo.*" 1914. *Standard Edition* 13: 211–238.
Gilman, Sander L. *The Jew's Body.* New York: Routledge, 1991.
Graetz, Heinrich. "The Structure of Jewish History" [1846]. In *The Structure of Jewish History and Other Essays,* trans., ed. and intro. Ismar Schorsch, 2d ed. New York: KTAV, 2002, 63–124.
Gsell Fels, Thomas [Dr.]. *Rom und die Campagna,* 7th ed. Leipzig and Vienna: Bibliographisches Institut, 1912.
Haddad, Antonietta, and Gerard Haddad. *Freud in Italia,* trans. Fabrice Olivier Dubosc. Milan: Xenia Edizioni, 1996.
Hall, G. Stanley. *Adolescence: Its Psychology.* 2 vols. New York: D. Appleton, 1904.
Hibbard, Howard. *Michelangelo.* New York: Harper and Row, 1974.
Jones, Ernest. *The Life and Work of Sigmund Freud,* vol. 1. New York, Basic, 1953.
Masson, Jeffrey Mousaieff, ed. and trans. *The Complete Letters of Sigmund Freud to Wilhelm Fliess, 1887–1904.* Cambridge, MA, and London: Harvard University Press, 1985.
Meige, Henry. "Le Juif-Errant a la Salpetrière." *Nouvelle Iconographie* 6 (1893): 277–291.
Paskauskas, R. Andrew, ed. *The Complete Correspondence of Sigmund Freud and Ernest Jones 1908–1939.* Cambridge MA, and London: Belknap Press of Harvard University Press, 1995.
Poliakoff, Michael. *Combat Sports in the Ancient World.* New Haven, CT: Yale University Press, 1987.
Roth, Joseph. *The Wandering Jews.* 1927. Trans. Michael Hofmann. New York and London: W.W. Norton, 2001.
Rudnytsky, Peter. *Freud and Oedipus.* w York: Columbia University Press, 1987.
Solomon, Solomon J. "Art and Judaism. *The Jewish Quarterly Review* 13 (July 1901): 553–566.
Thode, Henry. *Michelangelo: Kritische Untersuchungen über seine Werke.* Berlin: G. Grote, 1908.
Vasari, Giorgio. *La Vita di Michelangelo,* ed. Paola Barocchi, 5 vols. Milan and Naples: Documenti di Filologia, 1962.

Freud, Moses and Akhenaten
Florence Dunn Friedman*

During the 1930s Freud composed three essays that in 1939 were compiled as a book under the English title *Moses and Monotheism*. He had put pen to paper on the first essay in 1934, at the same time that a stinging piece of anti–Semitic screed was published by Jung (Yerushalmi 1991, 48–50), his one-time "son" and lapsed disciple; and just as the first Nazi racial laws were being issued in Germany. Freud opens the first essay with the following: "To deny a people the man whom it praises as the greatest of its sons is not a deed to be undertaken lightheartedly — especially by one belonging to that people" (1939, 3). The reader can assume that the essays that follow will inflict discomfort or disillusion on the people to whom he acknowledges he belongs — the Jews. But Freud discomfits, he says, in the pursuit of truth: "No consideration ... will move me to set aside the truth in favour of supposed national interests" (1939, 3). An apology (and a defensive one) is a strange way to begin a book. We readers are on guard: a "truth" is about to be revealed which may rob us of a cherished "lie." The analyst is doing his job.

The first two essays of *Moses and Monotheism* were published in 1937, in *Imago*, by which time the Nazi persecution of the Jews was under way. The last and longest essay of the book was completed in 1938, the year of the Anschluss, and published in 1939, when it was joined by the two previously published essays. Freud records two Prefatory Notes to the last essay. The first Note was written while still in Vienna, before March 1938, and the second the following June, after fleeing to London. During that brief interval, he says "the outer conditions of the author have radically changed" (1939, 69). His life had been permanently altered: Germany had invaded Austria, and the protection that he and psychoanalysis had enjoyed under the Church had vanished. With the move to London, his writing feels less constricted. He is freer to speak, he says, and so he expands on an earlier and provocative analysis of religion from *Totem and Taboo* (1913) that described religion as a form of neurosis (1939, 71; 91). He specifically looks at monotheism, Jewish and Christian, with statements that he knows will heap condemnation on him from the Church — the Church

---

*My thanks to Dr. Steven Sands for discussing portions of this paper with me. All responsibility for content, however, is my own.

that, once his protector, has now become "a broken reed" (1939, 69) before the Nazis.

Despite the title, the major theme of Freud's book is an attempt to make sense of anti–Semitism, which he does through an excursus on Moses and monotheism. But in this attempt, Freud sadly falls into a common trap of blaming the victim. "There must ... be more than one reason for a phenomenon of such intensity and lasting strength as the popular hatred of Jews," he says (1939, 115)[1] and proceeds to impute the causes of anti–Semitism to the "Jewish character" (1939, 134).[2] The Jews, in centuries of defying oppression, "developed special character traits, and, incidentally, earned the hearty dislike of all other peoples" (1939, 134). One cringes. Using a misguided "Lamarckian" model of phylogenetic transfer (Yerushalmi 1991, 52), not atypical for his day, he traces the origin of these unlikable traits to its alleged progenitor, Moses— impatient, stern (1939, 37), and ambitious (43). Moses, he says, was the person who "stamped the Jewish people" (134) with their "peculiar character," which includes believing themselves (he seems to distance himself) superior to others and united by the distinction of being "God's chosen" (158). This offensive talk is unworthy of Freud. Rather than accept anti–Semitism as irrational hatred, he spouts the distorted thinking of its perpetrators. But as dismaying as his words are, they are all the more poignant because they feel so propelled by the weight of fear. We are in 1930s Vienna.

Along with fear is ambivalence. On one hand, Freud "reduces religion to the status of a neurosis of mankind" (1939, 68), but maintains that "[t]o all matters concerning the creation of a religion — and certainly to that of the Jewish one — pertains something majestic" (1939, 164). He is drawn to Moses, liberator of the Jews but also progenitor of the despised "Jewish type" (1939, 51, n. 1). He both identifies with Moses and to some degree creates him as he writes (cf. Armstrong 2005, 230). As Moses' non-existent God is a reflection of Moses, Freud's Moses seems to be a reflection of Freud. Freud's ostensible interest in Moses, however, is in the spiritual/intellectual content of his monotheism. Freud is impressed with its "triumph of spirituality [Geistigkeit] over the senses" as it "subordinat[es] sense perception to an abstract idea" (1939, 144). Yet one wonders why Freud finds a more intellectualized form of cultural neurosis preferable to any other.[3]

In the pursuit of "truth," Freud is at pains to disabuse the Jews (including himself) of any claim to the origins of this spiritually elevated movement. The Jews borrowed monotheism from Egypt, he says, from the monotheist King Akhenaten, via Moses, so that it was ultimately Egyptian values that shaped the Jews' character "for good through the disdaining of magic and mysticism" (Freud 1939, 109). But what the Jews, unlike the Egyptians, did with these values was remarkable. They made unique cultural contributions due to their "instinctual renunciation" that allowed them to reach "ethical heights that had remained inaccessible to the other peoples of antiquity" (1939, 173). Freud's explanation for the origin of these contributions is, to the average reader, a surprise: it lay "in feelings of guilt due to the repressed hostility to God" (1939, 173).[4]

Mosaic monotheism, Freud contends, has wound into its very fabric features of guilt and hostility that are at the core of all father religions, and whose oedipal roots, if properly explored, can shed light, he believes, on the origins of anti–Semitism. Moses and monotheism are thus brought back to the central theme of the book. Freud's thesis is that just as one has inevitable but unexpressed hostility to one's father, so that hostility is projected onto the divine father. And since such hostility dare not be expressed, it can only be reacted to, resulting in guilt. It is the guilt that gives rise to repression and ethical restrictions but also great cultural achievements. The results, says Assmann, is that "Freud traced this 'undying hatred' [of the Jews] back to the 'hostility' inherent in monotheism as a religion of the father," concluding that "[n]ot the Jew but monotheism had attracted this undying hatred. By making Moses an Egyptian, [Freud] deemed himself able to shift the sources of negativity and intolerance out of Judaism and back to Egypt, and to show that the defining fundamentals of Jewish monotheism and mentality came from outside it" (1997, 167). While this analysis makes sense, it does not excuse Freud's slurs against the "Jewish character."

That Moses could not have been a Jew but an Egyptian is a logical suggestion made by others since antiquity (Yerushalmi 1991; Asssmann 1997). The name "Moses," despite a biblical attempt to make it Hebrew (Ex. 2:10), is derived from the Egyptian root, *msi*, "to bear, give birth to,"[5] and can be read "[the God x] is born." The truncated "Moses" with the God's name left out, may even lend some credence to Moses' historicity, since biblical myth-makers could more easily have given him a Hebrew name rather than going to the trouble of constructing a fanciful Hebrew etymology for an Egyptian one. Moses was one of Freud's early ego ideals (Shengold 1993). The Torah was regular reading for his secular father Jacob, who "established an atmosphere in which the young Freud acquired an enduring fascination with 'biblical history' of the Old Testament, when he had 'barely acquired the art of reading'" (Gay 2006, 6–7). But the church exerted influence, too. Freud lived his earliest years in Roman Catholic Freiburg, where, until the age of 2½, one of his most important figures was a devout Catholic nanny who took him to Sunday mass and instructed him in church teaching. She was a difficult personality, whom Freud's mother, with apparent jealousy, described as "elderly, ugly and clever" (Gay 2006, 7). But she was also a beloved mother figure for Freud, and her abrupt dismissal from the household, and incarceration, concurrent with his mother's absence due to the birth of his sister, was a sad, confusing and memorable event for Freud (Gay 2006, 7; see also Freud 1900, 247).

Given his early exposure to mass and religious instruction through the nanny, and given that he was living in a Roman Catholic country, Freud may well have been aware that the Moses of his father's Old Testament was, according to Church dogma, the most important Old Testament prophet who prefigured Christ. That "prefigurement" would be a concept consciously known to a tiny boy is very doubtful, though attempts to convert Jews of all ages typically drew on such parallels to illustrate the fulfillment of the Old Testament in the New. But Freud, as child and adult, may have been aware that Moses and Christ were parallel messianic figures (with only Christ the clear Jew here!). Both men defied authority (Pharaoh, for Moses; religious establishment, for Christ) to lead their followers out of bondage. Freud, of course, can be seen as a similar liberator, leading his followers out of the bondage of inner darkness into the light of self-awareness—but without God-myth.

Even as Freud dissociates himself from any religious connection to Moses, what is interesting is that faith, in its concerted absence, may have been a connection to the very thing it rejected. The subject provided a link to his secular but Bible-reading father, and a connection to and rejection of his Catholic nanny who both loved and "left" him. That his feelings about the Church were negative cannot be denied, insofar as it was the source of an ongoing, painful anti–Semitism, as well as posing institutional hostility to psychoanalysis (Freud 1939, 68). But that it may also have represented some ambivalence cannot be discounted, especially since Freud once had a protector in the Church.

Freud's attraction to the figure of Moses was life-long. He was impressed by Moses' construction of a deity that offered an alternative deity to the Levites' "rude," "violent," and "bloodthirsty" Jahweh (1939, 61) in the form of a "more spiritual conception of God, a single God who embraces the whole world, one as all-loving as he was all-powerful, who, averse to all ceremonial and magic, set humanity as its highest aim a life of truth and justice" (1939, 61). This noble God, Freud concludes, had been "taken ... over from his king Ikhnaton [Akhenaten]" (1939, 141), whom Moses either knew or was influenced by, and whose teachings he "forced upon the Jews" (1939, 142) (as Freud now forces a new "truth" upon his reader?). As to why Freud, the non-believer, should be concerned with *any* "noble God," he notes "that the conception of an Only God signifies a step forwarding spirituality," but that "this point ... cannot be estimated so very highly" (1939, 165). Yet one cannot but still wonder why belief in one deity as opposed to many deities has any spiritual advantage for an atheist? Freud seems torn: on one hand, there is no God, but on the other, Mosaic monotheism offers a prize in which he wants a claim. Freud is analyzing the past, but the reader is analyzing Freud.

When it comes to Akhenaten, Freud overvalues him as did others since James Henry Breasted had brought the king to worldwide attention at the end of the nineteenth and beginning of the twentieth centuries. Freud asserts that Akhenaten's "greatness as a founder of religion is proved without a doubt" (1939, 141), going so far as to associate himself with Akhenaten, in a letter to Karl Abraham, when he calls Akhenaten "our analytic Pharaoh" (Shengold 1993, 81).

Freud assumes, as have many, that the king's epithet, "living in/on Maat" (loosely translated, "truth"), meant that Akhenaten was a man of ethical worth. But this epithet, normally the Egyptian sun god's, we now know, had no moral dimension in Amarna religion (Amarna was Akhenaten's new capital) that focused almost exclusively on concrete, visible sense-perception (Assmann 1997, 190–191) without meaningful reference to ethics.

While Moses is a not a figure with any verifiable history, Akhenaten is. The king lived in the fourteenth century B.C. at a time when a body of textual and archaeological evidence for him and his reign, including part of an archive of Amarna letters, testify to his dealings with Near Eastern potentates and Egyptian officials. The literature and art of his reign suggest he was a monotheist, though there is immense cultural and academic attachment to, and debate about, what "monotheism" means. Did Moses know Akhenaten? Was Moses one of Akhenaten's followers; or, was Moses, sometime after Akhenaten's death, influenced by the king's monotheistic teachings that he then bestowed upon the Israelites?

Freud's genius was to lay bare aspects of the human self that no one had so clearly explicated before but that were hardly welcome news to many. The Oedipus complex is the most noteworthy. But Freud perhaps employed the Oedipus complex too liberally. He takes the story of Moses and applies the Oedipus complex, which others, in fact, like Ernst Sellin, had also suggested (Yerulshami 1991; Assmann 1997). Moses brings the message of monotheism to the Hebrew slaves; they ultimately reject it, and him, murder him, their "father," and are beset with a guilt that they then assuage by elevating his paternal memory to mythic proportions. This is the process that Freud had already outlined in *Totem and Taboo* (Freud 1913; Gay 2006, 332–333), and which, he believes, undergirds all religions where Gods serve as father figures writ large, "raised to the status of a deity" (1939, 166). Indeed, the attraction, hostility and guilt evoked by such father figure Gods can be an unsettling mix held in check, and relieved, by what feels like the steadying power of faith.

What is interesting, however, is that Freud, who spent his life dismantling fantasies, was eager to believe the fantasy of the monotheist Akhenaten as the noble, truth-seeking visionary. Freud naively accepts the Akhenaten presented by Breasted, but is quick to deconstruct the Moses presented in Scripture — and equally quick to embrace such givens as the "historical" Moses' bestowing on the Jews their alleged sense of being "God's chosen." Freud is correct that Akhenaten eliminated magic from religion, but what he chooses not to notice is that this king narcissistically assumes the focus of the new religion to an unparalleled degree in ancient Egypt, and to the detriment of any relationship between his God, the sun disk (Aten), and the Egyptian people. Akhenaten, unlike Moses, was "the ultimate goal of creation," "the one who is ultimately 'meant' by the cosmic process and ... the only one for whom it has meaning." Meaning, in this world, is something between God and king, not anything shared by the people" (Assmann 1997, 189). Mosaic monotheism, on the other hand—and this is one of its lasting contributions—is that it was a vehicle through which a caring relationship could exist between God and community, not just between God and one man. One might expect Freud, the analyst, to be concerned with the appearance or absence of the human dimension in Atenism vs. Mosaic monotheism. But he is looking less at differences than at broad similarities between the two, and puts a higher premium on abstract intellectuality than on human relationship.

To attribute the origins of Mosaic monotheism to Egypt is a daring thing for a Jew to do. But it makes sense: in the polytheistic world of antiquity, strict monotheism was, indeed, an alien concept, except in Egypt during the brief reign of Akhenaten. And that Moses borrowed the notion from Akhenaten specifically seemed to make sense, having read Breasted and his follower Arthur Weigall, whose books were among Freud's library (Gamwell and Wells, eds. 1989). Due to the more limited archaeological data of the period, however, and perhaps a desire to project fantasy on the past, Breasted and his followers idealized Akhenaten, in part, I believe, because *they* prized monotheism, and viewed Akhenaten as the discoverer of a higher spiritual truth. And since Breasted wrote his doctoral dissertation on the king's Hymn to the Aten, glorification of Akhenaten indirectly redounded to himself as well.

Before Akhenaten, no king had claimed exclusive claim to "the truth" to which others must submit. Polytheism, Egypt's traditional religious framework, was famously elastic, inclusive, and open to others' Gods. Monotheism (though this point can be overworked) is exclusive. It has the truth and (too often) brooks no other. But the leaders of these monotheistic movements could vary greatly. While Freud speculates that Moses was a father-figure and object of ambivalence for the Israelites, Akhenaten did not fill a commensurate role for ordinary Egyptians. He may have presented himself as an object of worship, but archaeology shows that the citizenry largely went on worshiping their traditional Gods in whatever way they could manage. The monotheism Akhenaten foisted on fourteenth century B.C. Egypt was unwelcome, resulting in a destabilization of political and economic life. After his reign, Egypt branded him a heretic and struck his name from their kinglists. Worse still, his reign was associated with a massive plague (possibly beginning under his father's reign [Kozloff 2006]) whose cause was attributed to the Asiatics, i.e., Semites. Amarna religious heresy disease thus became linked, with a new layer of prejudicial blame added later: "The Egyptian phantasm of the religious enemy first became associated with the Asiatics in general, and then with the Jews in particular. It anticipated many traits of Western anti–Semitism that can now be traced back to an original impulse. This impulse had *nothing to do with the Jews* but very much to do with the experience of a counter-religion [Akhenaten's monotheism] and of a plague" (Assmann 1997, 30; my italics). So the metaphorical "disease" of Akhenaten's monotheism and the literal disease surrounding his reign were, through a chain of later distortions, projected onto the Jews—and then the Jews' hero, Moses. Historical "fact" was irrelevant.

Unlike Akhenaten, Moses lives through biblical scripture, with no external historical verification. Even the story of the Exodus has yielded no firm archaeological support (Frerichs and Lesko, eds. 1997; but cf. Groll 1999). But Freud, attempting a historical analysis and assuming Moses a historic personage, speculates that the king must have been familiar with the teachings of Akhenaten as spelled out in the *Great Hymn to the Aten* allegedly written by Akhenaten himself and known to Freud through Breasted's translation. Indeed, the similarities in wording, phrasing and subject matter between the Old Testament's Psalm 104 and the Hymn to the Aten are striking—though not mentioned by Freud (Assmann 1997)—and suggest some sort of contact between Egyptian and Hebrew culture. But whether the Aten Hymn is a direct progenitor of the Psalm as opposed to their having a common source is still debated.

In the Hymn, Akhenaten addresses the Aten: the light-emitting sun disk and the king's one God and divine father, whose life-giving rays engender all flora and fauna, placing seed in women and sperm in man. In its detailed picture of the world as revealed by the Aten, the Hymn searches for first principles (Allen 1989): light, it determines, is the origin of everything. Only what sunlight reveals, only what is tangible in the light, truly exists (Allen 1996). The underworld, a major feature of traditional Egyptian religion, goes unmentioned since it is outside visible light. Freud was impressed with the image of an abstract universal God stripped of mythological trappings, including the afterlife, as opposed to other deities in the ancient world who were typically animal-headed local or state entities with bellicose and chthonic sides. Freud concludes that Moses, influenced by Atenism, was able to make the conceptual leap to a single, abstract deity.

Indeed, Moses did adopt a God like Akhenaten's Aten, in that both, most shockingly, are without a body or face, something unpalatable to most of the ancient world. But the Aten is also mute (Assmann 2001), and this is the most shocking feature of all, in my opinion. In traditional Egyptian art (Robins 1997), the Gods are shown speaking to their divine son, the king, as they face or embrace him. But Akhenaten silences his divine father, something clearly impossible for a son to do with his human father. Akhenaten may speak about him in the Hymn or other texts, but there is no dialogue. The Aten is depersonalized, silent and remote, an abstract disk, literally far from humanity in heaven. But Moses' God, though invisible,[6] listens and responds, and Moses feels free to express self-doubt and insecurity. Freud never mentions the distinctive absence of this personal dimension in the Amarna theology nor its presence in Mosaic monotheism (already fully present in Genesis exchanges, too, between God and Abraham, for example). This point of contrast between the Atenist and Mosaic Gods is noteworthy since Freud more than any other human being, perhaps, understood the deep, life-altering value of talking and listening. For the man who invented the "talking cure," his lack of attention to this point is puzzling.

The silence of the Aten throws the focus of Amarna religion on Akhenaten. In the Hymn, the king says to his divine father, "you (yourself) are not seen (except by your) sole [son] whom you have made" (Simpson 2003, 283), and "You (the Aten) are in my heart, And there is no other who knows you" (Simpson 2003, 283). The relationship with the Aten is exclusive to the king. Only he knows his invisible God and divine father. All creation has been raised up for him, the son — and, secondarily, for his wife, Neferititi (Simpson 2003, 283). In Amarna art, the Aten's hands, its only human feature, extend life (*ankh*) to her as well as to the king (and in a rare case to the king's mother Tiye, as in the Tomb of Huya), but only to them — not even to the couple's six princesses, much less the populace. So despite the hymn's egalitarian language about bestowing creation and benefits on all countries, Egyptian and foreign alike, and on all peoples, the only human beings the Aten visibly cares about are Akhenaten, and secondarily, his wife. Humanity, in fact, is meant to worship the three of them, Aten, Akhenaten and Neferiti, who form a new trinity in keeping with Egypt's long tradition of trinities comprised of a God, his wife and their child. But how much people truly worshiped the royal family in the dozen or so years at Amarna is dubious. What is important here is that Akhenaten's monotheism, first and foremost, focuses on himself, and that neither he nor the Aten is really concerned with community. This is quite the opposite of Moses and his one God.

Later considered a heretic, Akhenaten's name was erased from Egyptian king lists. But, as Freud suggests, his influence may have been repressed but not lost, only to resurface in the figure and teachings of Moses, through whom monotheism (in a related but different form) took root. "If monotheism was genetically Egyptian, it has been historically Jewish," notes Yerushalmi (1991, 53). But whether it actually was transmitted through Moses or was just "in the air" of the time, cannot be definitively proved even in light of the parallels of Psalm 104 with sections of the Aten Hymn. Freud's focus on oedipal claims are also at base unknowable. We cannot know if the Hebrews' oedipal feelings were inflamed to the point of murdering Moses. But we can suggest, based on actual data, that oedipal ambivalence is a relevant issue with regard to Akhenaten and *his* father.

This was a point that Karl Abraham made in a 1912 letter (Abraham and Freud, eds. 1965) and in an article on Akhenaten that he shared with Freud (Abraham 1955). While some of Abraham's suggestions may not hold up today, he did identify the oedipal issue: "[The king] despises his descent from his true father and replaces him by a higher one. As, however, he was in reality the son of a king, he could not raise himself above his father by the usual phantasies of royal parentage; he had to go even higher — to the Gods" (p. 272). Freud seems to have dismissed Abraham's insights in a cryptic response (Abraham and Freud, eds., 1965, 111–112). Even more oddly, decades later, in *Moses and Monotheism*, he neither references Abraham, nor his article, a "slip of the mind" (Shengold 1993, 63) that was perhaps the result of an unconscious denial related to Abraham's name — the name of the Jews' patriarchal father who preceded (had precedence over) Moses. "Freud had forgotten that, as with Moses, an Abraham had preceded him in Egypt. Indeed Freud's book neglects the biblical Abraham ... [with the result that] Moses replaces Abraham as the true father of the Jewish people" (Shengold 1993, 70; also 63–75; 81; 82). Freud seems to be denying two Abrahams, the ancient and the contemporary, and giving primacy to Moses (himself?).

Issues of primacy, denial and remembrance play out in the Akhenaten drama as well. Akhenaten's father was Amenhotep III, who reigned 39 years, celebrated three lavish sed-festivals (jubilees), and built extensively, especially at Egypt's religious capital of Thebes, where he founded Luxor Temple to the state God Amun. He ably controlled an empire from deep in the Sudan to northern Syria, with trade routes east into Mesopotamia and north into today's Turkey. While there has been much debate about whether he and Akhenaten ruled jointly in a coregency, recent research declares the coregency theory "disproved decisively" (Allen 2007, 8). This is an important point since coregency poses a situation in which there is inherent competition between two people, usually father and son. We can now assume that the father, Amenhotep III, died before his son's accession to the throne (cf. Reeves 2005, 80), after which Akhenaten ruled with the memory, not the physical presence, of his father, Amenhotep III. Akhenaten, in turn, did not have to live with competition from his own son. Though he tried to sire a son, even marrying several women in his own family (Allen 2007), he had only daughters.[7]

During the reign of Amenhotep III, a religious movement, termed by Assmann, The New Solar Theology (Assmann 2001, 201–208), characterized religious thinking and provided the context for the Amarna Theology of Akhenaten in the next reign. As revealed through hymns of the period (Lichtheim 1976, esp. 86–89), The New Solar Theology presented a kind of monotheism that gave preeminence to the visible sun (one aspect being Aten) as a force that absorbed the creative powers of all Gods and all natural creative processes. The sun, especially known under the name of Amun (abstract "hiddenness"), was understood as the hidden essence (Hornung 1995) that regenerated Gods and nature alike in a phenomenological understanding of the visible, tangible world that was described with little recourse to mythological language (Assmann 2001, 204; 1996, 212–213; Hornung, 1995, 19–20). This new form of theological thinking represents the latest and most profound form of solar monotheism — really, henotheism, which emphasizes one God but not to the exclusion of others — that had already been one of a number of hallmarks of Egyptian religion for a thousand years and that would resume after the Amarna period for another thousand (Assmann 2001, 201). By Amenhotep III's reign, the many Gods were all the more understood as aspects of the one sun God (Hornung 1995, 19–20) in what amounted to an "antipolytheistic movement" (Assmann 1997, 171). Amenhotep III apparently sensed a threat from the rising power of a single deity (Hornung 1995, 20) and cleverly redirected focus to himself.

In his first Jubilee, in his 30th year of reign, Amenhotep III declared himself the personification of all Gods (Johnson 1999, 45), including not only the most powerful state Gods, but also a variety of lesser, local ones (Hornung 1995, 20), in an equalizing process that slightly lowered the status of the many Gods and raised his own. He presented himself as the sun God, who incorporated all Gods in one, and was thus to be worshiped in multiple visible forms in what, art historically, has been called his "deification style" (Johnson 1990, 41). He was represented as Ptah-Sokar-Osiris, a triad of deities that combine creator and underworld Gods in one; as the reborn sun god, with the pudgy face of a young child; as a slumped and fat fertility God (not a usual way to show a king); or as Osiris, with exaggerated oblique eyes that were already foreshadowed stylistically under his father, Thutmose IV. But on a whole new level of grandiosity, Amenhotep III also had himself shown as a living man worshiping himself as a God (Freed 1999, 3). One can only suspect that he was at pains to display a power that felt compromised. Adding to this self-promotion, he gave himself a new appellation: "the Dazzling Aten," defining himself as the visible sun disk itself (Kozloff et al., eds. 1992).

Amenhotep III's son, Amenhotep IV, as Akhenaten was first called, starts his reign by depicting himself in the traditional Egyptian style that most kings used and which his father had used in his pre-deification style. But by his third or fourth regnal year (Allen 1996), Amenhotep IV appears with exaggerated features that exceed even those of his father's deification style. The features can only be described as grotesque: elongated face, slit eyes, drooping chin, sagging belly, effeminately swelling thighs and scrawny limbs. Is this an extension of Amenhotep III's deification style or a reaction to it? We don't know. If Amenhotep III had been alive, he would surely have been shocked, for his son, while reverently carrying on certain stylistic features of his father's images (like a slouchy paunchiness in select representations), is shown in a shocking new manner. In this early part of Amenhotep IV's reign, he also depicts his divine solar father, shown as a hawk-headed God, with some of the same expressionistic oddities that appear in his own representations. Identification of Amenhotep IV with this divine solar father seems to be the message (Redford 1976), while differentiation from his biological father, Amenhotep III, seems also to be at work. In Amenhotep IV's second regnal year, the king presents the Aten's name in cartouches, which are a feature otherwise reserved for kings' names. Furthermore, the Aten, like a king, now celebrates his own jubilee, that very rejuvenation rite that Amenhotep III had used to initiate his deification style. Under Amenhotep IV, king becomes more like God, and God becomes more like king. Boundaries blur between father-son and God-king, blurrings that had always been present in Egyptian religion, but which now become more pronounced.

Amenhotep IV soon eliminates all anthropomorphic images of the Gods— the very Gods his father had personified. In their place he depicts his solar father, the Aten, as a disk without body, face, or voice, from which emanates the light that creates all things. A few years later, between regnal years 9 and 11, the Aten receives a modified name in cartouches whose reading shows that the Aten was not just perceived as the sun's disk but as its very light (Allen 1996). Gone now are the traditional images of the Gods interacting with the king; gone, the expression of human relationship, of God and king nose to nose, as the God breathes life into his son. Except for its disembodied human hands that offer life and caresses to the king and queen, this Aten is a God of remote abstraction devoid of overt maternal/paternal features of former Egyptian Gods.

Evidence suggests that Amenhotep IV's feelings toward both his earthly and divine fathers were conflicted. From the start of his reign, we now know that he quickly erected temples at Thebes, not to Amun, the main God of his father, but to the Aten; that he did little for Amun at Thebes where his father and ancestors had done much; that he snubbed Amun, setting up a stone stela, for example, that ostensibly honored the God but with a text that ignored him (Murnane 1999, 307); and that he seems pointedly to ignore his own father, Amenhotep III, when he had plenty of time to erect the many temples to the Aten at Karnak, but none to finish a relief of himself on a structure there near his father's (Murnane 1999, 308). The son seems conflicted concerning his father and his father's main God (Amun). We are not told why. The answer may lie partly in Akhenaten's ambivalence toward his father, Amenhotep III, which was then projected onto the father's God.

Ambivalence is strongly suggested, for example, when also early in his reign, the king discards his name and that of his father, Amenhotep ("Amun is satisfied"), and takes the name Akhenaten. Names of kings, displayed in cartouches, were often added to in ancient Egypt, and sometimes changed, but always with a pointed political message. So what does the name Akhenaten mean? Most translate it as "He who is effective [akh] for the Aten," a translation that, while sound, misses a crucial point. It is true that in its most fundamental sense, akh means effectiveness. But the forms of effectiveness were both earthly and cosmic (Friedman 1981). On the earthly plane, the king is akh-effective in what he does for the Gods, providing offerings and building temples for them. And the Gods, in a typically reciprocal fashion, are akh-effective to the king by granting him life and the celebration of millions of rejuvenating jubilees. Akhenaten is called the "son of eternity who came forth from the Aten, being akh-effective for him (the Aten) who is akh-effective for him (the king)" (Sandman 1938, 91, ll.9–10). A quid pro quo relationship of reciprocity is at the heart of the father-son, God-king relationship, as it had been since earliest times. This reciprocal relationship was originally worked out in the

Horus-Osiris relationship, which is never referred to in the demythologized Amarna theology, but whose principle remained operative nonetheless in the Amarna Period (Friedman 1985; 1986).

But for the deeper meaning of Akhenaten's name, I think we have to turn to the meaning of akh in the cosmic sphere, where akh is the most effective substance in the universe: light. (Amarna inscriptions use "akh" in parallel with words that denote light [Friedman 1985; 1986, 100]). Akhenaten, I believe, through his new name, is saying that he is not just one who does akh-effective things *for*[8] his divine father, the Aten, but that he is the very akh-effective light *of* that father; that he is the gleaming essence of his Aten-father; that he is "The Akh of the Aten."[9] So while Akhenaten and his divine father act reciprocally for one another, being akh-effective for one another as father and son, they also, I believe, should be understood as consubstantial, being of one cosmic akh-substance of light. This double meaning, of being both pragmatically effective for one another and of one luminous substance is, I think, implicit in the king's name change.

The extreme claim, in my view, that God and king are consubstantial, is one that implicitly, I believe, Akhenaten used to elevate himself just a bit beyond the lofty perch once held by his father, Amenhotep III. The father may have been the "Dazzling Aten," but the son is the light-filled essence of that Aten. Akhenaten has either done his father one better — or drawn himself into deeper relationship with his father, in fact, with both fathers, earthly and divine. Quite cleverly, through the new name, Akhenaten ensures filial connection with both, since the Aten is at once Amenhotep III (the "Dazzling Aten") and the divine sun disk; and the king is the son of both. In this expanded filiation, Akhenaten, the king, manages to replace the national God, Amun. For as Amun, whose name means "hidden," had been the *hidden* essence of *all* Gods, Akhenaten, I suggest, has now become the *visible* (akh) essence of the *one* God.

In what may be a veiled rejection of the father, Akhenaten, as Freud knew, also moved the capital to an undeveloped no man's land, today called Amarna, a site untainted by association with any God, especially Amun, and far from Amenhotep III's monuments. Then, a few years later, he closed the temples to Amun at Thebes, including his father's Luxor Temple that had been the focus of the annual Opet Festival, in which the populace participated. Closing the temples robbed the people of contact with deity. This must have been a blow for those still in Thebes. Was Akhenaten motivated by hostility or just a desire to differentiate himself from his father? The contrast between father and son must have been striking. Amenhotep III knew how to manipulate religion and politics and how to keep an empire intact. Though Akhenaten was no pacifist, as Freud and those of his day mistook him to be, he was not adept at holding the empire together whether by military or diplomatic means. He neglected his father's empire (Kendall 1999, 160), alienated some of his father's base to the point that he was unable to entice enough of them to come to Amarna — or perhaps he dismissed them (the vizier Ramose, for example, did not come with

Akhenaten to Amarna), and in some cases was forced to rely on foreigners to fill administrative posts (Manuelian 1999, 146–7). He was apparently unable even to attract enough high quality relief carvers to the new capital (Barry Kemp in a September 27, 2006, interview at www.archaeology.org/online/interview/kemp.html.).

That Akhenaten is acting out against his father is most famously suggested by the fact that late in his reign, as Freud knew, he orders a campaign of expunging the name of the Amun from monuments, especially at Thebes, the city famous for Amenhotep III's monuments. Akhenaten does not expunge the names of all the other Gods. Most Gods' names, in fact, were not attacked. The destruction was selective in targeting Amun. There is even evidence that he had his men erase (castrate) the phallus from ithyphallic images of Amun (Fischer 1975). He also attacked any reference to the plural "Gods," an important point when remembering that his father had personified that very plurality. And the purging, we now see, was executed with brutality, not in the often careful manner that had happened a century earlier to the name of Hatshpesut (Dorman 2005; Roth 2005; Do. Arnold 2005). The purging included monuments in which the name of Amun was erased even in the name of Amenhotep III, his father. While Jung was inclined to excuse the hostility of this act "in comparison with the great deed of establishing monotheism" (Jones, 1955, 147), Abraham and Freud understood its oedipal thrust. In ancient Egyptian thinking, to eradicate a name was to eradicate the person. What Akhenaten ordered was tantamount to killing his own father.

But this is not simply a son's revolt against his father. For Akhenaten, as Ray Johnson has shown, treated other images of his human father Amenhotep III in quite a different way. Akhenaten apparently ordered that images of the God Amun in his father's funerary temple not be erased but rather recarved into images of the deified Amenhotep III, and into images of the very creator and resurrection Gods that his father had personified (Johnson 1999, 48–9). This strange exception to the standard purging contradicted the monotheism of the Aten. Using Freud's model (1939, 173), one wonders if this contradiction is a manifestation of the son's hostility transformed into an awareness of guilt. It looks like Akhenaten harbored ambivalence toward Amenhotep III, and even the Aten, that was apparently complex. But it also appears that the hostility that he perhaps dared not express toward his human father Amenhotep III was recast into worship of the divine (and all good) father; the Aten.

So is this Aten the one God taken up by Moses and "forced" on the Israelites? That a tendency toward solar monotheism had been in the air in Eighteenth Dynasty Egypt is indisputable, though it had been present for over a millennium, gaining added prominence under Amenhotep III, and given more radicalized treatment under Akhenaten. But Akhenaten need not, in my opinion, be invoked to explain monotheistic influence on Moses, if Moses indeed lived, for the notion of an abstract, universal God was in the air well before. And all the intellectualized values of monotheism that Freud attributed to Atenism do not negate the fact that its founder, Akhenaten, rejected his father's name, moved his father's religious capital to an unused piece of turf far from his father's monuments, alienated his father's officials, mutilated the image of his father's God, and expunged the name of "Amun" from his father's own cartouches, thus imperiling the survival of his father's soul for eternity. Nor does it take into account the narcissistic role played by Akhenaten, who presented himself as the universe's reason for being, the very akh-filled essence of the Aten's light (if I am right), and the focus of humanity's worship — feats of grandiosity unmatched even by his father, Amenhotep III.

And Freud, though he was searching for Egyptian roots in Mosaic monotheism, may have overlooked one of Mosaic monotheism's greatest contributions and one that differentiated it from Atenism: the fact that it modeled the critical elements of relationship — talking and listening, the very elements on which Freud based his own revolution of the talking cure, while Atenism, for all its intellectuality, offered only a remote deity silent before mankind.

And finally, how does all this relate to Freud? I don't think one can reliably apply the Oedipus complex to the followers of an ahistorical Moses, though it's not unreasonable, given the historical data, to assign oedipal conflicts to Akhenaten himself. Nevertheless, of the three men — Freud, Moses and Akhenaten — the only one about whom we have abundantly verifiable information is Freud. And *Moses and Monotheism*, is, at base, about Freud, about his identifications, his oedipal conflicts, perhaps, and his fears. This is not to say that his religious-historical excursions aren't fascinating and provocative. They are. But do they take us any closer to his quest for the origins of anti–Semitism? I don't think so. Freud is trying to ferret out of the historical past someone or something that is responsible for the enduring hatred which surrounds him. But the answer lies not in actual historical data of the past but in the projections and distorted memories of that past. How our past can profitably be mined for the origins of anti–Semitism, and how Freud's interpretations fit into a long chain of interpretations over millennia, are analyzed in Jan Assmann's *Moses the Egyptian: The Memory of Egypt in Western Monotheism*, where the author's focus is not the realm of history but, more appropriately, the sphere of memory — that cultural repository of projections and distortions that drive action with little if any relationship to truth.

References

Abraham, H. C., and E.L. Freud, eds. (1965). *A Psycho-Analytic Dialogue: The Letters of Sigmund Freud and Karl Abraham, 1907–1926.* New York: Basic.

Abraham, K. (1955). "Amenhotep IV: A Psycho-Analytical Contribution Towards the Understanding of his Personality and of the Monotheistic Cult of Aton (1912)." In Karl Abraham and Hilda C. Abraham, *Clinical Papers and Essays on Psycho-analysis*, pp. 262–290. New York: Brunner/Mazel.

Allen, James P. (1989). "The Natural Philosophy of Akhenaten." In *Religion and Philosophy in*

Ancient Egypt. Yale Egyptological Studies 3. W.K. Simpson, ed., New Haven: CT: Yale University Press, pp. 89–101.
_____ (1996). "The Religion of Amarna." In *The Royal Women of Amarna: Images of Beauty from Ancient Egypt*. Do. Arnold et al., eds., New York: Metropolitan Museum of Art, pp. 3–5.
_____ (2007). "The Amarna Succession." In *Causing His Name to Live: Studies in Egyptian Epigraphy and History in Memory of William J. Murnane*. Peter J. Brand and Jacobus van Dijk, eds., Memphis, TN: University of Memphis, pp. 1–17.
Armstrong, R. H. (2005). *A Compulsion for Antiquity: Freud and the Ancient World*. Ithaca, NY, and London: Cornell University Press.
Arnold, Do. (2005). "The Destruction of The Statues of Hatshepsut from Deir el Bahri." In *Hatshepsut: From Queen to Pharaoh*. C.H. Roehrig, ed., with R. Dreyfus and C.A. Keller, New York: Metropolitan Museum of Art, pp. 270–276.
Assmann, J. (1996). *The Mind of Egypt*. New York: Metropolitan.
_____ (1997). *Moses the Egyptian: The Memory of Egypt in Western Monotheism*. Cambridge, MA: Harvard University Press.
_____ (2001). *The Search for God in Ancient Egypt*. Trans. David Lorton. Ithaca, NY, and London: Cornell University Press.
Berman, L.M., ed. (1990). *The Art of Amenhotep III: Art Historical Analysis*. Cleveland, OH: Cleveland Museum of Art.
Dorman, P.F. (2005). "The Proscription of Hatshepsut." In *Hatshepsut: From Queen to Pharaoh*. C.H. Roehrig, ed., with R. Dreyfus and C.A. Keller. New York: Metropolitan Museum of Art, pp. 267–269.
Fischer, H.G. (1975). "An Early Example of Atenist Iconoclasm." In *Journal of the American Research Center in Egypt* 12, pp. 131–132, pl. XXXIX.
Freed, R.E., Y.J. Markowitz and S.H. D'Auria, eds. (1999). *Pharaohs of the Sun: Akhenaten, Nefertiti, Tutankhamen*. Boston: Boston Museum of Fine Arts.
Frerichs, E.S., and L.H. Lesko, eds. (1997). *Exodus: The Egyptian Evidence*. Winona Lake, IN: Eisenbrauns.
Friedman, F.D. (1981). *On the Meaning of Akh (3h) in Egyptian Mortuary Texts*. Unpublished doctoral dissertation. Brandeis University. University Microfilms.
_____ (1985). "The Root Meaning of 3h [*akh*]: Effectiveness or Luminosity." *Serapis* 8: 39–46.
_____ (1986). "3h [*akh*] in the Amarna Period." *Journal of the American Research Center in Egypt* 23: 99–106.
Freud, S. (1900). *The Interpretation of Dreams*. Standard Edition 4.
_____ (1913 [1946]). *Totem and Taboo*. New York: Vintage.
_____ (1939). *Moses and Monotheism*. New York: Vintage.
Gamwell, L. and R. Wells, eds. (1989). *Sigmund Freud and Art: His Personal Collection of Antiquities*. New York: Harry N. Abrams.
Gay, P. (1989). *Sigmund Freud and Art: His Personal Collection of Antiquities*. New York: New York State University Press.
_____ (2006). *Freud: A Life for Our Time*. New York and London: W.W. Norton.
Goring, E., N. Reeves and J. Ruffle, eds. (1997). *Chief of Seers: Egyptian Studies in Memory of Cyril Aldred*. London and New York: Kegan Paul.
Groll, S. I. (1999). "Historical Background to the Exodus: Papyrus Anastasi VIII." In *Gold of Praise: Studies on Ancient Egypt in Honor of Edward F. Wente*. SAOC No. 58, pp. 159–162. Chicago: University of Chicago.
Hornung, E. (1995). *Akhenaten and the Religion of Light*. Trans. by D. Lorton. Ithaca, NY, and London: Cornell University Press.
Iversen, E. (1996). "The Reform of Akhenaten." *Göttinger Miszellen* 155, 55–59.
Johnson, W.R. (1990). "Images of Amenhotep III in Thebes: Styles and Intentions. " In *The Art of Amenhotep III: Art Historical Analysis*, ed. L.M. Berman. Cleveland, OH: Cleveland Museum of Art, pp. 26–46.
_____ (1999). "The Setting: History, Religion, and Art." In *Pharaohs of the Sun: Akhenaten, Nefertiti, Tutankhamen*, R.E. Freed, Y.J. Markowitz, and S.H. D'Auria, eds. Boston: Boston Museum of Fine Arts, pp. 38–49.
Jones, E. (1955). *The Life and Work of Sigmund Freud. Vol. 2: Years of Maturity: 1901–1919*. New York: Basic.

_____ (1957). *The Life and Work of Sigmund Freud. Vol. 3: The Last Phase: 1919–1939*. New York: Basic.

_____ ed. (1949). *Selected Papers of Karl Abraham, M.D.* Trans. D. Bryan and A. Strachey. London: Hogarth.

Kendall, T. (1999). "Foreign Relations." In *Pharaohs of the Sun: Akhenaten, Nefertiti, Tutankhamen*, R.E. Freed, Y.J. Markowitz, and S.H. D'Auria, eds. Boston: Boston Museum of Fine Arts, pp. 156–161.

Kozloff, A. P., B.M. Bryan and L.M. Berman (1992). *Egypt's Dazzling Sun: Amenhotep III and His World*. Cleveland, OH: Cleveland Museum of Art.

_____ (2006). "Bubonic Plague in the Reign of Amenhotep III?" *KMT*, vol. 17, no. 3, 36–46.

Lichtheim, M. (1976). *Ancient Egyptian Literature. vol. II. The New Kingdom*. Berkeley, Los Angeles, London: University of California Press.

Manuelian, P.D. (1999). "Semi-Literacy in Egypt: Some Erasures from the Amarna Period." In *Gold of Praise: Studies on Ancient Egypt in Honor of Edward F. Wente*, E. Teeter and J.A. Larson, eds. SAOC No. 58, pp. 285–298. Chicago: University of Chicago.

Murnane, W.J. (1999). "Observations on Pre-Amarna Theology During the Earliest Reign of Amenhotep IV." In *Gold of Praise: Studies on Ancient Egypt in Honor of Edward F. Wente*, E. Teeter and J.A. Larson, eds. SAOC No. 58, pp. 303–316. Chicago: University of Chicago.

Redford, D.B. (1976). "The Sun-Disc in Akhenaten's Program: Its Worship and Antecedents, I." *Journal of the American Research Center in Egypt* 13: 47–61.

_____ (1999). "The Beginning of the Heresy." In *Pharaohs of the Sun: Akhenaten, Nefertiti, Tutankhamen*, R.E. Freed, Y.J. Markowitz, and S.H. D'Auria, eds. Boston: Boston Museum of Fine Arts, pp. 50–59.

Reeves, N. (2005). *Akhenaten: Egypt's False Prophet*. London: Thames & Hudson.

Robins, G. (1997). *The Art of Ancient Egypt*. Cambridge, MA: Harvard University Press.

Roehrig, Catharine H., ed., with Renée Dreyfus and Cathleen A. Keller (2005). *Hatshepsut: From Queen to Pharaoh*. New York: Metropolitan Museum of Art.

Roth, A.M. (2005). "Erasing a Reign." In *Hatshepsut: From Queen to Pharaoh*. C.H. Roehrig, ed. with R. Dreyfus and C. . Keller. New York: Metropolitan Museum of Art, pp. 277–281.

Sandman, M. (1938). *Texts from the Time of Akhenaten*. Brussels: Fondation Egyptologique Reine Elisabeth.

Shengold, L. (1993). *The Boy Will Come to Nothing: Freud's Ego Ideal and Freud as Ego Ideal*. New Haven, CT, and London: Yale University Press.

Simpson, W.K., ed. (2003). *The Literature of Ancient Egypt*. New Haven, CT, and London: Yale University Press.

_____ (2003). "The Hymn to the Aten." In *The Literature of Ancient Egypt*, W.K. Simpson, ed. New Haven, CT, and London: Yale University Press, pp. 278–283.

Yerushalmi. Y.H. (2006). *Freud's Moses: Judaism Terminable and Interminable*. New Haven, CT: Yale University Press.

Sigmund Freud in Exile
The End of an Illusion
FRANK MECKLENBURG

Freud's last publication, *Moses and Monotheism*,[1] which appeared in June 1939, generated lively debates about Freud's Jewish loyalties and adherence. However, one topic that seems to have been avoided, and not only within the context of this conference, is how this very question of Freud's Jewish identity, an aspect that seems so self-evident, has been shied away from. It seems to me that for us today, the question is radically different than it was in Freud's days. The Holocaust has reshaped the world and forced us to inquire in a different way. In the post–Holocaust world, the question of Jewish identity is not only posed from either within a Jewish perspective or from the traditionally Western non–Jewish perspective, but now we have a third point of view, which is that of humanity. The issues raised in the course of the International Nuremberg War Crimes Trials, that is, the more general questions of Human Rights and International Justice are now also relevant. In Freud's day, this was not so. This is obviously related to the claim of the Nazis that Jews were not to be counted as human beings. The absurdity of that claim, and at the same time the failure of the world community to reject that claim outright, has opened a third dimension, namely the re-affirmation of that self-evidential aspect of human existence, that is the universality of human identity. It seems to me that the pre–Holocaust issue of Jewish identity with its religious or rather transcendental notion, which opened up so easily to a pure racist rejection, that is, the innocence of the belief in the supreme truth of divine law, was challenged by the barbarism of the Nazi ideology in re-defining reality. The result of that claim made by Nazism was the fundamental shift in regard to that question, or to be more precise, the not posed question of human identity in the pre–Holocaust world, which instead became a question of ethics, the question of "the other," which is most clearly addressed in the works of Emmanuel Levinas. Freud's *Moses and Monotheism* is the key text to address this issue, that is, that the memory of the unspeakable deed needs to be repressed. Freud's text comes at a particular moment when the world is in transition from a pre–Holocaust to a Holocaust and subsequently a post–Holocaust era. Freud articulates and reacts to the rupture in the fabric of society that brings about the change in the question of identity. The universality of Freud's argument, which addresses, as he claims in *Moses and Monotheism*, not only the Mosaic religion but all religions — and consequently all systems that claim absolute truth — is also applicable to the situation he encountered at the conclusion of his life, which ends in exile and death.

Freud saw himself as a new "Moses," who had introduced the new (un)- "religion" of science and rationality to the chosen "tribe," the enlightened German-speaking Central European society. Jews belonged to this society as much as anyone else, notwithstanding complex internal conflicts of that society, such as conservative and anti-modernist anti–Semitic factions, first of all the Catholic Church. The dominant religious conflicts, the anti–Catholic forces in Northern Germany against anti–Protestant forces in Catholic areas had devastated Central Europe during the Thirty-Years' War, the echoes of which continue to this day. Freud was full of enthusiasm in receiving responses to his "revelation" in *Moses and Monotheism* that religion, in fact all religions, is illusion, "to be understood only on the model of the neurotic symptoms of the individual" (Freud 1939, p. 71). For him, this was a historically developed scientific fact, although for the Jewish religion it was the hardest to prove since he could find only one piece of hard evidence, that is, the quote from the Ernst Sellin book of 1922,[2] that Moses was killed by the Jews (Freud 1939, p. 71).

Freud's "discovery," however, that is, the publication of which, coincided with the verdict of the new dominant German political forces, i.e., the Jews as the instigators of modernity and as the declared enemy. Freud remarks that in contrast to the totalitarian rule in the Soviet Union and in Italy, "in the case of the German people, that retrogression into all but prehistoric barbarism can come to pass *independently of any progressive idea*" (Freud 1939, p. 67; my italics). This he stated in the pre–March '38 introduction to *Moses and Monotheism*, still written in Vienna and published only after he was safe in British exile. But this statement also carries a notion of irony as Freud, like many others, was left almost speechless, lacking for proper words, in his analysis of Nazism in Germany, which, in turn, was matched if not surpassed in its brutality by the events of March '38 in Vienna. The above statement is therefore rather to be seen as an expression of how perplexed and helpless he must have felt. Up to that point, he had regarded the Catholic Church as the force of resistance to his ideas and therefore the major enemy of the psychoanalytic movement. Yet the Nazis takeover of Austria (Anschluss) turned that situation upside down, and this seems to have come as a complete surprise to Freud. There is a notion of premonition when in the last sentence of the pre–March '38 introduction he already writes for future generations: "In darker days there lived a man who thought as you did" (Freud 1939, p. 69).

Is September 23, 1939, the date of Freud's death, an arbitrary date? Was Freud's cancer the only reason for his assisted suicide? Freud's Jewish identity was formed in the pre–Holocaust world, which allowed him to question the fundamental tenets of Jewish traditional identity expressed in the question, "was Moses an Egyptian?" The threat to Jewish identity was internal. And as a not unimportant aside, it would be interesting to see what the influence of his thesis was on the sources of Christianity. Is there a debate among Christian and/or Islamic scholars of Freud's thesis on Moses the Egyptian and the Jewish religion as a derivative of the Egyptian religion of Akhenaton? For Freud, this was not a threat to his understanding of Jewishness, rather he infused a rational historical concept as an element of debate into the traditional understanding of religious identity.

At the end of his life, Freud enjoyed a high degree of sensitivity through psychoanalysis and his historical studies, which can probably be described with Ernst Bloch's concept of anticipatory illumination (*Vorschein*), although in a reverse sense. The succession of events from 1933 to March and November of 1938, and, of course, June 1938, as he goes into exile is the most dramatic personal event which carried deep historical meaning for him. Freud's enlightened society of Central Europe would not have a place for another Exodus; but Freud and his ideas were rejected from his cultural environment. September 1, 1939, is the culmination point of his disillusion. With the beginning of open warfare in the East, being well connected as he was, Freud must have received information about the immediate onset of mass killings by the German invading armies in Poland. All this might have generated a sense of hopelessness in Freud which may have contributed to the decision to end his life. The publication of *Moses and Monotheism* in June 1939, featured, for instance, in "Books of the Times" for the month of June in the *New York Times*,[3] was definitely an uplifting event in Freud's life. He was looking forward to responses, positive and negative, and had great anticipation about the debate he was setting in motion. In light of the turn of events between June and September 1939, Freud's death serves as a signifier of the end of the pre–Holocaust identity of Central European Jews.

The exile experience is the most significant turning point in his development as an assimilated Jew in Austria, which had been a difficult position all along, but until March 1938 not an impossible position. However, as indicated in the two introductions to the *Moses* text, one from pre–March '38, the other dated June '38 in London, the escape to England marked the clear end of that dream. In the June '38 introduction he writes: "Then, suddenly, the German invasion broke in on us and Catholicism proved to be, as the Bible has it, but 'a broken reed'" (Freud 1939, p. 69). What he had regarded as the major force causing him to exercise restraint, that is, the Catholic Church, turned out to be a minor, feeble signpost of anti-modernity. "The certainty of persecution" (Freud 1939, p. 69) was a fact, and by what Freud had seen and heard, the Nazi persecution meant certain death, sooner or later, to his work and himself, and to his "race." Between June and September 23, 1939, the dramatic progression of events must have made clear to him that the destruction of the Jews was the real danger. Was he killing himself also as a substitute father, the primordial father of a new Jewish identity that no longer needed regressive religion? "That conviction I acquired a quarter of a century ago, when I wrote my book on *Totem and Taboo* (in 1912), and it has only become stronger since," extended to all forms of religion, although with "Jewish monotheism" he had the most difficulties to prove it (Freud 1939, p. 71). When he decided to "make public" (Freud 1939, p. 70) the last part of his essay (parts I and II were initially published in 1937 in *Imago*), he hoped to end the oppression and illusion of religion. He wrote that the people in English exile, "anxious to point me the way to Christ and to enlighten me about the future of Israel ... thus could not have known much about me." But then follows a peculiar sentence, in which he anticipates the exchange about his arguments and thesis, when he writes: "I expect, however, that when this new work of mine becomes known among my new compatriots I shall lose with my correspondents and a number of the others something of the sympathy they now extend to me" (Freud 1939, p. 70). This rather hopeful note, however, (hopeful in the sense that he expected people to react to his argument) is followed in the days of September by the news from Poland and the immediate beginning of the mass persecution and murder of the Jews. The October 1, 1939, issue of the German refugee paper *Aufbau*, which he wasn't able to read any longer but the reported news probably reached him, published the lead article under the headline "'Schm'a Yisroel!' Under the Hail of Bombs. How Death Ravages the Jews of Poland," in which "from the multitudes of news and the overabundance of unspeakable details and cruelties"[4] the mass killings and massive bombardments of synagogues and Jewish schools were reported. Even with the knowledge of the escalating brutality of the Nazi assault from 1933 onward, the invasion of Poland and the beginning of mass murder surpassed all negative expectations and must have been beyond comprehension, especially for all who not long before had maintained the belief that Central Europe was the cradle of modern enlightenment and humanity.

Freud's excitement at having published *Moses and Monotheism* and his eagerness for debate is broken when he realizes that the tenets of the enlightened society he grew up in are destroyed when the German armies invade Poland. Within a very short time it becomes clear that the mass killings of Jews (and of the Polish population in general) is on the minds of the Germans. September 23, 1939, the day of Freud's death, is Yom Kippur. The date of his death is no accident. Does Freud kill himself on that day to fulfill or symbolize the killing of the primeval father? Is there a greater degree of symbolism in Freud's death?

However, it comes as a surprise to realize that this fact of the date of death seems to have left little trace in the literature on Sigmund Freud. Either no particular attention is paid to the symbolic circumstances, or Freud's exile and death is simply ignored since it is not part of the body of psychoanalysis. What is his death date to signal? Is it the ultimate slap in the face of religion, or is it the recognition of his religious roots in light of the failure of Central European culture to accept Freud's discovery? Either one is embodied in this gesture. The German death threat cannot reach him since he is in the safety of the British exile. But as the Jewish people are being exterminated, he dies as the new "Moses" of the enlightened "religion" of rational science. At this moment, Freud's death questions the traditional Central European Jewish identity.

Notes

1. Freud, Sigmund, *Moses and Monotheism*. New York: Vintage, 1939 (reprint 1967).
2. Ernst Sellin, *Mose und seine Bedeutung fuer die israelitisch-juedische Religionsgeschichte*. Leipzig: Deichert, 1922.
3. See also the New York refugee paper *Aufbau* of April 1, 1939, announcing the publication two months in advance.
4. *Aufbau. Blaetter fuer das Judentum*. Herausgegeben vom German-Jewish Club, Inc., New York, October 1, 1939, under the title "'Schm'a Yisroel!' im Bombenregen. Wie der Tod in Polen unter den Juden rast," with a report from Warzaw from the end of September, p. 1.

References

Aufbau. October 1, 1939.
Bloch, E. (1986). *The Principle of Hope*. Cambridge, MA: MIT.
Freud, S. (1913–1914): "Totem and Taboo." *Standard Edition* Volume XIII: 1–255, Hogarth.
───── (1939). "Moses and Monotheism." *Standard Edition* Volume XXIII: 7–140, Hogarth.
Levinas, E. (1998). On Thinking of the Other: Entre Nous. New York: Columbia University Press.

"Leaving This World with Decency"
Psychoanalytical Considerations on Suicide in the Life and Work of Sigmund Freud

BENIGNA GERISCH

Introduction

To put an end to oneself is a monstrous act. Killing oneself is not a topic gladly discussed. It is frightening and unnerving, often rendering us speechless. And yet, as Albert Camus observed, there are, at least in thought, many who are familiar with an independent end — and such thoughts affect them greatly.

The extent of suicidal problems in the western world is not only extremely sensitive, it has also always been connected with strong empirical gender specifics (compare Gerisch 1998, 2003). Freud also developed his theories regarding the phenomenon of suicide predominantly on female patients.

I should like to begin by illustrating the extent of suicide with the aid of some straightforward figures, avoiding any interpretation because, eo ipso, epidemiological-universal interpretations must remain speculative.

In 2008 in Germany, 9,331 people died as a result of suicide. Of these, 6,971 were men and 2,360 women. More than twice as many men, therefore, commit suicide than women. In contrast, the attempted suicide rate among women is three times higher than among men. In Germany, we assume a figure of three to four hundred thousand suicide attempts each year. In the US in 2003, 31,484 people committed suicide: 25,203 men and 6,281 women. In the same year in New York, 1,169 people took their own lives: 928 men and 241 women. The suicide rate in the US, i.e., the number of suicides per 100,000 inhabitants is, at 10.83, slightly lower than in Germany, where it is around a figure of 13.5.

To think about suicide means attempting to grasp subjective causes and social conditions that enable such an act, or, which cannot prevent it. Debates on suicide therefore, at least ex negatio, reflect on which conditions are indispensable to make a life worth living. In this sense they are truly vital.

But irrespective of that, through the ages suicide has generally been held as taboo. It is strictly forbidden in all of the world religions, whether Judaism, Christianity or Islam: God alone gave life and therefore he alone may take it. There is neither space nor time here in this connection to discuss the currently delicate and burning issues surrounding acts of suicide, which draw apparent legitimization from the perpetrators' political-religious motivations. Mass murder as a consequence of suicide, and masked by the misuse of language stylizing it into acts of martyrdom in the Islamic world.

Even in the Bible, the book with the most diverse presentation of human fate and tragedy, portrayal of suicide is rare. In fact, there are only 10: 6 in the Old Testament, 3 in the Apocrypha and one in the New Testament. Depiction is generally short, factual and free of moral judgment. More detailed descriptions can be found in the stories of Samson, Rasi, Judas and Saul (compare Lindner 1999).

Philosophical opinion is divided on these religiously motivated judgments. Socrates is in agreement with those who reject it, whereas the Epicureans and the Stoics defend suicide as an expression of the human right to self-determination (compare Kettner and Gerisch 2004). Secular social-theorists, too, foremost the inventor of sociology, Emile Durkheim (1897), condemn suicide as unbearable self-empowerment.

As plausible as condemnation may appear from a religious and sociological perspective, it is confronted with an existential and individual experience in which pain, despair, helplessness and weariness of life can erode society's conventions and, even more strongly, the sense of self-preservation. "The world of the happy is another than that of the unhappy. And the world does not change with death, but ends." Jean Amery (1983) uses this quotation from Wittgenstein as the preface to his famous work "Hand an sich legen." And yet, a discourse on suicide by means of a written or spoken word can achieve a limited connection between the happy and the unhappy world, between the connectable world of the living and the "closed world of suicide." "As far as language can go," Amery (1983, p. 11) adds.

It is a fundamental fact that suicide debates have been conducted since the age of antiquity; almost all disciplines have been involved, on one hand in an attempt to develop understanding and explanatory models, while on the other, debates have always been affected by taboos, criminalization, politicization and pathologization (compare Gerisch 1998).

Freud's Theories on Suicide

I now wish to trace Freud's theories on suicide from his work.

As early as 1896, within the framework of his repression theory developed along the basis of hysteria, Freud postulated (1896) that a current cause only had a traumatic effect if it actualized a repressed and unconscious topic of conflict. In a comparison between hysteria and attempted suicide, Freud stated: "Not the final, in itself insignificant insult causes the sobbing, the despair, the suicide attempt, ignoring any proportionality of cause and effect; but this small, momentary insult arouses and triggers into effect so many previous and stronger insults, at the root of which is the memory of a serious insult in childhood that has never been overcome" (1896, p. 216).

Yet a psychoanalytic debate on suicide did not begin until 1910 at the "Symposium on Suicide" which was initiated by Freud as a result of a student's suicide in Vienna.[1]

At the 1910 congress introduced by Freud (Freud 1910, p. 231ff.), Adler, Stekel and Federn (compare Federn 1929a), among others, took part. The personality of a person who commits suicide was described generally as a "nervous character," and it was assumed that a constitutionally strong aggression drive was a precondition for suicide. While Adler, in particular, emphasized the significance of social factors, others stressed the tendency to suicide as an expression of a death wish intended for another person. In addition, the lack of human relationships was formulated as a causal factor for suicide.

In his conclusion, Freud again pointed out the initial unresolved question, namely, whether overcoming the drive for life was the result of disappointed libido, or whether there is such a thing as renunciation of ego assertion motivated by the own ego (Freud 1910, p. 232).

Even at that time, Freud suspected that a comparison of melancholia with the emotions of mourning would enable psychological access to the problem of suicide. It was not until 1917 that he revisited this topic in his work "Mourning and Melancholia," which is Freud's only systematic portrayal of the psychodynamics of the suicidal act, and is still today an invaluable tool in both clinical practice and theoretic conceptualization.

The Freud-Abraham Depression Model of Suicide

The classical psychoanalytic explanatory model, accepted as a suicide theory, was developed by Freud (1917) and Abraham (1912, 1924). According to Freud, the central difference between mourning and melancholia exists in the following phenomenon: "During mourning, the world is poor and empty, but with melancholia, it is the ego itself" (Freud 1917, p. 246).

The overall development of a melancholic syndrome, which is accompanied by emotional upset and a loss of self-respect is, therefore, connected to a pre-disposing condition and a triggering factor. The psychic disposition of a melancholic person is assumed to be a "primary narcissistic injury" (compare Abraham 1924), which was caused by the child experiencing its mother as a disappointment and failure, resulting in a basal "primal depression" (compare Abraham 1924). This encourages a pronounced ambivalence between loving and hating an object, as well as a tendency toward a narcissistic choice of object. The triggering factor is a real loss of object or a fantasized object loss due to disappointments, insults or rejections and experienced as a traumatic repetition of the primary disappointed love. The person pre-disposed to melancholia will react to this loss of object with a "wave of hate" (compare Abraham 1924), which must be warded off because the object is loved and, especially because of the ambivalence conflict, is experienced as indispensable. There is a narcissistic identification with the object enabling its retention despite the existing conflict. This was how Freud deciphered the "mystery of suicide tendency": "We knew that a neurotic person feels no urge to commit suicide unless an impulse to murder someone else is redirected against himself, but it was still unclear which power play enabled the intention to be carried out. The analysis of melancholia now teaches us that the ego is only able to kill itself if, by returning to occupying the object, it can treat itself as an object; if the hostility intended for an object can be directed toward itself representing the original reaction of the ego toward external objects" (Freud 1917, p. 251f.).

Furthermore, Freud (1917) wrote, although the object had lost its power over the ego due to narcissistic identification, in suicide the power is regained: "In the two contrasting situations, that of being extremely in love and that of suicide, the ego is overwhelmed by the object, albeit in totally different ways" (p. 252).

Considerations on the Suicidal Death Drive Theory

Following the introduction of the first psychodynamic deliberations on the problem of suicide by Freud (1917) and Abraham (1912, 1924), the significance of aggression and self-aggression was accepted as the central condition for suicidal acts, also within the psychoanalytic world. Three years later, in "Beyond the Pleasure Principle" (1920), when Freud developed the death drive hypothesis (also compare Freud 1923, 1924, 1930, 1940) and attempted to integrate it with the original suicide theory, the psychoanalytic world was split in two; into supporters and opposers of the death drive theory.

With the introduction of the death drive, Freud justified the second dualistic drive theory by combining the ego and sexual drives into a life drive ("Eros"), which he placed in contrast to the death drive ("Thanatos"). The aim of the death drive is to achieve total removal of tension and to return the living creature to an inorganic state. Freud (1940) assumed that the death drive is biologically anchored in every person and that from the very beginning it is in battle with the life drives. Murder is seen as an active expression of the death drive, whereas suicide is its passive and more extreme manifestation caused by a regressive de-mixing of libidinal and aggressive-destructive energies. According to Freud (1923), in melancholia, "the superego becomes a type of group venue for death drives" and so, "it often enough manages to drive the ego to its death" (p. 53). In "The Economic Problem of Masochism" Freud (1924) again discussed the drive mixture that fosters suicide, this time by understanding sadism directed at the self as a result of cultural drive repression. For this reason, Freud argued, self-destruction cannot take place without libidinal satisfaction because, in addition to the destruction tendency, an erotic component is also always present in sadism directed against the self (p. 169ff.).

"Brother Animal": Comments on Viktor Tausk's Suicide

I now wish to discuss the relationship between Freud and Viktor Tausk who committed suicide at the age of 40.

We may be familiar with Viktor Tausk as an enthusiastic follower of Freud in the infancy of psychoanalysis, but perhaps more so as Lou Andreas-Salomé's lover, although most people are unaware of his tragic end. Possibly one simply does not wish to remember the unhappy story, seeing as it touches on a less honorable episode in Freud's life and circle, although we are well aware of the numerous intense conflicts and broken relationships with once respected colleagues and friends. Viktor Tausk's suicide has been forgotten, or should I say repressed, perhaps because it occurred very soon after a vehement argument with Freud. It is thanks to Paul Roazen (1969, 1976) and his work that light has been shed on this unhappy biography, also revealing the strategies of denial.

It enables us to gain insight into the sources and development of taboos that have always enshrouded suicide, as the guilt, shame, feelings of responsibility, helplessness and defense that it generates—especially among the bereaved—compares with no other human experience.

But, to start at the beginning: Tausk grew up in Croatia, with an obsequious, loving mother and a tyrannical father. In 1897 Tausk began his law studies in Vienna, married Martha, returned with her to Sarajevo where they had two sons after their first child died at birth. The couple separated however, and Martha moved to Vienna and Tausk to Berlin where he continued his studies, worked as a journalist but increasingly suffered because of his perpetually unhappy love affairs which always ended in disaster, causing him to become ever more depressive. After many breakdowns he finally went to Vienna, turning to Freud for help. He was able to become more stable, read medicine and became a psychiatrist, which is when he concentrated on the study of psychoses. Being a brilliant thinker, he was initially accepted into Freud's circle. The start of his love affair with Lou Andreas-Salomé triggered the development of a curious *menage á trois*, which led to a confusing jumble of projected feelings by the various parties, such as jealousy, envy and rivalry. Freud was fascinated by Tausk's intellectualism, but also feared that Tausk could appropriate some of his unfinished ideas and complete them before time. Although Tausk knew that Freud felt increasingly uncomfortable in his presence, he still tried to persuade Freud to be his analyst. As was to be expected, Freud refused and at the beginning of 1919 sent him to Helene Deutsch, who herself was being analyzed by Freud for 6 hours each week. It appears typical for Tausk's personality structure that he not only needed to win people over permanently who maintained an independent distance, such as Freud, or who turned away from him, like Lou Andreas-Salomé but that, as if he were driven by an unconscious force, he continually reproduced disappointments and insults. And the Freud-Tausk-Deutsch constellation again produced such a reaction and a disastrous end, as had previously happened with Freud and Lou. In her analysis with Freud, Deutsch spoke only of Tausk, and Tausk spoke solely of Freud in his analysis with Deutsch so that, within three months, at the end of March 1919 Freud brought this incestuous interlocking to a radical end. He gave Deutsch a choice; either she end the analysis with Tausk or her own with him. As was to be expected, Deutsch obeyed and broke off Tausk's analysis immediately. In spite of much of it being his own fault, Tausk's feelings and the effects on him at having been dropped by two such significant people must have been catastrophic. This perhaps explains his sudden choice of affection for Hilde Loewi, in the sense of a substitute object, who was a concert pianist 16 years his junior. And, a particularly delicate point, she had once been his patient. However something within Tausk must have guessed that his desperate attempt to put order into his life was once again simply an unconscious acting out of inner conflicts. He did not, therefore, give notice of his intended marriage. Instead, in the early hours of July 3rd, 1919 he decided to end his life: "He tied curtain braid around his neck, placed his army pistol against his right temple and fired, hanging himself as he fell" (Roazen 1976, p. 317).

The different reactions within Freud's circle, and in Freud himself, are practically a textbook description of the after-effects of a suicidal act, where the question of guilt is implicitly or explicitly negotiated at the same time as defensive attempts are made by pointing out the victim's pathology. Freud did write an obituary praising Tausk, but admitted in a letter to Lou that he actually did not miss him: "For all his significant talent he was useless to us" (quoted from Gay 1987, p. 319). He then added his short and concise etiopathogenetic considerations in a letter to Ferenczi: "obscure, probably psychological impotence and the last act of his infantile battle with the ghost of his father" (quoted from Gay 1987, p. 391). Lou was quite horrified by Freud's coldness, but agreed with him in his evaluation of Tausk's fragile neurotic character. In contrast, Paul Federn saw the cause of Tausk's suicide entirely in Freud's rejection: "Within this tiny subculture," writes Paul Roazen, "Federn was not alone in his unquestioned belief that to be dropped by Freud could lead to a person's self-destruction. Exclusion from the revolutionary community was a worse destruction that any physical death" (Roazen 1976, p. 318).

Tausk's suicide was never again discussed in that community.

The shocking thing about this story is not just Freud's uncommendable behavior, and I am also not interested in a pointless discussion of guilt. But it makes one sad and thoughtful that only two years earlier Freud had developed the first etiopathogenetic overall psychoanalytical suicide theory which completely replaced the simplified equation of trigger and cause. Since then we have focused on the unconscious entanglement of external events with biographically influenced, mostly unconscious conflict topics in suicidality. And in all of its facets, Tausk's case exemplifies this understanding and explaining concept. Tausk's suicide was not Freud's fault; the fact that he turned away from him may have been the trigger, but also Tausk's own realization that he was not capable of a real, strong love relationship. These triggers fell on a fragile inner construct of brilliant intelligence on one hand, and emotional instability on the other, which most certainly would have had its roots in an earlier parental relationship experience. The fact that Tausk also repeated his unconscious conflicts with Freud—one of which was his traumatic fixation on a remote father—is additional proof that Freud was not at fault. It would however have been helpful if Freud and his colleagues had not contributed to his willingness to create unconscious destructive reproductions, but had provided him with the help that we are able to offer our patients today, which are especially thanks to Freudian conceptualizations.

Freud's Death: "Dying in Freedom"

To conclude, I should like to comment on the suicidality in Freud's life, and on his death.

As we know from his detailed biographies and self-portrayals, Freud suffered from numerous physical illnesses and neurotic symptoms all his life. He often mentioned cardiac disrythmia and breathing problems, depressive feelings and fear of death but also death desires, influenza, migraines, stomach aches, digestion disorders, a slight case of typhoid, angina and smallpox, etc. To claim that this list of symptoms suggests that Freud was chronically and latently suicidal his whole life would be crude speculation which could be negated by Freud's maxim—in a different context—to his biographer Fritz Wittels, that the probable is not always the truth.

However, there are many passages in which Freud sounds resigned, exhausted and gloomy. For instance, in his letter of February 1896 to Wilhelm Fließ: "I hope I will be filled with scientific interest until my life ends. Although I am hardly a human being any longer. In the evening, after ten and a half hours at the practise, I am tired to death" (quoted from Salber 2006, p. 174).

An even darker passage, and one which frequently occurs in letters, particularly at times of pressing exhaustion, is taken from comment to Emma Jung in 1911 when he, the man who described the consequences of restrictive suppression of drives, complains that: "marriage has long paid itself off, now there is nothing left but death" (Quoted from Gay 1987, p. 189).

We all know that Freud's (neurotic) fear of cancer over many years was bitterly confirmed when, in spring of 1923, he indeed fell ill with cancer of the gums and oral cavity which, as a result of many operations, finally led to the removal of part of his jawbone; from then on, in part because of the artificial jaw, he was never free of pain when eating and speaking.

Freud, the physician, surrounded by physicians, first turned to Felix Deutsch with his initial suspicions, the one person who found it most difficult to accept this truth and was therefore not capable of confronting Freud with the entire cruel reality. Peter Gay (1987) writes: "He worried that Freud's heart might not respond well to the truth. He had some hope that a second operation might eliminate all cause for alarm and let Freud live on without ever knowing that he had had cancer. But beyond that, Deutsch had been made uneasy by what he interpreted to be Freud's readiness for suicide; at their crucial meeting on April 7, Freud had asked Deutsch to help him *disappear from this world with decency*" if he should be condemned to prolonged suffering. Informed openly that he had cancer, Freud might be tempted to make his implicit threat a reality" (p. 473; my highlighting, B.G.).

In the end, it was not Felix Deutsch but Max Schur who wanted to help him die with decency.

In that year, Freud was not only confronted with his own death as never before, he also had to cope with the death of his daughter Sophie's youngest son, his beloved grandson Heinerle, who died of tuberculosis in June 1923. He spoke openly with Ferenczi about his actual lack of lust for life: "I have never had a depression before, but this now must be one." "This," writes Gay (1987), "is a remarkable statement: since Freud had been recurrently afflicted with depressive moods, this bout must have been exceptionally severe" (p. 422).

In letters to colleagues he admitted in various ways that he was becoming alienated from life, and felt he was a death candidate, unable to overcome the loss of the boy: "He meant the future to me and thus has taken the future away with him" (Gay 1987, p. 422). Certainly unusual words for a man with whom we are more familiar as unsentimental, sober, and more likely to be sarcastic and sharptongued. Heinerle's death had actualized all of his other losses, for instance the death of his beloved daughter Sophie, which, according to Freud himself, he had coped with well in comparison. Now however, Freud appeared to be overwhelmed by such powerfully painful feelings that his courage to face life was failing him.

But he lived on and continued to work, frequently to a point of total exhaustion. Between 1923 and 1928 he had to consult his surgeon 350 times. Worn out, Freud wrote in 1924: "The right thing to do would be to give up work and responsibilities, and to wait for a natural end in a quiet corner" (quoted from Gay 1987, p. 510).

In September 1930 Freud's mother died having survived her husband by 34 years. Until her death at the advanced age of 95 Freud called on her every Sunday although, as he once confessed, with feelings of ambivalence and stomach cramps. Freud, at 74 and seriously ill with cancer admits in a letter: "This great event had a strange effect on me, no pain, no sadness, which can probably be explained by the conditions involving her advanced age, sympathy with her helplessness at the end, and the accompanying feeling of liberation, of *being released*. Which I think I understand. I could not die as long as she was still living, and now I can. The value of life has shifted noticeably at some deeper level" (quoted from Salber 2006, p. 42; my highlighting, B.G.). Remarkably, Freud was not even able to attend her funeral: "I did not go to the funeral, Anna represented me" (ditto). "Losing one's mother must be something very strange, incomparable to anything else, and arousing impulses that are difficult to grasp," Freud had written the previous year to Max Eitington, his friend and colleague of many years, pointing to his own situation: "I still have my mother and she is obstructing my path to desired peace, to eternal nothingness" (ditto).

Fleeing from the Nazis, Freud reached London on June 5th 1938 after an escape to which he had finally agreed for the protection of his family, and: "to be able to die in freedom." At the end of August 1939, when the first air-raid warnings were heard in Maresfield Garden, Freud felt his end was near: he lay semi-consciousness, and read his last book by Balzac about the magically shrinking skin "Le Peau de chagrin." On September 21, 1939, Freud reminded his physician, Dr. Schur, that he should help him when the time came: "'Now it is nothing but torture and makes no sense.' Then, after a slight hesitation, he added, 'Talk it over with Anna, and if she thinks it's right, then make an end of it'" (Gay 1987, p. 651). She only hesitantly agreed to an injection of 30mg of morphine, which was repeated twice more on the following day. Freud did not awaken again. He died on September 23, 1939, at 3 A.M.

Anna Freud, who had not moved from her father's side, wrapped herself in her father's coat.

"Nearly four decades earlier, Freud had written to Oskar Pfister wondering what one would do some day, 'when thoughts fail or words will not come?' He could not suppress a 'tremor before this possibility. That is why, with all the resignation before destiny that suits an honest man, I have one wholly secret entreaty: only no invalidism, no paralysis of one's powers through bodily misery. Let us die in harness, as King Macbeth says.' He had seen to it that his secret entreaty would be fulfilled. The old stoic had kept control of his life to the end" (Gay 1987, p. 651).

Note

1. Austria, by the way, is traditionally seen as a country with high rates of suicide, which, from 1865 to 1986, rose to 28.

References

Abraham, K. (1912). "Ansätze zur psychoanalytischen Erfahrung und Behandlung des manisch-depressiven Irreseins und verwandter Zustände." *Zbl Psychoanal* 2: 302–311.
_____ (1924). "Versuch einer Entwicklungsgeschichte der Libido aufgrund der Psychoanalyse seelischer Störungen." In K. Abraham, *K. Gesammelte Schriften, vol. II*, pp. 32–145. Frankfurt a.M.: Fischer, 1982.
Améry, J. (1976). *Hand an sich legen: Diskurs über den Freitod*. Stuttgart: Klett-Cotta, 1983.
Durkheim, E. (1897). *Der Selbstmord*. Frankfurt a.M.: Suhrkamp.
Gay, P. (1987). *Freud: A Life for Our Time*. New York: W.W. Norton.
Gerisch, B. (1998). *Suizidalität bei Frauen. Mythos und Realität—Eine kritische Analyse*. Tübingen: edition diskord.
_____ (2003). *Die suizidale Frau. Psychoanalytische Hypothesen zur Genese*. Göttingen: Vandenhoeck & Ruprecht.
Federn, P. (1929a). "'Die Diskussion über 'Selbstmord,' insbesondere 'Schüler-Selbstmord' im Wiener psychoanalytischen Verein im Jahre 1918." *Z psychoanal Pädagogik* 3: 333–354
Freud, S. (1896). *The Aetiology of Hysteria. Standard Edition* 3: 189–221.
_____ (1910). The Suicide-Discussion. In *On suicide (Discussion of the Viennese Psychoanalytic Society). Standard Edition* 11: 231–232.
_____ (1917). *Mourning and Melancholia. Standard Edition* 14: 239–258.
_____ (1920). *Beyond the Pleasure Principle. Standard Edition* 18: 7–64.
_____ (1924). *The Economic Problem of Masochism. Standard Edition* 19: 157–170.
_____ (1940). *Compendium on Psychoanalysis. Standard Edition* 23: 139–152.
Kappert, I., B. Gerisch and G. Fiedler, eds. (2004). *"Ein Denken, das zum Sterben führt": Selbsttötung: Das Tabu und seine Brüche*. Göttingen: Vandenhoeck & Ruprecht.
Kettner, M. And B. Gerisch (2004). Zwischen Tabu und Verstehen: Psycho-philosophische Bemerkungen zum Suizid. In *"Ein Denken, das zum Sterben führt": Selbsttötung: Das Tabu und seine Brüche*, ed. I. Kappert, B. Gerisch, and G. Fiedler. Göttingen: Vandenhoeck & Ruprecht, p. 38–66.
Lindner, R. (1999). "Da nahm Saul das Schwert und stürzte sich hinein"—Der Suizid des biblischen Königs Saul aus psychodynamischer Perspektive. *Hamburger Ärzteblatt* 12: 532–537.
Roazen, P. (1969). *Brother Animal: The Story of Freud and Tausk*. New York: Alfred A. Knopf.
_____ (1976). *Sigmund Freud und sein Kreis. Eine biographische Geschichte der Psychoanalyse*. Bergisch Gladbach: Gustav Lübbe.
Salber, L. (2006). *Der dunkle Kontinent:. Freud und die Frauen*. Reinbek bei Hamburg: Rowohlt.

Freud's Jewish World
A Historical Perspective
STEVEN BELLER

In the preceding pages there has been much informed and informative discussion about the Jewish dimension to Freud's work and thus to psychoanalysis. Much of this discussion has concerned interpretation of Freud's *Moses and Monetheism*, and the origins of monotheism in Egypt, so much so that one might be forgiven on occasion for thinking that Freud's Jewish world was of 1400 B.C., not A.D. 1900. It is worth reminding ourselves that, whatever Freud might have preferred, his Jewish world was that of turn-of-the-century Vienna, and not that of ancient Egypt.

Freud was part, a very important part but still a part, of a larger cultural and intellectual world, of Vienna 1900. He was also a central figure in the, to my mind, most significant moment within that world, the response of Jewish individuals to the existential crisis that they experienced, brought on by the looming failure of emancipation and assimilation caused by the political and social success of antisemitism. Vienna around 1900 was a study in apparent contradiction. On the one hand its municipal government was in the hands of Karl Lueger and the explicitly antisemitic Christian Social Party; on the other it was home to one of the largest Jewish communities in the world, and Jewish individuals, such as Freud, were at the forefront of cultural and intellectual innovations that have given "Vienna 1900" in the eyes of many commentators the status of "birthplace of the modern world." The contradiction, however, is only apparent, because it was, in my view, precisely the problematic tension in the Jewish situation in Vienna that spurred individuals to attempt to look beyond the comfortable conventional thinking of the time, and to question and reject the false absolutes on which Viennese, and Austrian social and cultural norms rested. Jewish existence in Vienna, with its threatening antisemitic context, was under tension, but for many years, one could argue, this tension was not unbearable, and it could often be a creative and productive tension.

While one might debate what it means to be "the birthplace of the modern world," Vienna was undoubtedly a remarkably fecund center of innovative thinking, especially when it comes to what Allan Janik has termed "critical modernism." Jewish individuals were not the only participants in this critical approach to modernity and modernism, but they were its leading lights. In the world of literature there was Karl Kraus, a former ally of Freud turned opponent, who campaigned against the distortion of truth through the modern mass media, and restored an ethical criterion to the writer's vocation. Arthur Schnitzler, although no friend of Kraus, was also devoted to the unmasking the hypocrisies of conventional morality, sexual and otherwise. In philosophy, Ludwig Wittgenstein's thinking strove to show the limits to rational modern man's understanding, putting ethical and aesthetic values beyond the range of (scientific) language. Arnold Schoenberg was to take a similar idea about the inexpressibility of ethical truth through the aesthetic medium and turn it into the great "opera against opera," *Moses and Aaron*, a fascinating counterpoint to Freud's own approach to the same biblical theme.

Another Viennese "critical modernist" who merits more attention is Otto Neurath, a leading member of the Vienna Circle of Logical Positivism. Neurath was most famous, rather notoriously, for his militant campaign against the use of anything that smacked of metaphysics in philosophical language, but his ideas on how to achieve an "encyclopaedic" understanding of the world among the sciences, and about the need to base human social and economic rules on persuasion, negotiation and compromise, rather than on "iron laws" still offer many potentially productive paths of enquiry.

The "critical modernism" of figures such as Neurath, Kraus, Schnitzler, Schoenberg, and indeed Freud, was not confined to Vienna, but there was what amounted to a "tradition" of Jewish critical thinking, especially by Jewish individuals who were on the edge of Jewish traditional life, or rather between Jewish and non–Jewish worlds, connecting them, with a foot in both. Max Nordau, for instance, who himself had been an exponent of "critical modernism" in his *The Conventional Lies of Our Civilization* (1883), had as his Jewish intellectual heroes Baruch Spinoza and Heinrich Heine, both of whom left the Jewish religion.[1] Karl Marx, along with Freud the other great exponent of the "hermeneutics of suspicion," also fits quite well into this "critical modernist" tradition, as do, clearly, many of the socialist and left-radical thinkers of Jewish descent, including Ferdinand Lassalle, one of Freud's heroes, as he was one of Theodor Herzl's. The background to Freud's use as the epigram to *The Interpretation of Dreams* of the citation from Virgil's *Aeneid*: "Flectere si nequeo superos, acheronta movebo," is indicative of a certain non-conformist antagonism to the "compact majority" on the part of a certain group of ambitious Jewish men, and a sign (as Richard Armstrong would say) of the uses to which they put their classical *Bildung*. Not only was Freud avowedly inspired by Lassalle's use of the quote to describe his own political battles in Prussia, but Herzl used the *same* quote to describe his own struggles for Zionism — ironically against the Jewish banking establishment!

The critical, implicitly adversarial approach of Jewish individuals to the received social and cultural norms of (non–Jewish) society could also be celebrated in more popular, and rather unlikely spheres, such as operetta. In *Frühling am Rhein*, which had its premiere in November 1914, a Jewish merchant, Moritz Frühling is only half-acculturated but is clever and morally good: he has raised the daughter of a deceased non–Jewish friend, a German baron, as his own, and is devoted to her, Therese's, well-being. Her uncle, on the other hand, another German baron, is a case study in aristocratic aesthetic refinement, exquisite manners and good taste, but is completely amoral, only interested in his niece for the sake of getting control of her money. In order to protect Therese (Trendl) from her uncle, Frühling is prepared to cast opprobrium on himself by claiming that he substituted his own daughter for the deceased daughter of the baron and that Trendl is in fact his daughter, and not the baron's niece. In Act Two, once Therese has reached her majority, Frühling reveals that she is indeed the baron's daughter, and so can now enjoy her fortune and marry her longtime love, "Heini" Müller, captain of the *Loreley*, a steamer on the Rhine. Celebrating on board the boat, Frühling reveals his half-education by mixing up poetry by Heine and Goethe. Corrected by the completely *gebildet* Therese, and told that the poetry he had just quoted was actually by Goethe, Frühling responds: "Das ist auch von Goethe? Grossartig! Ich hab' geglaubt, von dem ist nur 'Nathan der Weise'!"[2] This little aside thus reveals to the audience, if they had not realized it before, that they were watching an operetta version of G.E. Lessing's classic plea for enlightenment and religious tolerance, whose hero was a thinly disguised version of Lessing's friend, Moses Mendelssohn, the father of the Jewish Enlightenment, or Haskalah, and hence the originator of the process of modernization, emancipation and integration of which many in the audience would have been products. In its use of the heroes of German *Bildung* to make a joke celebrating the success of a Jew against snobbery and prejudice, it also mirrors Freud's use, as described by Armstrong, of his classical education to criticize the non–Jewish world he inhabits.

The complexity of such a usage of various cultural and intellectual traditions, across the various supposed barriers between cultural traditions, should not be all that surprising, especially when it comes to questions of Jewish identity and Jewish patterns of thought, for, after all, there was a very long and very varied history of Jewish intellectual achievement, and thousands of years of intellectual and cultural *exchange and interaction* between the Jewish and non–Jewish worlds by the time Freud came to be thinking about the psyche. So much discussion of the Egyptian origins of monotheism, or the contrast between the "Greek" and "Hebraic" worldviews, in terms of how it influenced Freud's thinking about the mind and about his own Jewish identity, might lull us into forgetting that a great deal happened within Jewish thought between Akhnaten and Freud. One aspect of that Jewish intellectual history that we particularly need to recall in this respect is that the idea that "hellenization" of Jewish thought was something new around 1900 is belied, or at least heavily qualified, by the long tradition, going back into Antiquity, of the very profound interaction of "Greek" and Jewish thought that was extremely fruitful for both intellectual traditions, none more so when under the aegis of *Muslim* rulers in the Middle Ages. One of the greatest of Jewish thinkers, Moses Maimonides, resident in Egypt, derived his preeminence from his use of (Greek) philosophy and *logic* to *rationalize* Jewish belief. The idea of the *logos* had thus been incorporated into *Jewish* thought for centuries before Freud, especially since the Haskalah, and this fact should be remembered when one reads about *logos* somehow being Greek and hence not Jewish. It is just not that simple; rather Jewish religious thought had long incorporated concepts and modes of thought from many other sources, including Greek ones, and to think otherwise is to fall into the absolutizing, dichotomizing thinking that proved so fatal in nineteenth and twentieth century Europe.

That said, the Jewish intellectual heritage in the modern era was still markedly different from that of the non–Jewish world in several key respects. Moreover, many of these characteristic differences could indeed be traced back to Antiquity, with religious patterns of thought often paralleled in secular attitudes. A striking example is the reflection of the originary, ancient conflict between monotheism and polytheism in the Central European world of Freud's day, with an often strikingly dialectical interplay between universalist and particularist moments. Politically, for instance, Freud and his fellow acculturated Viennese Jews, were very much centralists, and suspicious of giving too much power to the particularist provinces of the Habsburg Monarchy. This was primarily because it was the constitutional and legal system, based on the central government in Vienna, that guaranteed Jews their equality before the law, in an era when the localities, including ironically the municipal government of Vienna itself (see above), were threatening to deprive Jews of their hard-won equal rights.

In more cultural and intellectual terms, the underlying strength of the monotheistic moment within the secular thought of Jews in Vienna 1900 and elsewhere was shown in their preference for what we now term pluralism over multiculturalism. Whereas multiculturalism denies that there are necessary commonalities, one unifying reality, "truth," shared by all humanity and underlying all human cultures and societies, pluralism assumes a unity of the human experience as the basis of human diversity. In the pluralist view, human cultures and societies, human individuals indeed, might respond to the human condition in many different ways, and there is not necessarily *one* right answer. Even individuals can face conflicts between two equally valid, equally good goals, but there *is* a human condition, and recognition of this must limit the possibilities of what we accept as ethically right or wrong. It is the acceptance of this fundamental unity of human experience that can then allow us to respect other humans as equally deserving of respect, despite their differing beliefs and values.

This pluralist dialectic between universalist unity and particularist difference was the hallmark of the Central European Jewry of which Freud was such a characteristic member. As David Sorkin has pointed out, the irony of the development of a new German Jewish identity, and the same can be said even more so for the somewhat broader Central European Jewish identity, was that the very universalist values by which Jews identified themselves as Germans, Austrians or Central Europeans, were seen by those who were not Jewish as marking Jewish particularism.[3] In other words, from this non–Jewish perspective: what made Jews Jewish was their perceived universalism, their belief in a set of universal human values of which national cultures were just differing interpretations, not absolute values, self-sufficient totalities in themselves. Whether it was the pluralizing juxtapositions of the music of Gustav Mahler, or the critical severity of the music of Arnold Schoenberg, paring away all convention and phraseology to form a musical language that would allow the individual composer to express his musical thought truthfully, both could be seen as "Jewish," because both challenged, and rejected as a form of "idolatry," the concept of the particular universal totality that lay behind the notion of nationalism and national culture. Both, in that sense, were challenges to the "compact majority," and as such "Jewish," no matter how much, in both cases, the individuals thought they were contributing to and participating in "German" or indeed "European" culture.

Freud's approach to the "compact majority" was, as we know, similarly adversarial. It is true that Freud has a reputation for being both patriarchal and authoritarian, when it came to his psychoanalytic movement. The frequent expulsions of dissenters from the ranks of Freud's followers are often interpreted as a sign of Freud's intolerance to criticism and it appears fairly clear that Freud thought he had found *the* secret to the human psyche, and that he had large, indeed totalizing ambitions for how much of human experience his psychoanalytic theory could explain and thus master. It is just as important to recognize, however, as Mark Edmundson has pointed out recently, the ways in which Freud's psychoanlytic theory was one aimed against totalizing systems, and against the authoritarian tendencies in mass society that Freud so astutely described in *Group Psychology and the Analysis of the Ego*.[4]

Freud might have been modern in his belief that a rational understanding of the mind could help individuals with their psychological problems, but he was very much a "critical modernist" in his assertion that there were limits—inherent in the civilizing process—to what modernity could achieve: that the best civilized humans could hope for was not constant happiness but rather the general avoidance of unhappiness, and a state of tolerable dissatisfaction. In his later years he saw the danger of individuals putting too much faith (libido-transference) into the doubt-free, truth-owning great leader, a human embodiment of the super-ego. Instead of approving of the psychological satisfaction available through such mass transference, Freud saw its immense dangers and its debilitating effect on the individual's power to think for him- or herself. He saw, in other words, the need for humans not to short-circuit the civilizational process by the mass libido-attachment involved in what we know as fascism, authoritarianism and totalitarianism, for *total* happiness was not possible, but rather the need for individuals to retain their distinct selves, resisting the temptation of melding in one communal self in the unitary self of the super-ego surrogate of the great leader. Not only did individuals need to keep their selves distinct from the mass, but, as part of the same process, needed to keep the components of their own selves, the ego, id and super-ego similarly distinct. The conflation of these components led not to happiness but to madness, both individual and collective.

This keeping the components of the self distinct is sometimes described in terms of a "divided" self, but it strikes me that this is not really how Freud saw the functional structure of the mind, or how he wanted it to be. There might well be the eternal conflict between Eros and Thanatos, but the mind in which this conflict occurs remains, after all, *one* mind. The ego is part of the same mind as the id, with the super-ego being in effect a product of the ego. The sane mind is not one where the components are divided from each other, but one rather where they are distinct yet connected in a relationship of *tension*, preferably creative tension. The sane mind is one, in other words, where the triumvirate of the soul rule together in a relationship of checks and balances, where the differing interests of each are satisfied through a process of negotiation and compromise, with sufficient space allowed for freedom of self-expression in the safety valves of dreams and, perhaps, the artistic imagination. The sane mind of balanced relationships between the id, ego and super-ego can then manage similarly balanced relationships with other individuals, in the "relationship of equals" that Siegfried Bernfeld saw as the ideal form of personal interchange.

Whether "orthodox" Freudians, including Freud, would agree or not, it seems to me that "object-relations" theory, as I understand it, has highlighted both the most productive and perhaps the most "Jewish" aspect of Freudian theory: its dependence for its structures, ultimately, on relations rather than systems. Systems are logical, whereas relational networks are inherently complex and not necessarily logical, in the way we usually think of this term. After everything said above about the dangers of making too great a distinction between the "Hebraic" and "Greek" models of thought, the irony is, nevertheless, that the Freudian concept of the mind, being one of relations between its components, is not, ultimately a clear-cut product of scientific, systematic, Greek *Logos*, but rather is only fully understood in terms of exigesis, of interpretation, and making *connections*. As the word "exigesis" would suggest, the interpretative mode of thought, with its implicit acceptance of diversity of perception, is not completely foreign to Greek thought either, just as the logical mode, with its assertion of just one logical answer, is not as foreign to Jewish thought as might appear from some of the other papers in this volume. It is, even so, striking that Freud, coming from the background of Talmudic, Ashkenazi, East European Jewry, should have created a practice of psychological therapy that relies so heavily on dialogue, conversation, verbal association, the patient-analyst relationship, and interpretation — on talking and not on writing. For this does reflect the forms of interpretative thinking that had become the mainstay of the Jewish intellectual tradition in Eastern and Central Europe, before the onset of modernity.

That Freud should attempt to meld this Jewish interpretative method with a "logical" theory is not something that should be seen as all that innovative or completely unheard of, within the Jewish tradition, for, as I have stressed, Jews had been adapting Greek modes of thought to their own purposes for millennia. What is perhaps striking is that, in the end, it is the Jewish side of psychoanalysis, the open, interpretative side rather than the totalizing, closed, systematic, theoretical side, that remained predominant, at least in Feud's mind, the side that did not claim the answer to all of the mind's mysteries, nor offered complete redemption, the side, as it were, that regarded the world as one for which the Messiah had not come, rather than one in which salvation was nigh. Freud's approach was ultimately one that rejected the idea of the dream of the complete disappearance of tension, and of conflict, and the solving of all of Man's problems, and in this he was in a very Jewish tradition of seeing the profound danger of worshipping "false Messiahs" and false Messianic dreams (even when some might see himself and psychoanalysis in such terms). In this sense it is perhaps doubly ironic that Freud is reputed to have advised Hans Herzl, Theodor Herzl's son, "finally bury your father — he was one of those people who have turned dreams into reality. They are a very rare and dangerous breed."[5]

Freud is to be understood not in messianic terms, but rather as an advocate of the creative consequences of difference, of tension and even of conflict within the human soul, also in human affairs, albeit within the bounds of sanity and civilized behavior. In this, his approach is echoed by other Jewish luminaries of Central European modern thought, such as, ironically given his criticism of psychoanalysis, Karl Popper, with his advocacy of "culture clash" as beneficial for societal and scientific progress, and Albert O. Hirschmann, with his notion of liberal democracy relying on the existence of difference of interests as the grist for its conflict-managing mill, or Isaiah Berlin, with his assertion that it is precisely the Jewish retention of their difference (along with other minority groups) which allows liberal democracy to exercise its fundamental nature as a guarantor of the freedom to be other.

It is such considerations that should give admirers and disciples of Freud a certain equanimity when it comes to the question of Freud's intellectual heritage. Recent literature on Freud, including such very general and introductory works as Anthony Storr's *Freud: A Very Short Introduction*, indicates that many of Freud's theses, and much of the psychoanalytic method have been challenged and found wanting, either theoretically, or in terms of cost-benefit analysis—faster forms of therapy, or drugs, appear the preferred choice these days, and much of Freudian theory has been criticized for being sexist, culturally imperialist, or worse, and generally passé. In a certain sense much of this is to be expected, and it would be remarkable if, a century or more after a theory's debut, scientific research and social and economic change would not have led to changes of perspective and advances (revisions) in that theory's conclusions. Nevertheless, it is evident that much of what Freud discovered and invented remains fundamental to most psychotherapeutic methodologies today, and a good part of their effectiveness, despite what the extreme crusaders for a purely pharmaceutical psychotherapy might want to think. Moreover, Freudian theory, and the very vocabulary of psychoanalysis has been so absorbed into Western culture that it still informs that culture, has become virtually an inherent part of the way we think and feel, especially as regards our culture's much more honest approach, despite many remaining repressions, to human sexuality.

How Freud's intellectual heritage will fare in the next century, or even the century after that, is an open question, but I suspect it will remain a major influence on human consciousness, though perhaps not in a form that we might readily recognize as such. Here, it is perhaps appropriate to return once more to the question of the Jewish aspect to Freud's life and his intellectual achievement, and through a Jewish joke, of sorts. At the time of Madeleine Albright's "discovery" of her Jewish descent, there was much discussion of what this meant, and how Jews should respond to it. One prominent liberal rabbi I spoke to on the issue said that Albright herself was not to blame for anything, but he could really not understand why her parents had converted to Catholicism. To him, the great achievement of Jews had been to go from worshipping many gods to just worshipping one God. In the modern era Marx and Freud had attempted to complete the process by going from one God to none. This, the rabbi said, was not something he agreed with, but at least it was understandable, as it was going in the right direction. What he could not understand was going from one God to three (the Catholic trinity).

Freud would have understood what the rabbi meant, and even approved, I suspect. Freud did think that there was something Jewish about himself; as Abigail Gillman quotes him, in 1934 he felt that it could be his "very essence." Freud added: "He could not now express that essence clearly in words; but some day, no doubt, it will become accessible to the scholarly mind." Interestingly enough, Karl Kraus, Freud's adversary and at one point an ardent assimilationist, ended up claiming more or less exactly the same thing, also in 1934. He wrote that he "thankfully recognizes in the spiritual [geistige] scorn which he possesses in liberal measure, in the veneration for desecrated life and defiled language, the natural force of an incorruptible Judaism, which he loves above everything: as something which, untouched by race, money, class, ghetto or the masses, in short by any sort of hatred between troglodytes and profiteers, exists in and of itself."⁶ Just as with Freud there is a sense that Kraus's Jewishness is something so abstract that it is beyond description in words, but it is there nonetheless. Something like that, in all likelihood, will be the fate of psychoanalytic thought in modern minds in the centuries to come.

Yet there is a possibility that goes beyond mere circumstantial analogy. Freud tried to articulate, in the years before he died, more precisely what the Jewish heritage meant to him, and he attempted this in the book whose text has turned up so many times in these pages, namely *Moses and Monotheism*. As Joel Whitebook has pointed out, the central irony of this book was that Freud saw himself, as in the "joke" above, in the direct intellectual lineage of Moses and his monotheism. Moreover, he saw the Jewish religion founded by Moses, with its concept of an abstract deity, as one of the great advances in abstract thinking, and as such of "intellectuality" (Geistigkeit) over sensuality, and by implication a vital step on the road to all subsequent scientific thought. His debt to the world of *Bildung* is still evident in his nod to the harmony of the Greek balance between the physical and intellectual worlds, a balance that he thought was denied to Jews, but, he asserted, in having to choose between "the cultivation of intellectual and physical activity" the Jews' "decision was at least in favor of the worthier alternative."⁷ The Jewish choice of intellectuality over sensuality thus made the Jews, in Freud's eyes, founding figures of the intellectual, scientific world view to which he subscribed. In *The Future of an Illusion*, Freud wrote of "Our God, Logos," as though this would put him on the side of the sensuous, totalizing Greeks; but this "god" is simply the expression of "man's intellect" and it is intellectuality, "the voice of the intellect" that will, Freud hopes, triumph over superstition and religious illusion. This is the same intellectuality that he saw as having been set free by the "instinctual renunciation" caused through the creation of the abstract God of the Jews.

It was therefore Freud's "very essence," his intellectuality, that he saw as originating in his Jewish heritage. At the same time, he saw psychoanalysis, with its individual psychological theory of the Oedipus Complex, and its collective psychological theory of the slaughter of the primal father as the basis of religion, and the murder by the Jews of the first Moses as the basis of the Jewish religion, as the possible salvation of Mankind from religion, and especially Jews from the Jewish religion. In other words, psychoanalysis, as the purely intellectual understanding of the human mind, was the true successor to the Jewish heritage, as well as liberating Jews from their repressed guilt about Moses, if they only would admit that they had indeed murdered "God" (as antisemitic Christians had always claimed). Whatever one makes of this rather bizarre thesis, it seems clear that Freud was positioning himself and psychoanalysis within the history of the *Jewish* heritage of intellectuality.

The strange thing is that in this claim for a transmission of the tradition of intellectuality from the Jewish religion to psychoanalysis Freud was more right than wrong. Psychoanalysis did, in Freud's case as in the case of most of the other early psychoanalysts, have its intellectual roots in habits of mind that reached back to the Talmudic tradition of East European Ashkenazi Jewry; and perhaps not accidentally, it was a theory that allowed a remarkable amount of intellectual investigation into the psychological reality that lies behind appearances, and the actual motivations, fears and desires that underlay the apparent morality and "truths" of modern society, especially those societies that have given themselves over to the worshipping of idols, whether they be Communism, Mammon, the Nation, Freud's particular *bête noire* of organized Religion, or indeed his hallowed Science. In this constant questioning of the conventional wisdoms and the mores of modern culture and society, the psychoanalytic movement and its Freudian heritage were worthy members of the "Jewish world" in which Freud found himself in Central Europe in the late nineteenth and early twentieth centuries, and as such they also have been worthy successors to the millennia-old tradition of critical Jewish intellectuality. I suspect that it is this tradition of intellectuality, ironically perhaps, that will also be psychoanalysis' longest lasting heritage.

Does that, then, make psychoanalysis a "Jewish science"? Yes it does; and that, its critical, questioning intellectuality, constantly seeking answers to what really, deep down, has made individuals and societies think and act the way they do, in order to bring them closer to psychic equanimity, self-understanding and the "truth" about themselves, is what makes psychoanalysis universally applicable, and still vitally relevant to our world today.

Notes

1. Michael Stanislawski, *Zionism and the Fin de Siecle* (Berkeley: University of California Press, 2001) p. 63.
2. Edmund Eysler (Text: Carl Lindau, Beda and Oskar Fronz), *Frühling am Rhein* (Vienna: Doblinger, 1914) Prompt and direction book. p. 104.
3. David Sorkin, *The Transformation of German Jewry, 1780–1840* (Oxford: Oxford University Press, 1987) pp. 173–78.
4. Mark Edmundson, "Who's Your Daddy?" *New York Times*, op-ed page, September 23, 2007.
5. Quoted in Ernst Pawel, *The Labyrinth of Exile: A Life of Theodor Hezl* (New York: Farrar, Straus & Giroux, 1989) p. 535.
6. Karl Kraus, "Warum die Fackel nicht erscheint," in *Die Fackel* (Munich 1973) vol. 39, end of July, 1934, xxxvi, No. 890–905, p. 38
7. See Sigmund Freud, *Moses and Monotheism*, in *The Origins of Religion*, vol. 13, *The Pelican Freud Library* (London: Pelican, 1985) pp. 358–363.

References

Cartwright, Nancy, et al. *Otto Neurath: Philosophy Between Science and Politics*. Cambridge: Cambridge University Press, 1996.
Edmundson, Mark. "Who's Your Daddy?" *New York Times*, op-ed page, September 23, 2007.

Eysler, Edmund. (Text: Carl Lindau, Beda and Oskar Fronz.) *Frühling am Rhein*. Vienna: Doblinger, 1914, Prompter's and Director's Book.
Freud, Sigmund. "Moses and Monotheism." In *The Origins of Religion*, vol. 13 of The Pelican Freud Library. London: Pelican, 1985.
Kraus, Karl. "Warum die Fackel nicht erscheint." In *Die Fackel* (Munich 1973) vol. 39, end of July 1934, xxxvi, no. 890–905.
Pawel, Ernst. *The Labyrinth of Exile: A Life of Theodor Herzl*. New York: Farrar, Straus and Giroux, 1989.
Sorkin, David. *The Transformation of German Jewry, 1780–1840*. Oxford: Oxford University Press, 1987.
Stanislawski, Michael. *Zionism and the Fin de Siècle*. Berkeley: University of California Press, 2001.

About the Contributors

Richard H. Armstrong is an associate professor of classical studies and fellow in the Honors College, University of Houston. He publishes on the reception of ancient culture, translation studies, and the history of psychoanalysis. His latest book is *A Compulsion for Antiquity: Freud and the Ancient World* (Cornell University Press, 2006). He is working on another book titled *Theory and Theatricality: Classical Drama and the Emergence of Psychoanalysis, 1880–1920*.

Steven Beller was born in London in 1958 of American and Austrian parents. He was educated at Cambridge University, where he was a research fellow from 1985 to 1989. Since 1989 he has lived in the United States. An independent scholar, he has written widely on Austrian, Jewish and Central European history. He lives in Washington, D.C.

Mary Bergstein is a professor, and the chair, of History of Art + Visual Culture at the Rhode Island School of Design. She has published widely on the art of the Italian Renaissance and the historiography of art. She has also written numerous essays on photography and culture. Bergstein was the Sigmund Freud Scholar of Psychoanalysis (Vienna) in 2005. Her book, *Mirrors of Memory: Freud, Photography and the History of Art*, will be published by Cornell University Press in 2010.

Harold P. Blum is a clinical professor of psychiatry and a training analyst at New York University School of Medicine, Department of Psychiatry. He is a distinguished fellow of the American Psychiatric Association; executive director of the Sigmund Freud Archives; president of the Psychoanalytic Research and Development Fund; and past editor-in-chief of the *Journal of the American Psychoanalytic Association*. He is the author of more than 150 psychoanalytic papers and several books and the recipient of numerous awards and lectureships including the inaugural Sigourney Award, Mahler, Hartmann, and Lorand prizes. He has delivered S. Freud lectures in New York, London, Vienna, and Frankfurt; and A. Freud, Hartmann, Brill, Friend, and Sperling lectures; and two plenary addresses to the American Psychoanalytic Association. He has chaired four symposia on psychoanalysis and art in Florence, Italy.

Florence Dunn Friedman is an Egyptologist who publishes on ancient Egyptian art and religion. Formerly the curator of ancient art at the Museum of Art, Rhode Island School of Design, she taught in the school's liberal arts division and at Brown University. She is a visiting scholar in the Department of Egyptology and Ancient Western Asian Studies at Brown and formerly an affiliate scholar at the Boston Psychoanalytic Society and Institute.

Benigna Gerisch is a psychoanalyst and member of the Center for Therapy and Studies of Suicidal Behavior at the University Hospital Hamburg-Eppendorf, Germany. She has published numerous papers and two books on suicidality and gender differences, and on suicidality in novels, films and theatre. She is a professor for clinical psychology and psychoanalysis at the International Psychoanalytic University in Berlin.

About the Contributors

Abigail Gillman is an assistant professor of German and Hebrew at Boston University. She is the author of *Viennese Jewish Modernism: Freud, Hofmannsthal, Beer-Hofmann and Schnitzler* (Penn State University Press, 2009), and of articles on German Jewish literature, Hebrew literature, Bible translation and cultural memory. She is at work on a history of German Jewish Bible translation.

Sander L. Gilman is a professor of the liberal arts and sciences as well as a professor of psychiatry at Emory University, where he is the director of the Program in Psychoanalysis and the Health Sciences Humanities Initiative. A cultural and literary historian, he is the author or editor of 80 books. His Oxford lectures *Multiculturalism and the Jews* appeared in 2006; his most recent edited volume, *Diets and Dieting: A Cultural Encyclopedia*, appeared in 2007. He has been awarded a doctor of laws (honoris causa) at the University of Toronto in 1997, elected an honorary professor of the Free University in Berlin in 2000, and made an honorary member of the American Psychoanalytic Association in 2007.

Ethan Kleinberg is an associate professor of history and letters at Wesleyan University and associate editor of *History and Theory*. He is the author of *Generation Existential: Martin Heidegger's Philosophy in France, 1927–1961* (2005) and is completing his second book, *The Myth of Emmanuel Levinas*. His research interests include European intellectual history, critical theory, educational structures, post-colonialism, and the philosophy of history.

Leo A. Lensing is professor of film studies and German studies at Wesleyan University. His scholarly work has focused on the literature and visual culture of fin-de-siècle Vienna. He has also written articles and essays on film history, the history of photography, and the history of psychoanalysis. He regularly reviews for the *Times Literary Supplement* and writes occasionally for the *Frankfurter Allgemeine Zeitung* and the *Süddeutsche Zeitung*. His current project is a biography of Karl Kraus.

Frank Mecklenburg has worked at the Leo Baeck Institute New York since 1984 and is the director of research and chief archivist. He has published in the areas of emigration history, Jewish community history and anti-Semitism, has worked as a translator and editor in the field of German philosophy and the history of socialism and is working on *The Politics of Memory and Historical Archives*.

Arnold D. Richards was editor of the *Journal of the American Psychoanalytic Association* from 1994 to 2003 and before that was the editor of *American Psychoanalyst*, the newsletter of the American Psychoanalytic Association. He is a training and supervising analyst at the New York Psychoanalytic Institute and on the faculty of the department of psychiatry at New York University. He is a former chairman of the board and a current director of YIVO and delivered the 50th Annual Leo Baeck Memorial Lecture in 2006. He is a psychoanalyst in private practice.

Marsha L. Rozenblit is the Harvey M. Meyerhoff Professor of Jewish History at the University of Maryland. She is the author of *The Jews of Vienna, 1867–1914: Assimilation and Identity* (State University of New York Press, 1983) and *Reconstructing a National Identity: The Jews of Habsburg Austria during World War I* (Oxford University Press, 2001). She has also co-edited *Constructing Nationalities in East Central Europe* (Berghahn, 2005) and has written 20+ scholarly articles on the Jews of Habsburg Austria.

Jill Salberg is adjunct clinical associate professor at the New York University (NYU) Postdoctoral Program in Psychotherapy and Psychoanalysis where she teaches and supervises. She is a member of the faculty at the Stephen A. Mitchell Center for Relational Psychoanalysis. She is also on the faculty of the National Institute for the Psychotherapies and a training supervisor at the Institute for Contemporary Psychotherapy. Her articles on Freud, gender, termination and Judaism and psychoanalysis have been published in *Psychoanalytic Dialogues* and *Studies in Gender and Sexuality*. She is a psychologist/psychoanalyst in private practice in Manhattan.

Eliza Slavet received her Ph.D. in literature from the University of California, San Diego, in 2007. Her book *Racial Fever: Freud and the Jewish Question* was published by Fordham University Press in 2009.

Index

Abraham, Karl 88, 151–52, 167
Adler, Alfred 167
"The Advance in Intellectuality [Geistigkeit]" 104, 107n25
Aeneid (Virgil) 41–43
aggression, and suicide 167–68
Akhaten, King 145, 147–57
Albright, Madeleine 182
Amenhotep III 152–57
Amery, Jean 165
"The Analysis of a Phobia in a 5 Year Old Boy," case study of Little Hans 85–88
analysts, as substitute fathers 46, 169–70
"And Rebecca Loved Jacob, But Freud Did Not" (Feldman) 16
Andreas-Salomé, Lou 99–100, 169
Anna O., case study of 67, 80–82
anti-Semitism 7, 16; bodily definition of Jewishness in 100, 102; conversion to avoid 84–86; effects of 41–42, 78–79; effects on Freud 35–36, 82; extent of 8, 23, 31, 82; Freud trying to understand 80, 86–87, 92, 145, 157; in Freud's case studies 78, 80, 90–94 (*see also* specific cases); Habsburg Monarchy as protection against 29; Jewish 15, 79, 85; Jewish responses to 8, 19, 27–28, 41–42; Jung's 88, 144; in medicine 71–73; origins of 86–87, 145–46, 149–50; racialization of Jewishness and 105; rise of 9–10, 79–80; stereotypes in 9, 83, 87, 91–92; in Vienna 24–25, 78–79
art: Freud's analysis of 126, 129; Freud's love of 136, 138–40; Jewish prohibitions in 136–38, 140
assimilation/acculturation 11, 27; attachment to Jewish identity *vs.* 26, 47, 115; classical influence as opposition to 40–41; of Freud and family 8, 10, 19; Jews' eagerness to 25, 79–80; Jews' longing for 2, 7, 44; Jews urged to 24, 85; methods of 36–37, 55; regional differences of 119
Assmann, Jan 99, 100, 109n55, 146, 157
attachment, of Freud and mother 13–14
Austria: central *vs.* provincial laws in 178; as dynastic state *vs.* nation-state 29; education in 38; influence of *Neue Freie Presse* in 60; Jewish attachment to 30–31; nationalist societies in 79–80; Nazi takeover of 160; *see also* Vienna
Austrian Israelite Union, opposing anti-Semitism 27–28
Austrian Republic: creation of 31
authoritarianism 179
authority and authorization: Freud *vs.* Levinas on 122
"An Autobiographical Study" 9

Baer, Abraham 61
Bauer, Ida *see* Dora, case study of
Bauer, Otto 83, 85
Bauer, Philip 70, 83
Beer-Hofmann, Richard 126–27, 133
Benedikt, Moriz 55–56
Benjamin, Jessica 17
Berg, Armin 54–55
Bergmann, Martin 6, 8, 17
Berlin, Isaiah 181
Bernays, Martha 35
Bernfeld, Siegfried 180
Bernstein, Richard 107n16, 112, 116, 118
Beven, William 67
"Beyond the Pleasure Principle" 128, 168
Bini, Lucio 66
Bloch, Joseph Samuel 28
Bnai Brith, Freud joining 80
Boyarin, Daniel 9, 11, 16, 99, 108n37
Braun, Heinrich 45
Breasted, James Henry 147–48, 150
Breger, Louis 12
Breuer, Joseph 37, 47, 67, 80–81
Breuer, Leopold 39
Buber, Martin 127
Burckhardt, Jacob 36
Buschan, Georg 71

cancer, Freud's 161, 172–73
castration: anti-Semitism and 86–87; in case studies 86, 93
Cerletti, Ugo 66
Chaim of Volozhin 122
Charcot, Jean Martin 67, 70
"A Childhood Memory of Leonardo da Vinci" 129

circumcision 86–87, 132
Civilization and Its Discontents 43
Clare, George 30
Clark, Ronald 53
Cohen, Gary 35
Cohen, Shaye 105
"The Conquest of the Jews Over the Germans" (Marr) 79
The Conventional Lies of Our Civilization (Nordau) 176
Cracow Platform of 1906, of Austrian Zionists 28–29
Cuddihy, John 19
culture: classical influence in 37–41; German 18, 24, 36–40, 179; German *vs.* Austrian 31; Greek and Jewish as antagonistic 136–37; Greek influence on 36–37, 136–37; influence of psychoanalysis on 182; Jewish 26–28, 37–40; Jewish contributions to Vienna's 22; Jewish relations with non-Jewish 43–44, 177, 181; Jewish *vs.* Gentile 10–11, 15, 19; Jews' comfort in German-Austrian 22, 30; pagan and Christian 40; pluralism *vs.* multiculturalism 178; race *vs.* 98; separate nationalities' in Austria-Hungary 29; transmission of traits 116–17; triangulation of 45–46; universalism *vs.* particularism in 178–79

Dawkins, Richard 116–17
death drive, and suicide 167–69
The Death of Georg (Beer-Hofmann) 133
Decker, Hannah 74–75
denial, in case study of Dora 83
depression: electrotherapy for 66, 75; Freud's 172; primal 167–68
Deutsch, Felix 172
Deutsch, Helene 170
Dido, in *Herr Aliquis* episode 41–43, 45
Diller, Jerry Victor 1
Doolittle, Hilda 15
Dora: case study of 70; Decker's book on 74–75; Jewishness in 82–85
dreams 19, 44, 83–84
Dreyfus, Captain 7, 82, 85
Durkheim, Emile 166
Dying Slave (Michelangelo) 139–42

"The Economic Problem of Masochism" 169
Edict of Toleration 24
Edmundson, Mark 179
education 47, 61, 83; anti-Semitism in 9–10, 35–36; in assimilation/acculturation 25–27, 36–37; classical 40, 44; Freud's 6, 36–37, 138; Jewish 37–39; Jewish professional 35, 41–42; Jewish self-differentiation in 40–41; Jews' secular 6, 80

ego, and suicide 167–69
Ehrentheil, Otto 30
Eilberg-Schwartz, Howard 102
electrotherapy: effectiveness of 68, 73–75; Freud abandoning use of 67–70, 72; history of 66–67; uses of 67–69
Elisabeth von R., case study of 69
emancipation: anti-Semitism and 7–8, 24–25; central *vs.* provincial laws in 178; effects of 11, 79, 81; life before and after 6–7; limitations of 24–25, 79
Emmy von N., case study of 69
England, Freud's exile in 80, 144, 162, 173
Epicureans, on suicide 166
Ethics, Levinas's focus on 120–21
Europe, anti-Semitism in 82
evolution 124n23; Lamarckian 137–38, 145; psychological influences on 116
exile, Freud's 80, 144, 162, 173

father neurosis 60
fathers 46; Akhaten's rejection of 153–57; in Egyptian religions 152–56; Moses as patriarch 138, 149; murder of primal 97, 104, 117–18, 163; in Oedipal myth *vs.* Freud's family 16–17; *see also* Freud, Jakob (father)
Federn, Paul 167, 170
Feldman, Yael 16
Ferenczi, Sándor 172
Feuerbach, Ludwig 114–15
fixations 128–29
Fleck, Ludwig 1–2
Fluss, Emil 35
"Fragment of an Analysis of a Case of Hysteria" 82
"Fragments of an Analysis of a Case of Hysteria" 70
Franz Joseph II, Emperor 24, 29–30, 38
free association, in *Herr Aliquis* episode 46–47
Freud, Alexander (brother) 41, 58, 140
Freud, Amalia (mother, née Malka Nathanson) 2, 8, 12–16, 173
Freud, Anna (daughter) 173
Freud, Emmanuel (half-brother) 8
Freud, Heinerle (grandson) 173
Freud, Jacob (father) 9, 13–14, 35, 87; assimilationism of 8, 19; influence of relationship with 6, 15–16; reading Torah 146; as unheroic 6, 8, 10–11, 15, 46
Freud, Martha Bernays (wife) 14, 87
Freud, Martin (son) 47
Freud, Minna (sister-in-law) 41
Freud, Phillip (half-brother) 8
Freud, Sophie (daughter) 172
Freud family 10, 23
Freud: A Very Short Introduction (Storr) 181

Freud and the Legacy of Moses (Bernstein) 112
"Freud: Darkness in the Midst of Vision" (Breger) 12
Freud's Moses (Yerushalmi) 99
Frieden, Ken 18
"From the History of an Infantile Neurosis," case study of the Wolf-Man 92
Frühling am Rhein (operetta) 177
Funkenstein, Amos 113
The Future of an Illusion 183

Gay, Peter 52, 126, 172
gender 67, 108n32, 165; Freud on femininity 15, 17, 43, 45; in Freud's theory of Jewishness 15, 43, 103, 108n37; influence of Freud's mother on theories 14–15; Jewish masculinity and 8–9, 93
Gender and Assimiliation in Modern Jewish History (Hyman) 7
gender relations 11, 83
gender roles, Jewish 10–11
The Genesis and Development of Scientific Fact (Fleck) 1–2
Germany: Jews as enemy in 160; nationalist societies in 79–80; *see also* Nazis
Gillman, Abigail 31n1, 182
Gilman, Sander 9, 15–16, 99
Glückl of Hameln 10–11
Graf, Max 59, 86–87, 107n13
Graf, Olga Honig 86
Greeks 92; culture of Jews *vs.* 136–37; influence of philosophy 18, 36–37; influence on Jewish thought 177–78, 180–81, 183
Group Psychology and the Analysis of the Ego 179
guilt: after suicides 169–70; Jewish 145–46, 183; in Oedipus myth 17

Habsburg Monarchy: Austria as dynastic *vs.* nation-state under 29; Jews' support for 22–23, 29, 31; universalism *vs.* particularism in 178
Hammerschlag, Samuel 36, 39–40, 57
Handelman, Susan 18
Hannibal, in Freud's fantasies 6, 45–47
Hasa, Abdima bar Hama bar 120
The Healing of the Cripple (Masolino) 139–40
Hegel, G.W.F. 53–54, 119–20, 124n23
Heidegger, Martin 114, 119, 121
Heine, Heinrich 176
Heller, Hugo 60
Heller, Judith 13
hermeneutics, Freud's development of 6
heroes 13; Freud identifying with 6, 12, 15; Freud's father not 6, 8, 10–11, 14, 46; Hannibal in Freud's fantasies 45, 47; Moses as 132–33, 146–47

Herr Aliquis episode 41–47
Herzl, Hans 181
Herzl, Theodor 28, 85, 176, 181
Heschel, Abraham Joshua 19
Hilsner case 82
Hirschmann, Albert O. 181
"The History of the Psychoanalytic Movement" 68
Hofmannsthal, Hugo von 127
Holocaust *see* Shoah
homosexuality, Kraus on 52
humanism, German 36
Hyman, Paula 7
hysteria 167; in case studies 69, 82–85; effects on voice 69–70; electrotherapy used on 68–70, 74–75; as inherited 72–74; Jews thought to be predisposed to 70–73; trauma and 67, 73

idealization, Freud's of father 6, 11
identification, Freud's, with parents 15
identity, Freud's: ambivalence and conflict over Jewishness 79; conservatism of 126; construction of heroic 12; as secular Jew 18–19, 114
identity, Jewish 31, 45, 127; achievements springing from guilt 145–46; ambivalence and conflict over 78–79, 87; anti-Semitism and 79, 120; circumcision and 86–87; effects of Holocaust on 162, 164; Freud linking with passivity and femininity 15, 43; Freud *vs.* Levinas in 112; Freud's 79, 160–62; Freud's as typical 22, 35, 114; Freud's attachment to 36, 80, 115, 127; in Freud's case studies 78, 81, 83–85, 88–90; German *vs.* 22; inferiority in 8–9, 85; influences on 30–31, 54–55, 177–78; intellectualism in 183–84; masculinity in 8–9, 11; origins of 113; persistence of 107n13, 107n20; repression of 81, 99–100; secular 37–39; superiority in 47; tripartite 29–31; universalism *vs.* particularism in 178–79; in Vienna 23, 26–31
identity, sexual 17
illnesses, Freud's 171–72
"Infant Sexuality" 74
intellectualism, Jewish 118; effects of 12, 120–21; in Freud's theory of Jewishness 15, 97, 102–3; Greek influence on 177–78, 180–81, 183; in heritage 183–84; in identity 2–3, 71, 73
The Interpretation of Dreams 12, 44–45, 52, 79, 128

Janik, Allan 175–76
Jauss, Hans Robert 40
Jellinek, Adolf 30
Jewishness: appearance of 139; biological

transmission of 97–98, 100, 103; bodily definition of 100–102; Freud questioning essence of 115–18, 127–29, 182; of Freud's Moses 96–97, 133; Freud's theory of 101–3, 105–6, 108n37; Greek culture as antagonistic to 136–37; Judaism vs. 99, 103; matrilineal vs. patrilineal transmission of 101, 108n32; persistence of traditions 97–100, 104–5; of psychoanalysis 181; racialization of 98–100, 102–3, 105, 107n15, 107n16; source of 98, 100, 103–4, 121; *see also* identity, Jewish
Johnson, Ray 156
Jones, Ernest 13, 52, 140
Judaism 115, 120; as compromise 130, 133–34; conversion and 104–5, 109n55; essence of 122, 123; Freud wanting psychoanalysis to be separate from 2, 19, 78, 118; Jewishness vs. 99, 103 *see also* religion
Juden auf Wanderschaft (*The Wandering Jews*, Roth) 55
Julius II, Pope 138–39
Jung, Carl 78, 88, 144

Kafka, Franz 127
Kierkegaard, Søren 119
Kramer, Michael 107n15
Kraus, Karl 176; on essence of Jewishness 182–83; Freud's relationship with 52–53, 58, 60–62, 63n2; *Neue Freie Presse* and 53–54, 56–57, 62; on power of the press 55; on psychoanalysis 51–52, 62–63; Wittels's criticisms of 59–60, 64n10

Lachs, Minna 24
Laius, as father of Oedipus 16
language 81, 128, 157
language disorders 75, 81, 150–51
Lanzer, Ernst *see* The Rat-Man, case study of
Lassalle, Ferdinand 44–45, 176
The Last Days of Mankind (Kraus) 55
Lear, Jonathan 18
Le Rider, Jacques 107n16
Leroy-Beaulieu, Anatole 71
Lessing, G.E., 177
Levenson, Edgar 18
Levinas, Emmanuel 112–13, 122, 160; influences on 114, 119–20; return to religion 118, 120–21
Life of Michelangelo (Vasari) 137–39
Little Hans, case study of 85–88
Loewi, Hilde 170
The Longest Hatred (Wistrich) 9
Lovett, Richard 67
Löwenfeld, Leopold 72–73
Löwy, Emmanuel 137
Lueger, Karl 7, 25, 80, 175

Mack, Michael 106n3
Mack, Ruth 91
Maimonides, Moses 178
The Man Moses and the Monotheistic Religion 112
Marr, Wilhelm 7, 79
Marx, Karl 176
Marxow, Ernst Fleischl von 67
matriarchy, transition to patriarchy from 101
Mayer, Sigmund 30
McNeil, William 117
medicine 140; Freud in 52, 57; race and 70–73, 75; use of electrotherapy in 66–67, 69–70
melancholic syndrome 167–69
memory: Jews' of Mediterranean 137–38; recollection of 128; repression of 97, 104, 118, 128–29, 160; resistance to 132–33; tradition as 134
Mendelssohn, Moses 177
mental illness: electrotherapy used for 66–67, 74–75; Jews thought to be predisposed to 70–73
Meyerhöfer, Annette 52–53
Michelangelo: *Dying Slave* by 139–42; *Moses* of 29–32, 137–39
Möbius, Paul 68
modernism: critical 175–76, 179; Jews as enemy for instigating 160; Viennese 24, 126, 134–35, 175–76
monotheism: effects of 183; as Egyptian 116, 145, 147–54; of Judaism vs. Christianity 120, 136, 144–45; of Moses vs. King Akhaten 116, 150–51, 156–57; origins of 146–54; solar 152–53, 156
Moravia, Jews immigrating to Vienna from 23–24, 35
Moser, Fanny *see* Emmy von N., case study of
Moses 147; and birth of monotheism 103–4; as Egyptian 146, 162; as father-figure 149; Freud as 160, 164; Freud blaming Jewish character traits on 145–46; Freud vs. Levinas's uses of 113–14, 120–23; Freud's feelings about 145–47; Freud's image of 2, 129–30, 132–35; Jews and 114–15, 118, 145–46, 160, 183; lack of historical evidence of 148, 150; Levinas's focus on ethics and 120; monotheism of 96–97, 150–51; murder of 113, 117–18, 151; tradition of 134
Moses (Michelangelo) 2, 129–32, 137–39
Moses and Monotheism 80, 112, 126; Abraham ignored in 151–52; as compromise 133–34; examining all religions 97–98, 160, 163; Freud's technique in 129–30, 132, 134, 144; on Jewishness 96–97, 100; publication of 162; timing of 115–16, 144

"The Moses of Michelangelo" 126, 129, 131–32, 134, 136
Moses the Egyptian (Assmann) 157
mothers 86, 146, 167–68; *see also* Freud, Amalia (mother, née Malka Nathanson)
"Mourning and Melancholia" 167

narcissism, of the Wolf-Man 91
narcissistic injury 167–68
nationalism: Jewish 133; societies promoting 79–80
Nazis 160; Church not protecting Jews from 144–45, 162; Freud fleeing 173; ideology of 93–94, 97; Jews and 160, 163
Neue Freie Presse: Freud avoiding debates over 61–62; Freud's articles in 57, 62–63; Freud's habitual reading of 53, 55–56; Kraus and 53–54, 56–57, 62; reading in Jewish identity 54–55, 60; Wittels's analysis of 60–61
Neurath, Otto 176
neurosis 67, 86; cultural 116–17, 145; Jews thought to be predisposed to 70–73
The New Solar Theology 152–53
New York Psychoanalytic Institute 2
newspapers: habitual reading of 53–54, 58; influence of 55, 61–62; in *The Psychopathology of Everyday Life* 58–59
Nordau, Max 11, 102, 176
"A Note on the Mystic Writing Pad" 128

object-relations theory 180
occupations: anti-Semitism and 41–42, 82; Jews in professions 36, 57, 79; traditional Jewish 25–26, 35
Oedipus complex 79, 85–86, 146, 148, 151
Oedipus myth 16–17
On the Concept of the Science of Judaism (Wolf) 115
Oppenheim, David 61–62
Oppenheim, Hermann 71–72
Ostow, Mortimer 18

Pankejeff, Serge *see* The Wolf-Man, case study of
Pappenheim, Bertha *see* Anna O., case study of
paranoia, in Schreber case study 93–94
Patent of Toleration, Jews purchasing to live in Vienna 23
patriotism, of Austrian Jews 30
Pfister, Oskar 18–19, 173
"Place and Utopia" (Levinas) 120
Plagues and Peoples (McNeil) 117
politics: anti-Semitic parties in 25; Austria-Hungary's paralyzed 29; Jews in 45, 178; Zionist parties in 29
Pollak, Ludwig 137

Popper, Karl 181
poverty/wealth, of Jews in Vienna 22–27
Prince, Morton 68
Professor Bernhardi (Schnitzler) 133
"Project for a Scientific Psychology" 17–18
psychoanalysis 62–63, 167, 179; analyst as substitute father 46, 170; anti-Semitism ignored in literature of 80; Church's hostility to 147, 160; criticisms of 181–82; dynamics within 168–70; efforts to remove Judaism from 2, 19, 78, 92; Freud wanting to be science 17–18, 92, 101–2, 115; Jewishness of 122, 181, 183–84; Kraus on 51–52, 62–63; logic's influence on 180–81; as savior from religion 183; of socio-cultural prejudice 86–87, 92; on voice and language disturbances 74–75
Psychoanalytic Congress (Paris) 107n25
"Psychoanalytic Notes on an Autobiographical Case of Paranoia" 93
The Psychopathology of Everyday Life 41–45, 57, 58–59

race 9; culture *vs.* 98; Jewishness and 79, 96–99, 102–3, 105, 107n15, 107n16; medicine and 70–73, 75
Raising of Tabitha (Masolino) 139–40
The Rat-Man, case study of 88–90
rationalism 7, 14–15, 18, 180–81
reality, and mass media 53
religion 15, 166; art and 136, 138–40; Church not protecting Jews from Nazis 144–45, 162; conversion among 84–86, 89, 104–5, 109n55, 182; in Egypt 152–54 (*see also* Akhaten, King); Freud rejecting 14, 18–19, 22, 114, 118, 147; Freud's analysis of 14–15, 97–98, 109n51, 144, 160, 163; Freud's familiarity with Catholicism 146–47; in Freud's interpretation of *Herr Aliquis* episode 46–47; intellectualism as temptation away from 120–21; Jewish community of 27–28; during Jews' assimilation 25–26; Oedipus complex in origins of 146, 148; origins of 115, 162; psychoanalysis as savior from 183; in The Rat-Man case study 89–90; relations among 88, 120, 160; *see also* Judaism; monotheism
Remak, Robert 70
renunciation, in Freud's theories 17
repression: Freud's 20; of memory of murder of primal father 97, 104, 118; return from 105–6; sexual 74
Revolution of 1848, liberalization after 23
The Road into the Open (Schnitzler) 133
Roazen, Paul 169, 170
Roith, Estelle 10, 15
Rome, Freud's obsession with 137–38
Rose, Jacqueline 103–4

Roth, Joseph 55
Rozenblit, Marsha 35, 39
Russia 30, 71–72

Sadger, Isidor 61
Schalit, Isidor 28
Schnitzler, Arthur 126, 128, 176
Schoenberg, Arnold 176
Schorskie, Carl 7, 16
Schreber, case study of 93
Schur, Max 172–73
science: Freud wanting psychoanalysis to be 17–18, 78, 92, 101–2, 115; Freud's faith in 15, 122, 160; Freud's theory of Jewishness as 101–2; of Judaism 115; race in 9, 105
The Selfish Gene (Dawkins) 116–17
Sellin, Ernst 160
Selling, Ernst 148
sexuality 53, 58, 69, 74, 137; in Freud's case studies 83, 85–86, 91; infantile 61, 85–86
shame 9, 19
Shavit, Ya'acov 37–38
Shoah 122; effects of 118–20, 160, 164; Freud's Jewish identity formed before 161–62
Silberstein, Eduard 35
Sloan, Samuel 73–74
Socrates 18, 166
Solomon, Solomon J. 136
Soyka, Otto 62
Sperber, Manès 24
Spielrein, Sabina 88
Spinoza, Baruch 176
Spitzer, Daniel 56
splitting 15, 90
Stekel, Wilhelm 61–62, 167
Sternberg, Julian 57
Stoics, on suicide 166
Storr, Anthony 181
Stricker, Robert 29, 31
Studies in Hysteria (Breuer and Freud) 5–6, 80
subjectivity, Freud's 5
suicide: extent of 165; Freud's assisted 161, 163–64, 172–73; Freud's theories on 166–67; Tausk's 169–71

talking cure 67, 69, 181
Talmudic Institutes in Vilna 118–19
Tausk, Viktor 60, 169–71
"The Temptation of Temptation" (Levinas) 120
Three Essays on Sexuality 62
Timpanaro, Sebastiano 42
Torah and Talmud: Freud's father as scholar of 9, 146; presentation of 114, 120; Talmudic Institutes in Vilna 118–19; textual analysis of 6; transcendence through 119–20, 122
The Torch (Kraus's journal) 52; critiques of psychoanalysis in 62–63; on *Neue Freie Presse* 54, 56; Wittels analyzing 59–60
Totality and Infinity (Levinas) 119
Totem and Taboo 115, 148, 163; Freud's preface to Hebrew translation of 127, 129; on murder of primal father 117–18; on religion 97–98, 144
transcendence 114, 118–20, 122
transference: counter-transference and 86, 92; mass 179–80
trauma, and hysteria 69, 73
Tucholsky, Kurt 53–54, 55
Tuesday Lessons (Charcot) 70

unconscious: Freud's conception of 18–19; in *Herr Aliquis* episode 46–47; Michelangelo's *Dying Slave* personifying 141–42
Unheroic Conduct (Boyarin) 9
universalism, *vs.* particularism 178–79

vagal nerve stimulation 75
Van Herik, Judith 17
Vasari, Giorgio 137, 138–39
Vienna: anti-Semitism in 7, 24–25, 78–80, 175; creativity of cultural scene in 2, 22, 175; Jewish community in 27, 35; Jewish culture in 22–24, 26–30, 37–38; sexual moral code in 11, 51, 53; sources of Jews immigrating to 23–24, 39; Zionism in 28–29; *see also* modernism, Viennese
Vienna Psychoanalytic Association 2, 78; discussion of the press and 61–62; Wittels and 52, 59–61, 64n10
Viennese Jewish Modernism (Gillman) 31n1
violence, in birth of monotheism 103–4
Virgil, in *Herr Aliquis* episode 41–43
voice: disorders of 66, 68, 72, 74–75, 81; hysteria and 69–70, 75

Wagner-Jauregg, Julius 68–69
Wechsberg, Joseph 24
Wistrich, Robert 9
Wittels, Fritz 52, 59–61, 64n10
Wittgenstein, Ludwig 165, 176
Wolf, Immanuel 115
The Wolf-Man, case study of 90–92
women, psychoanalytic views of 2; *see also* gender
World War I 29–30
Wulfing-Luer, Georges 71

Yerushalmi, Yosef Hayim 3, 99, 107n20, 112, 116, 151
YIVO Institute for Jewish Research 1, 3

Zakkai, Jochanan ben 3
Zionism 11, 28–29
Zweig, Stefan 30

www.ingramcontent.com/pod-product-compliance
Lightning Source LLC
Chambersburg PA
CBHW032100300426
44116CB00007B/833